THE JOURNAL OF INDUSTRIAL ECONOMICS

437

VOLUME XVI

1967-68

BASIL BLACKWELL

OXFORD

Printed in Great Britain by
Alden & Mowbray Ltd
at the Alden Press, Oxford

CONTENTS

VOLUME XVI

Number 1, November 1967

PAGE

Galbraith and Consumer Sovereignty, by MAURICE ZINKIN 1

Firms' Exit Rates and Their Determinants, by MATITYAHU MARCUS 10

The Firm in the Czechoslovak Economy, by MONIKA ŠESTÁKOVÁ 23

Advertising and Concentration: An Empirical Investigation, by H. M. MANN, J. A. HENNING and J. W. MEEHAN, JR. 34

Regulation of International Liner Shipping and 'Freedom of the Seas', by DANIEL MARX, JR. 46

The Need for Product Market Analysis: A Case Study of the Feasibility of Import Substitution in Nigeria, by PHILIP C. PACKARD 63

Concentration and Price-Cost Margins: A Comment, by HASKEL BENISHAY 73

A Note on 'Measuring Shopping Costs', by ROBERT BACON 75

Number 2, April 1968

Dynamic Programming Extensions to the Theory of the Firm, by T. M. WHITIN 81

A Note on Mergers and the Business Cycle, by C. J. MAULE 99

Cyclical Behavior of Manufacturing Plants, by T. Y. SHEN 106

The Regional Significance of I.C.F.C., by G. DAVIES 126

The Determinants of Steel Prices in the U.S.: 1947–65, by RICHARD MANCKE 147

Number 3, July 1968

Limit Price and the Market Share of the Leading Firm, by B. PETER PASHIGIAN 165

The Relation of Profit Rates to Operating Rates, by REED MOYER 178

Private Capital Investment: A Case-Study Approach towards Testing Alternative Theories, by C. M. Cannon 186

Entropy, Markov Processes and Competition in the Brewing Industry, by Ann and Ira Horowitz 196

Vertical Integration and the Market for Repair Parts in the United States Automobile Industry, by Robert Crandall 212

GALBRAITH AND CONSUMER SOVEREIGNTY

by Maurice Zinkin

Professor Galbraith, one suspects, finds economics somewhat boring. His heart is with aesthetics. Both in *The Affluent Society* and in the Reith lectures the central suggestion is that the problems of scarcity and uncertainty have now been solved, and that our attention should be given to the beauty of our cities, the cleanliness of our air, and the quality of our education. The need is no longer to satisfy the individual desires of the consumer, but to improve the amenities of the community.

In so far as Professor Galbraith is making a value judgment about the good society, we can all go part of the way with him. We might all get more total satisfaction if we spent more of our resources on getting rid of pollution, on providing more and better education, and on making the centres of our northern towns attractive. We are all tempted to spend too much on those commodities which satisfy a strong immediate want, like alcohol or tobacco, and too little on those which improve the environment in which we live, like parks and safety.

We even recognize this limitation in ourselves. As voters, we express our mistrust of ourselves as consumers. We support a policy which taxes beer and petrol and toilet soap in order to make education free. Yet, if we could trust our own sense of perspective, it might be simpler for most citizens to pay for the education of their children with the money they would save by not having to pay taxes on their beer and petrol and toilet soap. It is because we are not sure that we would use the money saved to buy education, and not more and more beer and petrol and toilet soap that we go through all the administrative contortions of subsidizing education and taxing beer and petrol and toilet soap.

One can of course argue about who constitutes 'we' in this context; to some extent the subsidy is not just from petrol or beer or toilet soap to education, but from one section of the community to another. Most people, however, both pay the taxes and get the subsidy, yet the idea of basing the supply of education upon the demand for it, as expressed by the fees parents would pay, has not been accepted by any political party of importance in the western world. Obviously, there are some things which, at the straight market price, we would buy more of than we think is good for us, and others of which we would buy less. So we use our power as voters to impose something of our definition of the good life upon ourselves as consumers.

If Professor Galbraith had confined himself to this simple proposition, if by his contrast between private affluence and public squalor, he had meant merely that we are liable to over-indulge some of our wants and to stint others, there would have been no cause to quarrel with him.

He has, however, backed up this value judgment with a model of the working of the economy which appears to be in large part untrue, though the way in which the economy works is still sufficiently often obscure for it to be impossible to be dogmatic about how untrue.

Professor Galbraith's model is a subtle and complex one, which contains many minor theses of great interest. He has, for instance, a view of the importance of the committee as against the individual in the large organization which does not coincide with my experience. His doctrine would, however, appear to rest essentially on three propositions. First, the economy is now dominated by a limited number of large firms, and this is new. Secondly, these firms (whether public or private) are now in a position to organize their research and marketing in such a way that they can impose upon the consumer the products they make, many of which he (or she) does not really want at all. Thirdly, these firms need the State only to perform those tasks they cannot do themselves, like managing demand, or would find uneconomic, like providing higher education.

Between the big firms and the State, there is thus no conflict of interest. Society is affluent, the big firms never make losses. The market can be left to them to run. The State can turn its attention to the higher pursuits, like the beautification of our cities.

This may sound like the perfect world of the new managerial class. It uses all their technical skills. It does not require from them entrepreneurial intuition and the capacity to live with uncertainty, gifts which are much less highly correlated with the possession of a university degree than is the ability to do, say, operational research. In this world, it would be foolish of bureaucrats and politicians to try and interfere very much with the managers, and, if they do try, then they are liable to find their monopolies commissions and their anti-trust legislation a mere 'charade'—the word is Professor Galbraith's.

Better still, the values Professor Galbraith prefers to the mere satisfying of the consumer's choice fit in very well with the values of the managerial class. They too would like the centres of our cities to be beautiful; they usually work there, and quite often live there.

They too would like their air clean, and changing away from open fires is relatively not expensive for them. They too like their countryside quiet and their children well taught. Their values are not very different from those of professors.

There is only one snake in this Eden. The world is not like this idealized picture of it.

Big firms are not a new phenomenon, and it is more than doubtful whether in the essential respect of innovation, they dominate the economy.

Consumer's choice remains. Firms, however big, however impressive their advertising, do not have the capacity to impose their products upon the consumer. Firms which misjudge the consumer's desires can still make losses.

There is no necessary harmony between the needs of free enterprise and the objectives of politicians; it is very often true that what is good for General Motors is good for the United States; but especially in socialist and semi-socialist countries, it is surprising how often politicians do not think so.

It is true that in every developed country the top few hundred firms control a large part of the economy. But so they did in 1910. United States Steel and the Great Western Railway were not small then.

The difference between decision-making in the Ford Motor Company today and decision-making in Ford's when Henry Ford was young is quite as enormous as Professor Galbraith alleges. A big organization normally decides through many people, relatively slowly; the problems it faces are usually complex. It cannot decide with the off-the-cuff simplicity of a single individual manning a jobbing shop. However, though this may be new for the Ford Motor Company, it is not new as a historical phenomenon. Governments and armies have been large organizations making their decisions in a complicated way and with considerable forward planning for a very long time. Amongst commercial organizations, the Dutch and British East India Companies had a highly complex mode of decision-making in the eighteenth century; there was nothing of the early Henry Ford about them.

The real change in scale came not in the twentieth century, with the large corporations, but in the nineteenth, with the railways. Indeed, in country after country, no body of private individuals was sufficiently powerful to raise the capital and create the organization required to build and run railways. The State had to do it. There are not many characteristics of the Galbraithian corporation, from the importance of its managers to the exercise of deliberate influence upon the consumer's choice, which one cannot find in the railway of 1900, whether its ownership was public or private.

The main issue is, therefore, not whether the large corporation is getting larger—as the economy grows it must be expected to get larger—but whether a few hundred of such large corporations, perhaps even a hundred or two, can be expected one day to dominate the whole economy of major countries, perhaps even of the whole world.

It is fashionable to give the answer 'yes'; and if it is once accepted that the large corporation can impose upon the consumer its idea of what the consumer ought to want, then the answer is plausible, though only for manufacturing industry. In the services, which are an even larger part of most Western economies, the economies of scale are often small, and the problems of management can be very large. The independent hairdresser or pharmacist can compete very well with a chain (as indeed Professor Galbraith concedes). The grocer who joins a voluntary group, the girl with a sense of fashion who opens a boutique, may be perfectly competitive. And it is not obvious that General Motors are more important to the consumer than her hairdresser and her dress shop.

In the service industries it is obvious that the talent which most effectively changes the consumer's tastes and best responds to the consumer's desires, lies in the small firm rather than the big. Mary Quant has had more effect on fashion than all the department stores put together. It was the relatively small travel agencies, not the great airlines, which invented the package holiday. The idea of high quality food on a limited menu was invented by new firms like Angus Steak Houses and Golden Egg, not the old-established J. Lyons. It was the owner-driver with a lorry or two, rather than the large haulage firms, who originally took the traffic away from the railways. Even the major supermarket companies are largely new; many of the old multiple retailers were slow to see the possibilities of this new form of retailing.

In manufacturing, too, the list of firms at the top very frequently changes as the market changes. In 1910, the biggest quoted firm apart from the railways was J. & P. Coats. Such household names as Thorn Electrical and Marks and Spencer, to name only two, are largely creations of this generation, and both were built up by individuals to an extent which does not fit Professor Galbraith's model at all.

Not only are a lot of big firms new; not only is there no reason to think that other big firms will not grow from small beginnings in the future as these have in the past; but also there is nothing to make one think that size in itself confers any sort of immunity from the vagaries of the market. Positive losses, in these days of full employment, are admittedly rare, though they have happened in the recent past to some of the giants of steel and shipping and shipbuilding. But poor profits in good years are fairly frequent, and they leave the management nearly as open to takeover, or reorganization, or other equally unpleasant remedies as positive losses. There is a large smattering of big British firms whose record does not suggest the effective planning of the Galbraithian model.

The reason for these frequent failures to earn a proper return may be incompetence. It is more often some shift in consumer choice. The consumer becomes less enthusiastic for travel by passenger liner, or he keeps his old television set longer than expected, or he changes his preferred size of motor car. When this happens, it may also happen that some firms, by no means necessarily the biggest in the industry, or perhaps in some quite different industry altogether, have anticipated and encouraged the changes; but they did not normally create it.

Here we should perhaps introduce a qualification. Whether one considers that the firm creates the demand, or responds to it, depends upon how one defines the word 'create'.

If, by 'create', one means produce a demand which was not there before in that form, then firms, big and small, very often do create demands. One could not want the latest style of the hairdresser round the corner before he had conceived it. One could not want a television set before somebody had invented it. In that limited sense, the demand for any invention is a creation of its inventor.

If, however, the argument is pressed further, if it is implied that the new want is 'created' in the sense of being artificial, then this is normally not true. The new want is nearly always an old want but satisfied in a new way.

This is clear for all the inventions which have produced major new industries. Man has always wanted mobility; the Indian peasant will spend months going on a pilgrimage in a bullock-cart. The motor car did not invent this desire; it merely satisfied it on an unprecedented scale; any surrogate for male virility it may also have provided was quite accidental. Nor did the aeroplane invent the love of speed, or the helpfulness of talking face to face with colleagues and customers far away; it did provide a means of going fast, and of conducting negotiations in other continents, which had not previously existed. Can one doubt that George Washington would have flown to London for discussions if the aeroplane had existed in 1776, even though it was before the days of mass advertising?

Not many will argue that motor cars and aeroplanes are created wants. The aeroplane after all was supported for many years by its obvious military value; and nobody has alleged that this was a value created by advertising. The motor car was not a heavy advertiser until it was well-established. When Ford was selling black model Ts, nobody talked of the motor car as a symbol of power and aggression; they merely recognized that it gave the farmer or the salesman a better means of getting to town or to their customers than they had ever had before.

The motor car and the aeroplane are more typical of the new products which have revolutionized our time than any of the heavily advertised consumer goods.

A very interesting example is computers. Ever since man discovered arithmetic, he has wanted an easier way of doing calculations. Calculation is frequently necessary; except perhaps to a child revelling in the sense of power conveyed by a newly learnt multiplication table, it is never amusing. The abacus, the adding machine, the electronic adder, the comptometer are so many tributes to man's—and woman's—reluctance ever to do a sum that they can get a machine to do for them. The computer's merit is that it does more and bigger sums, and does them quicker. It has not needed a great advertising campaign. On the contrary, it has been urged on a sometimes reluctant industry by the massed voices of politicians, journalists and professors. It has been seen not just as a convenient way of solving certain mathematical problems, but as a symbol of national Keeping up with the Joneses.

It has made IBM one of the world's great firms. Yet nobody who knows the history can believe that IBM *planned* the advance of the computer. As late as 1950, indeed, it is said that none of the computer companies believed the computer to have any future outside scientific research; nor was this, in the state of the art as it then was, a ridiculous view. Moreover, IBM was not a firm whose skills lay in electronics. None of the fundamental ideas came from IBM. The idea of a machine which could calculate in this way comes from Babbage, a Victorian Cambridge professor. The idea of a logical algebra comes from Boole, another Victorian professor, this time Anglo-Irish. The transistor was invented in the Bell Laboratories. The Index Register was conceived by a Manchester professor. Other firms are ahead of IBM in micro-circuitry.

This does not mean that IBM have made no research contribution to computers. Their contribution has been considerable. It does mean that the computer is not something they decided to invent, then invented, and then sold to the public. On the contrary. At the beginning there were other firms who produced computers just as good as theirs. The reason IBM went ahead was something they did not plan at all. It was the simple fact that, since they were already in the office machinery business, they understood particularly well what their customers wanted to use the computer to do. Their machines were no better than other people's; but at the crucial time in the late '50s and early '60s their software—the programmes and the standard procedures which enabled their customers to use the machines—and their willingness to spend time on the individual customers' problems, *were* better, or so at least their customers thought.

It may be argued that, however helpless the manufacturer may be over cars and aeroplanes, he can at least work his will on that frail creature, the housewife. Let us then take a few examples from consumer goods.

Chocolate is one of the success stories of the last hundred years. When Queen Victoria came to the throne, nobody ate chocolate. Today everybody does. It is true that chocolate is heavily advertised. But it is also true that the consumption of sugar has been rising steadily in the Western world, even without advertising, for over 200 years; and it is one of chocolate's main attractions that it is sweet. And most of us remember from our childhood that the enthusiasm for chocolate antedated the ability to read advertisements.

An even more typical example is soap and detergents. Anybody who wishes to complain about heavy advertising always begins with the detergent firms. Yet it can hardly be seriously suggested that the desire to be clean has been created by Unilever and Procter and Gamble. In so far as they have encouraged this desire, Professor Galbraith would doubtless agree that they have performed a public service. But the idea of cleanliness as next to godliness antedated not merely the advertising, but the very existence of the detergent firms.

As for that other favourite Aunt Sally, drink, the advertising has been considerably higher since 1900 than it was before, but the consumption per head in the U.K. has halved. Price, availability, and the general social attitude to drunkenness have been more important than anything the brewers and the distillers could do.

In short, as every manufacturer knows to his cost, there is no way of planning the housewife. She follows her own desires, desires created by the whole social environment, of which the manufacturer's marketing is only a small part This does not mean that bankruptcy stares every firm in the face. The consumer may be sovereign; she is not therefore arbitrary. Her consumption of bread may be declining; she does not stop eating bread altogether overnight. Her consumption of coffee may be rising; she does not therefore suddenly give the children coffee for their tea,

The sensible manufacturer works with the environment, not against it. He tries to satisfy desires, latent or patent, the consumer already has; it is much cheaper than creating new ones. The manufacturer, therefore, follows a rather different, less predestined, course than that postulated by Professor Galbraith.

First, he tries to identify these desires. To do this he now has all the aids of marketing research, but real success still requires intuition. If he only researches into which detergent the consumer considers to wash cleanest, he may miss the fact that the consumer now also wants her detergent to be pleasantly perfumed. If he only tries to find out which variety of chocolate the consumer considers to be best value for money, he may miss the fact that many consumers will pay more for chocolate with honey and almonds.

That is why so many of the new products even of the biggest firms fail miserably in test market. It is rarely because they are poor products technically. It is because there is something in their mix of qualities which fails to appeal to the consumer, and which perhaps at some later stage, when the consumer has more money or has changed her tastes, will make the product a roaring success. The British consumer today wants more varieties of ice cream than she did a dozen years ago; frozen food today sells in Germany where fifteen years ago it did not. One can always find rationalizations for such changes after the event; beforehand, the manufacturer painfully often does not see them coming, let alone plan them.

Once the manufacturer has found out what he thinks the public wants, he has to embody it in a product. This is a planned process, but one where the plans very frequently go wrong. With some sorts of applied research, it is possible to estimate that it will take so many people so long to make the necessary discoveries. With others, one is heavily dependent on luck. The scientific key may prove very hard to turn; or one may find an answer which is scientifically perfectly satisfactory, but too expensive for the consumer. Every motor car manufacturer can see that there is a market for an electric car. Many of them have planned large-scale research. What they have not been able to do hitherto is to produce an electric car at a reasonable cost. One can doubtless make the guess that one day this century some firm (and it may not be a motor car manufacturer) will find an answer; but a guess of this vagueness hardly ranks as planning.

When the manufacturer does find an answer at a reasonable price, he still has to sell it to the public. He may think the answer will work; he may feel the price to be reasonable. He does not know whether the public will see it as he does.

Even if he has the right answer, the manufacturer still has to be able to persuade the consumer that it is right. To some extent this is something that can be planned. The manufacturer usually knows what terms will induce the retailer to stock his brand, and—with a rather wider margin of error—what promotions will induce the housewife to try it, though even here he quite often goes wrong. Artificial flowers have proved more successful, and Indian dolls less successful, with the British housewife than one would have predicted.

The chanciest part is the advertising. It must tell the right story. The consumer will not be persuaded unless the quality in the product which the advertising emphazises is one she considers to be important and relevant. It would be no good advertising Blackpool for a holiday on the ground that its inhabitants were regular churchgoers, though that might well be a consideration for someone contemplating buying a house there. There are children in the breakfast food advertisements because much breakfast food is eaten by children but a child drinking whisky would not sell much whisky.

If one resorts to the consumer's deeper drives, one may find it more difficult still to get the answer right. Girls with nothing on may attract the manufacturer's young men; they may be much less exciting for the middle-aged women who actually buy his product.

At every turn, in the market research, in the product development, in the setting of the price, in the marketing, the manufacturer may, and more often than not does, go wrong, so much so that one is driven to the reluctant conclusion that Professor Galbraith's lovely world does not exist. The businessman still lives in the classical world of risk and uncertainty, where he makes money if he guesses right and loses it if he guesses wrong. More often than not, he guesses wrong; but fortunately, his competitors do the same. So he survives.

What Professor Galbraith's model does remind one of is universities. Faculties can plan their courses, and how many students they will take, and how many they will fail. They can make their customers, the students, attend lectures and write essays, and punish them if they do not. Harvard and Oxford can, to a surprising extent, control their future; they can leave to the State the bit they do not want to do, namely finding the money. But even professors should not be too complacent. Is not the demand for a student share in power a manifestation of the desire for consumer choice? Is not the student a consumer who wants to be able to reject lectures and tutorials for reasons as flimsy—or as good—as those for which he rejects toilet soap?

London

FIRMS' EXIT RATES AND THEIR DETERMINANTS

by Matityahu Marcus*

The effect of entries and exits on the competitive performance of firms occupies a prominent role in theoretical discussions of industry behaviour. Unfortunately, comprehensive statistics on entry and exit rates are seldom available, thereby denying students of industrial organization the benefits of such information.[1]

In the first part of this paper we suggest a simple model for explaining exit rates. Tests of the model against available data on firms' mortality rates indicate that it has considerable predictive value.

The key variable of the model is the proportion of loss firms as reported regularly by the income tax authorities. In Part II we investigate what determines the probability of becoming a loss firm. Our conclusion is that much of the variation in this factor can be explained by postulating the operation of size and age effects which are common to all industries.

I. THE DETERMINANTS OF EXIT RATES

A. Theory

It is a basic proposition of economic theory that a firm would leave the industry if it is incurring losses, namely, if its realized rate of return falls short of its opportunity rate of return. This does not mean that *all* loss firms exit, or that those which leave do so instantaneously.

Clearly, even in an industry with no exiting firms some will experience losses at any time due to the presence of various sorts of disturbances. These may be errors in judgment and execution, or the experience of external adversities such as weather-inflicted damages. Thus, although we cannot predict whether a particular

* Completion of this study was facilitated by a national Science Foundation Post-Doctoral Fellowship during 1964–65. I am grateful to George H. Borts for helpful comments on an earlier draft of this paper.

[1] Most empirical studies of entry and exit rates have usually relied on changes in listings of industry directories. This approach is laborious and not fully satisfactory since (*a*) many industries do not have regularly updated directories, and (*b*) directories give incomplete coverage to new and small firms—the groups that must not be omitted in studies of entry and exit rates. Some specific problems arising when directories are used are discussed by E. Mansfield, 'Entry, Gibrat's Law and the Growth of Firms', *The American Economic Review*, Vol. LII (December 1962), p. 1046. More general statistical treatment of the problem, technically referred to as incomplete frames, can be found in Frank Yates *Sampling Methods for Censuses and Surveys*, New York: Hafner Publishing Co., 1960.

loss firm will exit without knowledge of the specifics of its situation, we would expect differences in exit rates among large groups of firms to be related to their differences in the proportion of loss firms.

This hypothesis requires several qualifications. First, the relevant PLF (proportion of loss firms) for inter-industry comparisons should be the one computed over an economic period. Clearly, an industry subject to sharper cyclical fluctuations will have a larger PLF in the trough than an industry with milder cyclical fluctuations, and yet it will not necessarily display a larger exit rate. Also, a given PLF will result in differing exit rates if the expected profits in the event of success are larger in the one case than in the other. In other words, some firms may undertake more trials given the same odds because the prize is larger.

If a firm decides to leave, the length of departure period will be determined by its cost mix, in particular, by the ratio of variable to sunk costs. The lower the ratio of variable to sunk costs, the greater, ceteris paribus, is the likelihood that part of sunk costs is being recovered and the less likely is the firm to shut down immediately. Therefore, for a given proportion of loss firms, we would expect exit rates to be negatively related to the ratio of sunk to variable costs.

In summary, I would expect the rate of exit to be determined by the PLF with appropriate qualifications based on expectations of future profits and the structure of costs.

In order to obtain exact estimates of the PLF we would need to know the proportion of firms earning less than their 'opportunity' rate of return. This would require information on the distribution of firms' rates of return. It is common knowledge that such distributions are scarce and of questionable value. The major reason for doubts about their reliability is that for computing rates of return one first needs to obtain the value of a *stock* of capital goods—an estimate which is fraught with statistical as well as conceptual pitfalls.

As a measure of the PLF we propose to use the proportion of firms earning zero or negative income as reported by the Internal Revenue Service. These statistics are available annually for the corporate sector in the United States, and since 1957–58 also for the non-corporate sector at the three-digit industry detail.

The inclusion of firms with zero income as a component of the PLF presents no problems. These firms are loss firms in the economic sense because IRS does not consider charges on owners' equity deductible. Hence, true costs are always underestimated and reported zero income can be regarded as negative income.

A discrepancy between the true PLF and the one reported by the

IRS may result from the fact that the latter excludes firms which realize positive, though less than 'alternative' rates of return. I believe that the size of this group is small, and that its omission is of little consequence in predicting exits. More on this when the statistical tests are described.

Given the industry PLF, we argued earlier, the exit rate will be modified by profit expectations. As a measure of these expectations, we use next period's *realized* rate of return. This assumes no forecasting error which, in the absence of information on actual expectations, is not an unreasonable assumption.

Last, it was suggested that the cost structure will also affect the exit rate. Since we cannot compute the ratio of sunk to variable costs, we use the capital-output ratio. It is reasonable to expect—on *a priori* as well as on empirical grounds—that the capital-output ratio measures the degree of capital intensity in production, and is therefore a good proxy for the ratio of sunk to variable costs.

We can now specify our model fully:

$$EX_{i_t} = \alpha_0 + \alpha_1 PLF_{i_t} + \alpha_2 K/O_{i_t} + \alpha_3 r_{i_{t+1}} + u \qquad (1)$$

Where EX_{i_t}, PLF_{i_t}, K/O_{i_t} refer, respectively, to the i industry exit rate, proportion of loss firms, and the capital-output ratio all in period t, and where $r_{i_{t+1}}$ is the realized rate of return in the t + 1 period.

B. The Data and the Statistical Results

Tests of the suggested model are limited to the data available. I know of only two comprehensive sets of exit rate estimates, and the hypothesis is tested against both.

1. *Crum's Data*

The first estimates, prepared by Crum as a part of a wider study on corporate behavior and age, provide the number of corporate exits in 1964 by year of incorporation.[2] Briefly, in 1945 and again in 1946 the IRS presented the distribution of all corporations by year of incorporation. By considering decreases in the number of corporations from 1945 to 1946 as corporate deaths, Crum was able to compute exit rates for 17 age groups.

The only information reported for each age group in 1946 is the

[2] William Leonard Crum, *The Age Structure of the Corporate System* (Berkeley: University of California Press, 1953), Ch. 7.

PLF; no other data for these age groups are given, and therefore we could test only the effect of the PLF on the exit rate.[3] The results are:

$$EX_k = \underset{(.029)}{.390}\ PLF_k - \underset{(.062)}{.042} \qquad \bar{R}^2 = .918,\ n = 17$$

Where EX_k is the exit rate for the k age group, and PLF_k is the proportion of loss firms in the k age group.

These results indicate that on the basis of 1945–46 data, variations in the PLF explain (after adjusting for degrees of freedom) about 92 per cent of the exit rate variability. We also find that a 10 per cent change in the loss ratio is expected, on average, to cause a 3.9 per cent change in exits. Finally, the constant term in the equation suggests, though with little confidence because of its substantial sampling variability, that even with no exits one would expect, on average, 11 per cent of all firms to realize no income.

2. *OBE Data*

A second, and more recent, set of exit estimates was prepared by the Office of Business Economics (OBE).[4] These estimates are five-year (1951–55) annual average rates, given at a 2-digit industry detail for the combined noncorporate and corporate sectors. They are based on the Bureau of Old Age and Survivors' Insurance (BOASI) tabulation of employers filing Social Security tax returns.

In the OBE study, exits are defined as all businesses ceasing operation for whatever reason. Thus, they include firms ceasing operations voluntarily as well as firms discontinuing operations involuntarily following bankruptcy proceedings.[5]

[3] As noted earlier, our PLF omits firms which realize positive though lower than 'alternative' returns. I believe that this omission does not bias the regression estimators. For, with no knowledge about the distribution of profit rates and the value of the 'alternative' rate, we may assume no correlation between the PLF and the omitted group. This assumed independence cannot be tested directly. However, it was possible to compute the degree of correlation between the PLF and the percentage of firms earning 0–2 per cent profits (on sales); the coefficient of rank correlation for twenty-one manufacturing industries was low and statistically insignificant (−.245). This indicates that there is no correlation between the percentage of industry firms which earn low positive profits and the proportion of loss firms.

We also must consider the possible simultaneous equation bias entering into the estimation of equation (1). Specifically, one might argue that the PLF is a function of the exit rate. Consider firms which exit *in anticipation* of realizing losses. These will register as exits, and, since they leave while realizing profits, the reported PLF would be lower. Hence, the larger this group of exits, the lower the PLF.

I would think that this group of firms is exceedingly small relative to all exits and that the bias introduced is therefore minimal. It may be emphasized that for all *loss* firms the causality hypothesized in equation (1) strictly holds. This is true regardless of the time of exit. No matter how early in the year a loss firm decides to exit, it still files a tax return which is, in turn, reflected in the reported PLF.

[4] Betty Churchill, 'Rise in the Business Population', *Survey of Current Business*, May 1959.

[5] This definition is more comprehensive than the one used by Dun & Bradstreet in the compilation of their Business Failure Statistics; there, coverage is limited to instances

In addition to exit estimates, the OBE study provides data on transfers. These are defined as firms which are sold to, or otherwise acquired by, new owners. They also include firms which have undergone change in legal form of organization from, say, partnership to corporation. It thus appears that the transfer group is quite heterogeneous: it includes 'proper' exits, i.e. loss-induced exits, as well as sales of profitable firms for any reason and mere changes in legal form. We would therefore expect our suggested exit model to have little relevance for the transfer group.

Using OBE data on exits we test hypothesis (1). The results are presented in Table I.

TABLE I

REGRESSION RESULTS: EXIT RATE ON SEVERAL VARIABLES (SEVENTEEN MANUFACTURING INDUSTRIES, 1951–55)*

Equation	PLF_t	K/O_t	r_{t+1}	*Constant*	$\bar{R}^2$
1.1	.223	−.016	−.208	.320	.532
	(.085)	(.031)	(.104)	(3.87)	
1.2	.249		−.210	.096	.556
	(.068)		(.101)	(.301)	

* The following are the data sources for the variables used. The exit rates are OBE five-year (1951–55) annual average discontinuance rates referred to earlier. The PLF are five-year averages derived from the appropriate *Corporation Income Tax Returns*. The profit rate is a five-year average (1956–60) based on the *Corporation Income Tax Returns*. Finally, the capital-output ratios are for 1953. See, D. Creamer, *Capital Expansion and Capacity in Postwar Manufacturing*, National Industrial Conference Board Studies in Business Economics Number Seventy-two, Table 3.

The OBE statistics are available for nineteen industries of which seventeen are used in our study. We excluded miscellaneous because of its heterogeneous nature (tobacco was included in it). Lumber was also excluded because of its atypical nature. The exit rate reported for the lumber industry (18.2 per cent) is far outside the range of all other industries (2.7 per cent to 10.8 per cent). This inordinarily high exit rate can be probably ascribed to the many small firms which enter in order to undertake specific, limited contract jobs in logging with the expectation of terminating operations at the end of the job. I thought it best, therefore, to omit lumber from the sample. If lumber is included, we obtain the following results:

$$EX_t = \underset{(.135)}{.419}\, PLF_t + \underset{(.040)}{.097}\, K/O_t - \underset{(.177)}{.337}\, r_{t+1} - \underset{(.639)}{.470}; \quad \bar{R}^2 = .503$$

We note that the regression results support the model. All the coefficients have the expected signs, and the PLF is significant at the

involving possible loss to creditors. Also, D. & B. failure rates are computed on the basis of listings in their Reference Book, and may not be representative of the industry-wide experience.

1 per cent level. When K/O is omitted (equation 1.2), the regression results improve and r_{t+1} now becomes barely significant at the 5 per cent level.[6]

In a later section (p. 19) we discuss the possibility that the reported PLF for small-size firms are biased upwards. If such a bias exists, it is quite possible that the PLF used in our regressions are artificially higher for industries with disproportionate concentrations of small firms. To guard against this we adjust the PLF so as to eliminate the small-size reporting bias. The adjustments are described in the Appendix. The same regressions were then run with the adjusted PLF as the dependent variable. These yielded, for all equations, PLF coefficients larger by about 15 per cent than those reported in Table I. In all other respects the findings are substantially unchanged.[7]

In conclusion, we note that the estimators of the PLF coefficient arrived at on the basis of Crum's and OBE data are reasonably close considering differences in the sources of the exit rate estimates, in periods of study, and in industry coverage.

Our findings cast the proportion of loss firms as a significant predictor of exit rate differences. We next proceed to investigate the determinants of the PLF.

II. DIFFERENCES IN THE PROPORTION OF LOSS FIRMS AMONG INDUSTRIES

A. Causes of Differentials

Recalling that the PLF is the proportion of firms earning zero or negative income, we suggest that the proportion will vary among industries in accordance with differences in market conditions. Specifically, the higher is demand relative to industry capacity, the lower will be the PLF since more firms are expected to cover their costs and realize profits. We would therefore expect a negative association between the industry profit rate and the PLF.

In addition, I would also expect the PLF to depend on the proportion of weak, performance-wise, firms in the industry. Two groups that should be considered in this context are the 'small' and the

[6] As expected, the model performs poorly for the transfer group.

$$TR = -.076\ PLF - .018\ K/O + .054r + .665\ ;\ \bar{R}^2 = 0.042$$
$$\quad (.062) \qquad (.022) \qquad (.075) \quad (.281)$$

[7] The regression results are:

$$EX = .250\ \hat{PLF} - .019\ K/O - .206 + .248\ ;\ \bar{R}^2 = .522$$
$$\quad (.099) \qquad (031) \qquad (105) \quad (.387)$$

Where $\hat{PLF}$ is the industry PLF adjusted to eliminate the small size reporting bias; all other terms retain their previous meanings.

'young'. Specifically, we suggest that variations in the PLF are influenced by the proportion of 'small' and 'young' firms in the industry. It should be emphasized that age and size are two distinct factors which merit separate analysis. For, although most 'young' firms are 'small', the one does not imply the other.

The above does not imply that other factors, such as the natural abilities of the owner, are unimportant in explaining the probability of loss. I would think, however, that these factors can be regarded as randomly distributed among different industries thereby leaving our estimators unbiased.

We can now state our model briefly:

$$PLF_i = \alpha_0 + \alpha_1 \hat{PLF}_i^S + \alpha_2 \hat{PLF}_i^A + \alpha_3 r_i + u \qquad (2)$$

That is, the i industry proportion of loss firms (PLF_i) is a linear function of the size- and age-predicted proportion of loss firms ($\hat{PLF}_i^S$, $\hat{PLF}_i^A$), of the industry profit rate (r_i), and an error term (u).

The derivation of the size- and age-predicted PLF will be described fully later. Suffice to say here that they are derived on the assumption that a given size/age structure has the same effect on all industries (an alternative assumption is discussed in section D). Several hypotheses will now be suggested in support of the assumption of common effects.

We point to two explanations underlying common age effects. The first is based on the role of on-the-job-training. We expect such learning to be important in all industries in the first years of the firm's life since it is in the course of these years that the entrepreneur is faced with many new problems whose first-time solution constitutes learning.

A second-hypothesis relies on the assumption that, in all industries, a fraction of newly formed firms is failure-bound. These are firms which enter the industry on the basis of erroneous evaluations of their entrepreneurial capacity, and therefore face a high probability of failure. One would expect the virtual weeding-out of these firms in the course of several years and a subsequently falling PLF with age.

What would rationalize the hypothesis of common size effects? The first argument we would cite is that prices of some factors faced by small firms are higher; in particular, the cost of capital. Assuming that small firms sell at the same price, this implies a lower profit rate and a higher probability of incurring losses given identical market risks.

A second hypothesis for the presence of common size effects may be termed the migration hypothesis. According to it, profitable firms experience, on average, positive growth rates. This implies the migration of profitable firms into larger size groups and the subsequent inverse relationship between the PLF and size of firm.

In the next section we describe the derivation of the size and age effects. The usefulness of these effects in explaining variations in the PLF as specified by our model is tested in section C.

B. The Age and Size Effects

Statistical and data difficulties arise when one tries to derive the age and size effects. Although the distribution of corporations by size is available annually, one cannot relate the PLF to size alone because size and age are positively correlated, and changes in the PLF with size also reflect systematically varying proportions of 'young' corporations.

Age distributions are provided at long intervals. The one we are using in this study—which is also the most recent—is for 1959–60. Prior to this, the age distribution of corporations is available for 1945 and 1946. Even for 1959–60 a cross-classification of corporations by age and size is given only for 'all active corporations'; no industry detail is provided.

We hypothesize that there are independent size and age effects and that these are common to all industries. These assumptions permit us to obtain estimators of the size and age effects from data on all corporations. Specifically, we use the mean PLF for the j size group—computed from observations across the different age groups—as the estimator of the common size effect for the group. This estimator is denoted as $PLF^*{}_j{}^S$. Similarly, the age effect is the mean PLF for a given age group computed from observations across the different size groups. It will be denoted as $PLF^*{}_k{}^A$.[8] The estimators are presented in Table II.

Looking first at the age effect (Table II, panel A) we note that

[8] Restating the above in more compact notation, we have:

$$(1)\ PLF_{jk} = PLF_j{}^S + PLF_k{}^A + u_{jk} \quad j = 1, 2, \ldots 14 \quad k = 1, 2, \ldots 17.$$

That is, PLF (loss ratio) for the j size and k age group consists of a size effect $PLF_j{}^S$ and an age effect $PLF_k{}^A$ and an error term u_{jk}, where $E\,(u_{jk}) = 0$; $E\,(u_{\grave{j}\grave{k}}\, u_{jk}) = 0$, for $j \neq \grave{j}$ or $k \neq k$.
Using these assumptions we get:

$$(2)\ E(PLF^*{}_j{}^S) = \frac{1}{17} E \sum_k PLF_{jk} = PLF_j{}^S + \mu PLF^A$$

$$(3)\ E(PLF^*{}_j{}^S) = \frac{1}{13} E \sum_j PLF_{jk} = PLF_k{}^A + \mu PLF^S$$

where μPLF^A and μPLF^S are the mean age and size effects respectively. We thus see that the expected value of $PLF^*{}_j{}^S$ is the true size effect plus a constant, and the expected value of $PLF^*{}_k{}^A$ is the true age effect plus a constant.

the PLF declines sharply to age five (year of incorporation 1954). Thereafter no consistent relationship between it and age is observed: changes are small in magnitude and are about equally divided between positive and negative values.[9] We thus conclude the economic childhood is limited to six years, of which the first two present the greatest hazard. Survival past six does not appear to reduce loss prospects further.

TABLE II

AGE AND SIZE EFFECTS ON THE PROPORTION OF LOSS CORPORATIONS (ALL ACTIVE CORPORATIONS, 1959–60)

A		B	
Year of incorporation	*Age effect* (PLF*A)	*Size (Total assets) in dollars*	*Size effect* (PLF*S)
1959	·445	1–25,000	·563
1958	·438	25,000–50,000	·410
1957	·336	50,000–100,000	·332
1956	·333	100,000–250,000	.262
1955	·311	250,000–500,000	.246
1954	.274	500,000–1 million	.224
1953	.265	1–2.5 million	.228
1952	.270	2.5–5 million	.236
1951	.267	5–10 million	.251
1950	.265	10–25 million	.270
1945–49	.247		
1940–44	.260	25–50 million	.246
1930–39	.267	50–100 million	·197
1920–29	.247	100–250 million	·175
1910–19	.262	250 million and over	.089
1900–09	.267		
1899 and prior*	·304		

Source: Statistics of Income 1959–60, Corporate Income Tax Returns, Tables 16 and 24.

* Consists of the three age groups 1880–99, 1860–79 and 1859 and prior. These were combined because for some size groups no breakdown was reported.

Turning to the size effect (Table II, panel B), we notice that initially the PLF declines sharply: from .563 in the first to .262 in the fourth size group. Using the earlier regression findings on the relationship of exit to the PLF, this suggests that growth to $100,000–$250,000 in assets can be expected to reduce the probability of exit by 7.5–11.5 per cent. With further increases in size to the $25–50

[9] The single exception is the positive—and relatively large—increase in the PLF of the oldest age group.

million group, the ratio first rises and then declines, but both movements are very mild (the range of variation is from .276 to .224). Finally, in the giant size groups ($50 million and over) the PLF resumes its decline falling perceptibly in the largest size group.

When interpreting the sharp initial decline in the PLF we must bear in mind that the reported losses for the smallest corporations may be biased upwards. This is because small corporations are more likely—due to the closer identity between owners and officers—to pay their officers excessive salaries in order to minimize their corporate tax liability.[10] If this is so, the reported costs of these corporations are exaggerated and through them so are the loss proportions. Therefore, any conclusion about the true size-PLF relationship requires a prior estimate of this bias. After investigating this question for manufacturing, I believe that the bias is important only in the three smallest groups, and that it is in the order of 20 per cent of the reported ratios. The procedures and data on which these estimates are based are presented in the Appendix.

It can be readily seen that a reduction in this order of magnitude if applied to the first three size groups in Table II, panel B, would reduce the range of variation substantially, and would bring the ratio of the third size group within the middle range. It would still leave the ratios of the first two sizes higher than those of other groups. We would conclude, therefore, that the size effects reveal significant disadvantages only for the smallest size groups.

C. Tests of the PLF Model

In 1959, for the first time, the Internal Revenue Service reported separately the size and age distribution of firms for 2-digit industries. Based on these, we compute for each manufacturing industry size-predicted loss proportion ($\hat{PLF}_i^S$). and age-predicted loss proportion ($\hat{PLF}_i^A$). The former is the average of the size effects weighted by the share of the different size groups in the industry, and the latter is the average of age effects weighted by the shares of the different age groups in the industry.

The tests of hypothesis (2) are presented in Table III. Regression 2.1 includes all variables as specified in the model, whereas regression 2.2 omits r since it is found to be statistically insignificant from zero when included (equation 2.1).

When we examine the magnitudes of the regression coefficients,

[10] This problem has been recognized by many. See, for example, William Leonard Crum, *Corporate Size and Earning Power* (Cambridge, Mass.: Harvard University Press, 1939), pp. 306–16; S. S. Alexander, 'The Effect of Size of Manufacturing Corporations on the Distribution of Rate of Return,' *Review of Economics and Statistics*, XXXI (1949).

we note that the size effect on manufacturing industries is close to the expected effect, i.e. the value of the coefficient is close to unity. The age coefficient, on the other hand, differs significantly from unity. Thus, while changes in the regression-predicted ratios are related, significantly, to changes in the age-expected ratios, they are not equal: a one per cent change in the age-expected ratio is associated with about three per cent change in the regression-predicted ratio. Thus, the higher the age-expected PLF, the larger its deviation from the regression line.

This may be explained on the grounds that the higher the age-predicted PLF the younger the average age, and the higher in the

TABLE III

REGRESSION RESULTS OF PLF ON SEVERAL VARIABLES
(TWENTY-TWO MANUFACTURING INDUSTRIES, 1959)

Equation	$\hat{PLF}^S$	$\hat{PLF}^A$	r	*Constant*	$\bar{R}^2$
2.1	.936 (.286)	2.998 (.872)	−.080 (.174)	−.843	.738
2.2	.898 (.268)	3.118 (.773)		−.894	.749

indicated risk of the industry. This higher risk may well result in a systematic upward shift of the PLF from the one expected on the basis of standardized age effects.

D. Concluding Remarks

We saw that a readily available statistic—the proportion of loss firms—can be used for estimating exit rates by industries. Proceeding to investigate the determinants of this ratio, we hypothesized that size and age effects are common to all industries. Based on this assumption we estimated the magnitudes of these effects and reached the conclusion that only the smallest size groups (assets to $100,000) face a substantially higher probability of incurring losses. This is in broad agreement with findings on the relationship of profitability and size.[11] We also saw that the disadvantage of young age—estimated independently of the size effect—vanishes after the first five years.

The absolute effects hypothesis, in particular with respect to size,

[11] See Sidney S. Alexander, 'The Effect of Size of Manufacturing Corporation on the Distribution of the Rate of Return', *The Review of Economics and Statistics*, Vol. 31 (1949), p. 234; H. O. Stekler, *Profitability and Size of Firm*, Berkeley: Institute of Business and Economic Research, University of California, 1963.

may appear extreme. Indeed, it was forced upon us by the data. An alternative approach which might seem more reasonable on *a priori* grounds should be mentioned. It would propose that the effects of size are not absolute, but dependent on the *industry* characteristics. Specifically, it might suggest that size of firm is relevant only when considered with respect to the industry's optimal size. An empirical evaluation of this hypothesis would require that a testable version be specified; this would necessitate that we specify both 'the optimal scale' and the assumed functional relationship of size effects to deviations from the optimal size.[12] Needless to say, we had no information to permit us to do this for the wide group of industries treated in this paper.

Though we cannot say whether, and to what extent, the inclusion of industry-specific size variables would improve our understanding, it is clear from the findings that *absolute* size should be considered a most important determinant of the performance of small firms.

RUTGERS, THE STATE UNIVERSITY, NEW BRUNSWICK

APPENDIX

Following recent (1958) revisions in the Internal Revenue Code, some corporations—designated as small business corporations—can elect to be taxed through their shareholders if they meet several qualifications. These corporations file Form 1120-S. The eligibility requirements for filing under this law are intended to insure that the corporation does not have, or is not a part of, a complex corporate structure. Some of these requirements are: it cannot have more than ten stockholders; it must be domestic; it can have only one class of stock and cannot be a member of an affiliated group eligible to file a consolidated return. These corporations are not subject to the corporation income tax and therefore do not have the alleged incentive to take part of their profits in the form of officers' salaries. We therefore consider PLF based on the reported income of such corporations to be unbiased. This enables us to gauge the extent of the bias in the PLF for all corporations on the assumption that the two filing groups (1120 and 1120–S), for a given industry, differ only with respect to this reporting bias.

[12] An interesting testable version of this hypothesis is presented by Mansfield in a study of exit rates. He uses some of Bain's estimates of optimal size (available for twelve selected industries) and assumes, specifically, that the exit rate is related exponentially to the ratio of the firm's size to the industry's optimal. See Edwin Mansfield, 'Entry, Gibrat's Law, Innovation, and the Growth of Firms', *The American Economic Review,* Vol. LII (December 1962), pp. 1028–30).

The information on the reported PLF for the two groups is contained in the following table:

TABLE IV

PROPORTION OF LOSS FIRM: ALL MANUFACTURING INDUSTRIES (1959–60; BY SIZE OF CORPORATION)

Size of corporations (In thousands of dollars)	PLF *Corporations filing* 1120	*Corporations filing* 1120–S	*Number of Returns Corporations filing* 1120	*Corporations filing* 1120–S
0–25	.637	.529	26,218	2,306
25–50	.433	.326	17,551	2,035
50–100	.357	.303	21,400	2,603
100–250	.247	.255	29,637	2,917
250–500	.198	.151	18,023	1,279
500–1000	.185	.199	11,869	417
1000–2500	.141	.090	8,390	100

Source: Source Book of Statistics of Income, 1959–60.

* The comparison could not be carried beyond the $1–2.5 million group since in the next two groups only eight corporations filed on Form 1120–S. No corporation with assets of more than ten million dollars filed Form 1120–S.

Since industries differ in their size distributions, it was necessary to check for possible distortions in our earlier regression results (Table I). This was done by running the OBE regressions with PLF adjusted to eliminate this source of bias. The complete adjustment is now described.

We first compute the 'true' PLF for 1959 2-digit manufacturing industries. These are obtained using the equation:

$$PLF_i^t = \sum_j PLF_{ij}^r w_{ij} - \sum_j (PLF_{ij}^r - PLF_{ji}^t) w_{ij}$$

where PLF_{ij}^t is the 'true' loss ratio for the j size group in the i (two-digit manufacturing) industry; PLF_{ij}^r has the same meaning except that it is the reported ratio, and w_{ij} the weight of the j size group in the i industry. Since we do not know $PLF_{ij}^r - PLF_{ij}^t$ for every industry (many industries did not have a sufficiently detailed breakdown of their 1120–S returns by size), we used the known values for 'all manufacturing' presented in the table above. Using these values and the appropriate weights, the PLF for the individual industries was computed.

With possession of unbiased PLF for 1959 2-digit manufacturing industries, we adjust the 1951–55 reported PLF for the corresponding industries assuming the same ratio of true to reported PLF for the two periods.

THE FIRM IN THE CZECHOSLOVAK ECONOMY

by Monika Šestáková

I. THE FIRM IN THE NEW ECONOMIC SYSTEM

1. *Background*

The former centralized model of the socialist economy did not recognize the firm as an independent legal and economic unit, as a decision-making centre. The enterprise was a physical unit only, a pure tool in the centrally planned and managed system of resource allocation and production. All details—volume and structure of output, rise of labour productivity, the amount of wage funds, etc., and of course prices of all goods, were determined by the central authorities. Sometimes these obligatory indicators were in mutual contradiction, and the enterprise made use of such a situation in a way which resulted in negative social consequences (lowering the quality and technical level of the products, hiding reserves, struggling to get lower targets in the plan, etc.).

In such conditions the application of the market mechanism was only formal. There was no space for the regulatory function of the market.

The shortcomings of the centralized model became very apparent when the extensive sources of economic growth were exhausted and the new factors in the development of our economy were coming to the fore. The quantitative and volume-of-physical-product aspects of development now step into the background and the qualitative and value factors come into the foreground. They are reflected best in market relationships. Therefore it was necessary to change the relation between the central plan and the market and to strengthen the function of the market mechanism in all spheres of our economy.

The market mechanism can work effectively only in some kind of decentralized model. Therefore the principal feature of our new economic system lies in the decentralization of decision-making to the individual firms. The firm will choose the structure and volume of its output, set prices of its products, determine wages, finance capital investment (from its internal funds or from credit granted by the State Bank or by other firms), etc.

This new system was experimentally introduced in some industries during the years 1965–66 and from January 1st, 1967 some principal features of this system were introduced in the whole economy. But the system we really have now is still far from the theoretical ideal—the project we plan to reach in the 1970s. We are now in a transitional period, during which, we hope, our enterprises will learn how to behave rationally, so that it will be possible to make full use of the competitive relations between the firms as one of the moving forces of our economic system.

2. '*The Rules of the Game*' *between the Firm and the Central Authorities*

'The rules of the game' in the transitional period ought to encourage initiative and rational behaviour of our enterprises (lead them to make the most effective combination of production factors, etc.). What kind of rules of the game we shall have in the final model we do not know exactly. The principal idea is to establish for our enterprises a *uniform criterion* of effectiveness and thereby make them feel the effect of their efficiency in their revenue.

Currently our enterprises are allowed to make freer combinations of production factors (although this choice is limited by the insufficient supply of some factors) and in most cases to choose the structure and volume of their output and set prices within certain limits. The opportunity for independent policy for our firms will increase from year to year.

All firms must pay from their gross revenue (profit + wages) the following payments (taxes) to the state budget: 1. a payment for fixed assets (6 per cent of their value after amortization); 2. a payment based on gross revenue (in 1967—15 per cent). There are also some suggestions to establish payments from wage funds—to limit the rise of wages. But there is no definite solution to this problem.

The proportion of the payment from fixed assets will gradually decrease and will, in the final solution of our model (after all the fixed assets originally received from the state have been depreciated), be dropped completely. The payments based on gross revenue will probably have a continuous tendency to rise.

The credit policy of the State Bank will be one of the important instruments of influencing centrally the investment policy of our enterprises. Decisions concerning the grant of credit will be made on economic criteria (which do not apply to the old model), the principal criterion being the expected investment efficiency. Moreover the credit policy of the Bank will be based on the targets of the national plan. When making decisions concerning the conditions for granting a credit, those industries will be preferred the development of which is in accordance with the planned targets.

3. *Some remarks concerning the current pricing problems*

The problems which have to be faced at present in Czechoslovakia when determining prices can be divided into two basic groups:

(a) problems of the mutual relationship between the wholesale and retail price levels;

(b) problems of actual price relations of various commodities.

These two basic problems reflect the shortcomings of the centralized model and of the price system associated with it. A substantial intervention in the price system which would, at least, show the way to find a solution of both sets of problems, is an inevitable condition for introducing successfully the new economic model in Czechoslovakia.

The whole logic of the old model caused a considerable difference between the levels of wholesale and retail prices. In the strictly centralized model of the socialist economy the consumption goods market was the only real market, only the consumption goods retail prices were able to reflect objective market conditions (even though they did not always do so). Real market relations did not exist between manufacturing firms (or between manufacturing and wholesale firms).

The wholesale price system was actually isolated from the world market price level as well as from the retail price system within the country itself. Wholesale prices had been in most cases passively adapted to the production costs in the particular industry and were practically independent of the demand for the respective commodity. This, naturally, considerably biased the wholesale price relations of various commodities (as compared with the respective retail price relations). Moreover the 'rule of the game' implied in the centralized model—according to which the major part of enterprise profit was transferred to the central funds (and therefore was not included in the wholesale price)—caused a considerable difference in the absolute level of the wholesale and retail prices.

The main objective of the wholesale price reform was to abolish this double price level and help to establish such a price system as would reflect the actual conditions of the home market and would at the same time relate our prices to the world market prices. Only in this way is it possible to create objective criteria of economic efficiency which is an inevitable condition for the successful operation of the new model.

Naturally this objective is a long-term one and it is impossible to attain it by introducing single measures taken by the central authorities. The new wholesale prices, valid since January 1st, 1967, were intended to do away with the unfounded differences in the profitability of various commodities and so create uniform 'rules of the game' for all firms. But it is impossible to expect that any price reform, carried out by the central authorities, would be perfectly consistent with the market logic. The central authorities will never have sufficient information to be able to accomplish this.

The wholesale price reform was only intended to prepare the 'environment' for the successful starting of the new model, and create conditions enabling the market mechanism to operate effectively. In the future, firms themselves will set prices of their products, taking into account the actual market conditions.

The type of price[1] used as a basis while reforming wholesale prices was the so-called production price. Principally the price was calculated according to the formula

$$p = c + v + \rho K,$$

where c = material costs, v = wage costs, ρ = rate of profit, K = funds-intensity coefficient.[2] The 'normal' production costs in the respective industry and the principle of an equal rate of profit in all industries served as a starting point.[3] (The actual rate of profit which a particular firm reaches is different—depending on the cost conditions of the respective firm.)

II. SOME UNSOLVED THEORETICAL PROBLEMS CONNECTED WITH THE ECONOMIC AND LEGAL POSITION OF A FIRM

The new Czechoslovak economic model brings very radical changes in the economic structure, and raises a lot of new theoretical and practical problems. To some of these problems we have no definite answer and we are only in the stage of searching for an adequate theoretical explanation, which could help us to formulate

[1] The basic types of prices in the socialist economy have already been the object of long discussions in Marxist economic theory. It is possible to summarize the substance of the problem in the following manner: every price consists of three basic components —material costs, wage costs and profit. (For simplification purposes the theoretical model abstracts from the distribution margin, various taxes, etc; all non-cost components are included in the 'profit'.) The various price types will then be distinguished according to the way the profit is being included in the price (in what proportion to the costs or individual cost components, etc.).

[2] The price calculation problem is indeed much more complicated. For a more detailed explanation see: Hejl, Kýn, Sekerka 'Price Calculations', in *Czechoslovak Economic Papers* (1967) No. 8.

[3] Naturally it is impossible to make absolute the principle of an equal profitability of various products. Before the competitive pressure begins to affect the firms in the sense of increasing their efficiency, it has been necessary to allow, to a certain extent, for different profitability of individual commodity groups, in accordance with the efficiency of their production (taking into consideration the ratio between the world and home prices).

some norms for our economic policy. I should like to mention two groups of such unsolved problems—which are now in the centre of our theoretical discussions.

1. *Who will be the economic agent in the decentralized model? To whom can we delegate decision-making in our firms?*

This group of problems is very closely connected with the concept of ownership. Is the decentralization of decision-making to the individual firms compatible with the socialist ownership of the means of production? This is the principal question very often raised in theoretical discussions in all socialist countries and extremely important in our present situation. The orthodox opponents of our new economic model answer this question negatively.

There are two main alternatives giving a positive answer to this question, connected with two alternative concepts of the economic agent, goals of its activity, etc.

The first alternative is based on a concept of *collective ownership*. All the employees of a firm are regarded as collective owners of its assets and hence also as the economic agent in the decentralized model of the socialist economy. This concept leads to a certain type of market syndicalism. Some proposed 'rules of the game' for the firms in our new economic model—especially the gross-revenue-maximization as a goal of their activity—are similar to those of market syndicalism. Will the firms under such conditions behave rationally? Will the results of their policy be at least the same as in the capitalist system?

Nine years ago Mr. Ward in a model of an 'Illyrian firm'[4] which bears a close resemblance to the real position of the industrial firm in Yugoslavia, showed that there was a great difference in the market behaviour of a worker co-operative on the one side and its capitalist twin on the other. The difference follows from the position of a socialist worker who is a producer and an entrepreneur at the same time. Assuming that all employees of a socialist enterprise have a share in the profit (dividend), they would be interested to accept new employees (which in Ward's pure model is the only way of increasing output) only in the case that their present share in the profit would not be reduced. The response of a worker-co-operative to changes in the fixed costs, and in the price of the output is on this view quite contrary to that of its capitalist counterpart. A change in the fixed costs of the Illyrian firm leads to a change in its output in

[4] B. Ward, 'The Firm in Illyria: Market Syndicalism', in *American Economic Review*, September 1958.

the same direction and a change in price leads to a change in output in the opposite direction. The equilibrium output of the Illyrian firm is smaller than the output of its capitalist twin. (The only exception is the zero-profit-point where the equilibrium position of both firms coincides.)

Of course, Mr. Ward concludes that the difference between the market behaviour of a socialist worker-co-operative and that of its capitalist twin is directly proportional to the relative weight of labour in the firm's inputs. In a highly mechanized firm, where labour does not enter significantly into the production function as a variable input, the socialist firm would behave in the same way as its capitalist counterpart (p. 581). But this was not the case of typical Yugoslav firms in 1950, although it could be the case of some Czechoslovak enterprises where labour is a very scarce factor and the increase of output is possible only with technological innovations.

More recently Mr. Domar in his model of a Soviet Collective Farm[5] (which could be considered as a general model of the socialist worker-co-operative) confirmed Mr. Ward's findings and made some of his results more definite.

The conclusions derived from both models are very sensitive to changes in their assumptions. In order to make these models more realistic it would be necessary to change these assumptions.[6] In particular the assumption that the whole sum of profit is distributed as a wage bonus (which follows from the static character of both models) is very unreal. The same applies to the assumption that labour is a homogeneous factor and that profit is therefore equally distributed among all employees (no distinction is drawn between workers and managers, etc.).

Nevertheless the real development of the Yugoslav economy showed some tendencies very similar to those which could be derived from the above mentioned models. The profit-per-worker maximization as a typical policy of a worker-co-operative resulted in a situation which was far from being optimal. In this case it is not possible to rely upon one remedy only—the interference of central authorities. From the experience of our centralized model we realized that central bodies cannot be informed in detail about the production function and demand conditions of all enterprises and that under administrative central management a highly developed economic system cannot work effectively.

[5] E. D. Domar, 'The Soviet Collective Farm', *American Economic Review*, September 1966.

[6] I am not discussing here some obvious inadequacies of the marginalist approach applied in both models which significantly reduce the relevance of Ward's comparisons (neither capitalist firm would behave in the way assumed in Ward's and Domar's models).

There is another solution of the problem raised by Mr. Ward—a solution in some aspects similar to Mr. Domar's Model II (with a fixed number of co-operative members or with the possibility of discrimination among the members). This solution was proposed recently by two Czechoslovak economists.[7] It is proposed to discriminate among the workers according to the time of their employment in the same firm. The longer the time of employment in the same firm, the higher would be the dividend. The market behaviour of such a firm is very close to profit maximizing policy. Under such conditions old employees would agree with the increase in the number of employees if the increase of the total profit would be greater than the sum paid out to the new members.

Of course, these conclusions were derived from an abstract model. In reality the situation is a much more complicated one. Although the older employees would be interested in profit maximization we can throw in doubt their ability (or the ability of some council elected by the workers) to make rational economic decisions. Experience shows that even in those cases where we have real co-operatives (small enterprises, especially in the sphere of services and in some industries with a high degree of product differentiation) the collective of co-operative members does *not* fulfil the functions of an entrepreneur. Practical decision-making is entrusted to the director and managerial team. In big firms decision-making (both strategic and operative) is much more complicated, and it cannot be entrusted to any committee elected by the workers. Absolute democracy and lack of hierarchy in production management could effect very negatively the economic efficiency of our production units. This follows from the technological and economic characteristics of all industrially developed systems.

Another—and I think more appropriate—alternative results in some type of 'managerial socialism'. In this case the collective of employees is not regarded as a legal owner of the enterprise. Practical decision-making is entrusted to a team of managers with approximately the same rights (although with a somewhat different preference system) as have the managers of capitalist corporations.

Of course nobody goes so far as to say that managers are owners of the enterprise in the legal sense of this word. The ultimate owner of all resources is society. But the separation of ownership from direct control is accepted as one of the principal features of a developed economic system.

We must now develop an institutional structure which would not

[7] R. Kocanda, P. Pelikán, 'Socialistický podnik jako účastník trhu' (Socialist enterprise as a participant of the market), in *Politická ekonomie* (1967), No. 2.

only be compatible with our new economic model, but which could also play a stimulating role in its functioning. If we consider our new economic system as some kind of 'managerial socialism' we must find some socialist counterpart to the controlling function of shareholders in a capitalist economy. We must establish an organ which could control the behaviour of managerial teams, and represent in the micro-economic sphere the interests of the society as the ultimate owner of all resources in the socialist economy. Traditional central authorities cannot play this role. Their interference is acceptable in the macro sphere only.

Several alternative schemes for such an institution were drawn up by our economists and lawyers. I cannot say now which one will be accepted. It is possible that the composition of such organs would be different in various industries. Most probably it would be a council, members of which would be representatives of superior authorities (e.g. Manufacturing Economic Organization), experts from the Planning Commission, State Bank and various research institutions etc. Of course, top managers would be *ex officio* members of such councils. These representatives would be nominated by the respective organizations for a relatively long period. Their rewards (e.g. in the form of bonuses) would be conditioned by the economic results of the relevant firm.

According to some proposals the Trade Unions and Party Organization of each firm ought to participate in the work of these councils too. But their rights and responsibility are not yet clear. Nevertheless we think that these representatives ought to be elected by the members of the respective organizations and that their post should be an honorary one.

It is clear that the success of our new economic model hinges to a great extent upon the ability of our managerial and administrative personnel. Managers of the necessary 'ability quotient' are really a scarce factor in our country. But the situation is not so bad as it seems from the paper by Mr. Shaffer, published recently in this Journal,[8] e.g. our statistics, quoted by Mr. Shaffer, make no difference between the directors of the firms of various size. Directors of our most important big enterprises usually have university education (or finished courses in technical institutes). But a university degree is not a necessary condition for becoming the director of a small enterprise—with less than 50 employees. Further, we cannot identify managers with the directors only. In the cases where the director did not have the necessary education, there was a managerial team (vice-directors,

[8] H. G. Shaffer, 'The Enterprise Director and the New Economic Model in Czechoslovakia', in *The Journal of Industrial Economics*, November 1966.

etc.) with highly qualified and trained members to whom in reality operational decision-making was entrusted (as far as it was possible within the centralized model). These groups can be (and are) the main source of highly qualified enterprise directors in our new economic system.

2. *Monopoly and competition in the Czechoslovak economy*

The concepts of monopoly and competition did not appear in the economic theory of socialism for many years. But in reality the centralized model implied various monopolies (state monopoly of foreign trade, monopoly power of producers practically in all markets, etc.) and competitive relations also existed. The operation of the centralized model eliminated or weakened competition among producers (meaning those spheres where competition can and must play a very progressive rôle), and sharpened competition among consumers—with several negative consequences.

The problem which is very real in our present situation is not whether competition is desirable or not. Effective competition is a necessary precondition of the successful operation of our new economic model. But difficulties begin when we try to answer the question, what kind of competition and what degree of competition we really want, what kind of market performance is desirable, and whether the existing structure of our industries is compatible with these desirable results.

The structure of our industries is marked by a contradiction between the high degree of administrative, organizational concentration and much lower, insufficient 'genuine' concentration—the concentration of the production process.[9]

We have now two principal types of industrial organizations (Manufacturing Economic Organizations):

1. Associations of enterprises—similar to horizontal trusts in western countries;
2. Leading firms, with or without subsidiary enterprises.

Type 2 is not in contradiction with genuine concentration. In this case we have typical monopolies and oligopolies, and probably various forms of anti-monopoly policy (especially measures against an excessive price increase, or against attempts to lower the quality of the products, etc.) will be applied to ensure the desired performance. The main means of this policy will be stimulation of entry or increasing

[9] For further information about these problems see: Z. Kodet, 'Monopoly and Competition in a Socialist Economy', in *Czechoslovak Economic Papers* (1966), No. 6.

the competition of foreign products. In some exceptional cases it might be decided to use a direct price control.

Much more complicated is type 1, covering the majority of our enterprises. Organizations of this type are artificial and were established by applying the sector principal in a too simplified and schematic manner. Under such an organizational structure there was no possibility of vertical concentration.

In the first version of our New Economic Model these organizations were regarded as a decision-making centre, and practically no room was given for independent policy in the individual firms—members of these associations. This model would lead to some kind of absolute monopoly in every industry, with many negative consequences. For that reason it was criticized in our discussions.

The latest version of our Model shows some signs of an opposite extreme. Each of the enterprises—even the smallest one—is regarded as an independent legal and economic unit, although sometimes geographical conditions and production programmes of several enterprises predestine them for integration. Under such conditions the associations of firms are becoming purely formal administrative bodies and their economic function is not clear.

The latest discussions contain proposals according to which associations of enterprises should become the actual result of a 'genuine' economic concentration. The firms should be permitted to choose their membership in the association on the basis of a consideration of their own advantage (this applies to the horizontal as well as vertical integration), or may, as the case may be, leave the association.

But it is not certain whether the firms themselves—mostly it is the question of small production units—will have sufficient information to be able to make really rational decisions concerning their membership in an association.

Perhaps market mechanism will create some stimuli towards economic concentration, but this process will be very slow and for a relatively long period we shall have enterprise of significantly suboptimal size. Our society now has an opportunity to choose the organizational structure of our industries and it ought to make use of this opportunity in order to create decision-making units of optimum size. But the current state of the theoretical background of our New Economic Model does not provide criteria for such a choice.

In the sphere of pure theory the latest version of our Model implies the concept of perfect competition. It is hoped that the market behaviour of our firms will result in a situation approximating to the Pareto optimum. But in reality our markets are far from being perfect and in the most important industries we have typical monopolies and oligopolies. What we really need as a theoretical background for our policy of competition is a theory which could show as practically attainable social configurations (compatible with socialist economic relations) under which competition could work effectively.

ECONOMIC INSTITUTE OF THE SLOVAK ACADEMY OF SCIENCES

ADVERTISING AND CONCENTRATION: AN EMPIRICAL INVESTIGATION

by H. M. Mann, J. A. Henning and J. W. Meehan, Jr.*

The existence of product differentiation in a market means that buyers will rank the outputs of competing sellers differently. One consequence, economic theory suggests, is that the degree of product differentiation will be positively associated with seller concentration.[1] The empirical evidence concerning this prediction conflicts. On the one hand, Joe Bain found, in a sample of twenty manufacturing industries, that as product differentiation became an increasingly important characteristic of the market, seller concentration rose.[2] On the other hand, Lester Telser found that '. . . the correlation between concentration and advertising is unimpressive'.[3]

The purpose of this paper is to present additional evidence on this hypothesis. As our measure of the degree of product differentiation in each of the industries included in the study, we take traceable advertising expenditures as a percentage of sales revenue. This measure should be, according to the hypothesis, positively correlated with a measure of seller concentration. Our results agree with Bain's findings and tend to support the theoretical prediction referred to earlier.

I. CHARACTERISTICS OF THE SAMPLE

Forty-two firms were chosen from the list of advertisers which *National Advertising Investments* (NAI) compiles in order to report

* The authors thank Harold Petersen for helpful comments.

[1] Economic theory is not clear about the 'cause and effect' aspect of the relationship. On the one hand, it can be argued that the general adoption of sales promotion expenditures by all firms in some initial size distribution may change the distribution such that the sellers whose products attract consumer allegiance will expand their share of the market, while those whose efforts fail to attract buyers will lose their market share. Some empirical support for this reasoning is offered by Leonard W. Weiss, 'Factors in Changing Concentration', *The Review of Economics and Statistics,* February 1963 (70–7). In this paper, Weiss found that increases in concentration between 1947 and 1954 were significantly related to the kind of industry which relies on style or model changes as a means of competing, e.g. consumer durables. On the other hand, high seller concentration may be a necessary condition for intensive sales promotion efforts, for only in situations of market dominance may sales promotion expenditure appear a superior form of rivalry to price competition. Whichever the direction of causation, however, a positive association has significant public policy implications.

[2] Joe Bain, *Industrial Organization,* New York, John Wiley & Sons, Inc. 1959, p. 236. Also see P. K. Else, 'The Incidence of Advertising in Manufacturing Industries', *Oxford Economic Papers,* March 1966, pp. 88–110.

[3] Lester G. Telser, 'Advertising and Competition', *The Journal of Political Economy* December 1964, p. 544.

total advertising expenditures in three media.[4] These firms were assigned to fourteen four-digit industries defined by the Standard Industrial Classification (SIC). In all cases, the firms were dominant in the markets in which they were classified.

The average amount of advertising undertaken by each of the selected firms as a percentage of their sales revenue was computed for the years 1952–56, 1957–61, and 1962–65. From these figures an industry average was obtained which could then be related to the four-firm concentration ratios of the fourteen industries in 1954, 1958 and 1963, as reported by the Bureau of the Census. (See Table I, Appendix.)

Since NAI data cover only three media, *Printers' Ink* and *Advertising Age* data,[5] which include a larger number of media, were also employed as sources for advertising expenditures. These publications, however, report advertising for only the 100 largest advertisers,[6] which meant that sample size could not be kept constant for the three years involved. Many of the firms which were among the 100 largest advertisers in the 1950s were not so placed in the 1960s. The result was that the sample was reduced from fourteen to twelve industries and from forty-two to thirty-one firms for 1963. (See Table 2, Appendix.) These sources, though, permit an alternative set of tests to be made on the relationship between concentration and advertising intensity.

One major limitation of our sample is its size. As an alternative, a larger sample could have been obtained by following Lester Telser's procedure and using the ratios of advertising expenditures to sales revenue obtained from income tax return data. Since the industry classification for these data is that of the Internal Revenue Service (IRS), concentration ratios would have to be constructed by taking an average, weighted or unweighted,[7] of the four-digit SIC industry concentration ratios relevant to the IRS data.

Two considerations favored the smaller sample which permits the use of data at the four-digit SIC level rather than the larger sample using IRS data, requiring aggregation over several such industries. First, there is considerable doubt that the broad IRS industries correspond to economically meaningful markets.[8] The four-digit

[4] The criteria used for selection were that the firms did not produce in regulated industries, employed advertising as the principal means of sales promotion, and were not highly diversified. The latter two criteria, as explained below, reduce the chance for measurement error in the independent variable.

[5] *Printers' Ink* ceased its coverage in 1962.

[6] In 1966, *Advertising Age* started to compile expenditures for the largest 125 advertisers.

[7] Telser employed a weighted average.

[8] The broadness of the IRS industry relative to economically meaningful markets is a point made by Richard D. Heflebower in, Sub-committee on Antitrust & Monopoly, U.S. Senate, *Economic Concentration,* Hearings Part 2, Washington, 1964, p. 790.

industry, on the other hand, though it sometimes tends to be too narrow, represents more closely the theoretical concept of a market or industry.[9]

The second consideration which led to our choice of the smaller sample was the gain achieved in minimizing measurement error in the independent variable. Our estimate of the importance of product differentiation is subject to the following sources of measurement error:

1. The ratio of advertising to sales revenue will tend to understate the intensity of promotional effort where relatively heavy reliance is placed on means of sales promotion other than advertising. An attempt was made to select only those firms which appear to employ advertising as the principal means of influencing consumer preferences, but complete success may not have been achieved.

2. The data on advertising expenditures are understated to some degree because they include only national space and time and do not include all media in some years.

3. All the firms in the sample are diversified. This means that the advertising to sales revenue ratio will be understated in those cases where the advertising is directed only at a part of a firm's product line. For most of the firms, well over 50 per cent of the sales revenue came from the product of the industry to which the firm was assigned. For those firms which had a ratio closer to the 50 per cent, there may be some serious understatement of their advertising effort.

The effect of errors like the above in the independent variable is to cause a downward bias in the estimate of the slope of the least-squares line.[10] At the IRS level of industry classification, it seems likely that measurement error in the advertising to sales revenue ratio will be increased when compared with the four-digit level, particularly because many markets are being combined, only a few of which may be the object of advertising effort.

II. PRESENTATION OF RESULTS

Three regressions using the *NAI* data were computed in order to estimate the relationship between market shares and product differentiation. The first regressed the 1954 concentration ratios on

[9] Joe Bain, *Industrial Organization,* pp. 112–13. Note especially footnote 2, pp. 113–14.

[10] J. Johnston, *Econometric Methods,* New York, McGraw-Hill Book Company, Inc., 1963, pp. 148–50.

the average advertising to sales revenue ratios for the leading firms over the years 1952 and 1956 for fourteen four-digit industries. The second regressed the 1958 concentration ratios on the average advertising to sales revenue ratios for the leading firms over the years 1957 to 1961 for fourteen four-digit industries. The third regressed the 1963 concentration ratios on the average advertising to sales revenue ratios for the leading firms over the years 1962 to 1965 for fourteen four-digit industries.

Table I shows the results.

TABLE I

REGRESSIONS OF CONCENTRATION RATIOS, Y, AND ADVERTISING EXPENDITURES AS A PERCENTAGE OF SALES REVENUE, X, FOR FOURTEEN FOUR-DIGIT INDUSTRIES, 1954, 1958 AND 1963*

Year	*Regression of* Y *on* X	*Correlation coefficients*	*Coefficients of determination*
1954	Y = 42.01 + 8.95 X (3.55)	·59	·35
1958	Y = 36.23 + 10.80 X (2.97)	·72	·52
1963	Y = 35.87 + 9.64 X (3.04)	·68	·46

* Y = four-firm concentration in per cent; X = advertising expenditure divided by sales revenue in per cent.

Table II contains the results for the three regressions, using data from *Printers' Ink* and *Advertising Age*.

The correlation coefficients and the regression equations in Tables I and II show a positive relationship between concentration and the proxy for product differentiation, average advertising to sales revenue ratios for the leading firms over a period mostly closely corresponding to the concentration ratio employed. In Table I, the slopes of the least square lines are significant at the .03, .01, and .01 levels for 1954, 1958 and 1963, respectively, using a two-tailed test. In Table II, the levels of significance are .15, .04, and .08 for 1954, 1958 and 1963, respectively, using a two-tailed test. Since the hypothesis concerning the related variables indicates that the association will be positive, a one-tailed test can be used. The results in Table II are then significant at the .075, .02, and .04 levels in 1954, 1958 and 1963, respectively.

The significance of the above statistical analysis is further augmented by the fact that the three regressions in Table I are quite similar to one another. This similarity also characterizes the three regressions in Table II. Such similarity can be interpreted to mean that the separate regressions are repetitive experiments from the same population which increases the likelihood that Tables I and II measure a systematic and persistent relationship between concentration and the advertising sales ratios of the leading firms. To confirm this, a well-known test[11] of the hypothesis of a common regression was applied to the data in each of the tables. In each case, the hypothesis of repetitive sampling from the same population could

TABLE II

REGRESSIONS OF CONCENTRATION RATIOS, Y, AND ADVERTISING EXPENDITURES AS A PERCENTAGE OF SALES REVENUE, X, FOR FOURTEEN FOUR-DIGIT INDUSTRIES, 1954 AND 1958 AND TWELVE FOUR-DIGIT INDUSTRIES, 1963*

Year	*Regression of* Y *on* X	*Correlation coefficients*	*Coefficients of determination*
1954	$Y = 44.88 + 4.23\,X$ (2.69)	.41	.17
1958	$Y = 37.05 + 4.81\,X$ (2.04)	.56	.31
1963	$Y = 38.03 + 3.12\,X$ (1.53)	.54	.29

* Y = Four-firm concentration in per cent; X = advertising expenditure divided by sales revenue in per cent.

not be rejected; that is, the observed differences among the regression equations can easily be due to sampling error.[12]

Both sets of equations in Tables I and II show a marked relationship between concentration and advertising intensity, particularly in view of the fact that the data employed would have a tendency to bias the regression coefficients toward zero. The coefficients of determination suggest that enough of the variance in concentration is explained by advertising intensity to raise an issue for public policy.[13]

III. CONCLUSIONS

Economic theory predicts that product differentiation will be positively associated with seller concentration. Joe Bain confirms

[11] C. R. Rao, *Linear Statistical Inference and Its Application,* New York, John Wiley & Sons, Inc., 1965, pp. 237–9.

[12] The critical F-value for rejection at the .05 level was 5.74 and 5.73 for Tables I and II, respectively. The F-values obtained were only 1.54 and 1.49, respectively.

[13] Joe Bain finds that product differentiation is probably the most important barrier to entry into the twenty manufacturing industries which he studied. Joe Bain, *Barriers to New Competition,* p. 216. Furthermore, note Donald Turner's (Assistant Attorney General in charge of the Antitrust Division, Dept. of Justice) concern with advertising as a barrier to entry. 'Justice in a lather over soap ad outlays', *Business Week,* November 5th, 1966, p. 44.

the prediction by an inspection of the relationship between seller concentration and a qualitative ranking of the importance of product differentiation in twenty manufacturing industries. Lester Telser's finding that concentration and advertising intensity are not closely related suggests no support for the hypothesis.

This paper employed the same kind of variables as did Telser, but measured them in a way which probably reduces the chance of measurement error. The results support Bain, indicating that the intensity of sales promotion efforts must receive high priority from any general policy which seeks to establish competitive markets.

BOSTON COLLEGE

APPENDIX

TABLE I

NAI DATA

FOUR-FIRM CONCENTRATION RATIO AND AVERAGE PERCENTAGE OF TRACEABLE ADVERTISING[a] TO SALES REVENUE[b] FOR THE LEADING FIRMS IN FOURTEEN 4-DIGIT INDUSTRIES, 1952 TO 1956, 1957 TO 1961, AND 1962 TO 1965

Industry and firm	*Four-firm concentration Ratio, 1963*	*Average annual percentage of advertising to sales revenue 1962–65; 3 Media*	*Four-firm concentration Ratio, 1958*	*Average annual percentage of advertising to sales revenue 1957–61: 3 Media*	*Four-firm concentration Ratio, 1954*	*Average annual percentage of advertising to sales revenue 1952–56: 3 Media*
Chewing Gum	90		88		86	
Wrigley (Wm., Jr., Co.)		1.48		1.00		2.56
American Chicle[c]		—		5.33		4.32
Beech-Nut Life Savers		2.55		3.79		.58
Soap	72		90		85	
Procter & Gamble		4.25		4.11		4.74
Colgate-Palmolive		4.33		5.29		5.95
Pens	48		51		57	
Parker Pen		3.20		2.31		4.05
Sheaffer		2.74		5.00		5.55
Scripto		2.62		2.17		2.65
Cigarettes	80		79		82	
R. J. Reynolds		3.92		3.26		3.33
American Tobacco		4.38		2.86		2.72
Liggett & Meyers		6.85		4.72		3.73
Philip Morris		5.82		4.26		3.77

TABLE I (*Contd.*)

Liquor	58		60		64	
Distillers-Seagrams		3.96		3.74		2.75
National Distillers		1.56		2.15		2.15
Schenley Industries		2.07		1.84		2.89
Hiram Walker		2.68		2.60		1.64
Biscuits	59		65		71	
National Biscuit		2.34		2.31		1.01
Sunshine Biscuit		0.38		0.65		0.35
Canned Fruits & Vegetables	24		29		28	
California Packing		1.48		1.16		1.10
Libby-McNeil		0.93		0.78		0.58
Stokely-VanCamp		0.58		0.63		0.74
Tires & Tubes	70		74		79	
Goodyear		0.97		0.82		0.59
B. F. Goodrich		0.53		0.48		0.42
Firestone		0.43		0.44		0.42
U.S. Rubber		0.52		0.30		0.24
Cereal	86		83		88	
Kellogg		5.54		5.05		4.10
Quaker Oats		2.85		2.69		2.34
Brewing	34		28		27	
Anheuser-Busch		0.93		0.97		0.56
Pabst Brewing		0.38		0.83[d]		0.89[d]
Falstaff Brewing		3.11		1.08		1.19
Schlitz		2.28		2.70		2.32[d]
Soft Drinks[g]	62		55		53	
Coca Cola		1.73		1.17		1.82
Pepsi Cola		2.22		2.18		3.05
Canada Dry		2.87[e]		2.19		1.65
Flour[h]	70		75		73	
General Mills		3.71		4.13		3.15
Pillsbury		2.70		2.67		2.36

TABLE I (*Contd.*)

Industry and firm	*Four-firm concentration Ratio, 1963*	*Average annual percentage of advertising to sales revenue 1962–65: 3 Media*	*Four-firm concentration Ratio, 1958*	*Average annual percentage of advertising to sales revenue 1957–61: 3 Media*	*Four-firm concentration Ratio, 1954*	*Average annual percentage of advertising to sales revenue 1952–56: 3 Media*
Baking	23		22		20	
Continental Baking		0.10		0.19		0.57
Interstate Bakeries		0.07		0.11		0.06[f]
Meat Packing	31		34		39	
Armour		0.63		0.42		0.24
Swift		0.15		0.21		0.30
Wilson & Co.		0.20		0.09		0.08
John Morrell		0.10		0.07		0.11

[a] The years 1952 to 1954 include the advertising expenditure in 4 media, while the years 1955 to 1965 include only 3 media.

[b] The sales revenue figures for the cigarette, liquor and beer companies are net of excise taxes.

[c] American Chicle merged with Warner-Lambert Pharmaceutical Company in 1962.

[d] Advertising data were available for the years 1956–65. For Pabst, advertising expenditures were unavailable for 1959.

[e] Advertising expenditures were unavailable for 1963.

[f] Advertising data were available for the years 1954–56.

[g] The four-digit class 'flavoring' was used rather than 'bottled soft drinks' because the former more closely represents the facts on actual concentration in the market. See Lester G. Telser, 'Advertising and Competition', *The Journal of Political Economy*, December 1964, p. 545.

[h] The four-digit class 'blended and prepared flour' was used rather than 'flour mills' because it is the former product which the flour companies principally advertise.

Sources:

Advertising Expenditures: *National Advertising Investments, Annual Issues*, 1952–65.

Sales Revenue: *Moody's Industrials.*

Concentration Ratio: Subcommittee on Antitrust and Monopoly, U.S. Senate, *Concentration Ratios* in *Manufacturing Industry* 1963, Washington, 1966.

APPENDIX

TABLE II

PRINTERS' INK—ADVERTISING AGE DATA

FOUR-FIRM CONCENTRATION RATIO AND AVERAGE PERCENTAGE OF TRACEABLE ADVERTISING[a] TO SALES REVENUE[b] FOR THE LEADING FIRMS IN FOURTEEN 4-DIGIT INDUSTRIES, 1952 TO 1956, 1957 TO 1961 AND 1962 TO 1965

Industry and firm	*Four-firm concentration Ratio, 1963*	*Average annual percentage of advertising to sales revenue 1962–65: 7 Media*	*Four-firm concentration Ratio, 1958*	*Average annual percentage of advertising to sales revenue 1957–61: 7 Media*	*Four-firm concentration Ratio, 1954*	*Average annual percentage of advertising to sales revenue 1952–56: 7 Media*
Chewing Gum	90		88		86	
Wrigley (Wm., Jr., Co.)		15.6		9.1		7.5
American Chicle		12.3		9.4		5.1
Beech-Nut Life Savers		10.2		—		—
Soap	72		90		85	
Procter & Gamble		11.1		7.6		6.1
Colgate-Palmolive		10.5		7.8		8.0
Pens	48		51		57	
Parker Pen		—		7.4[c]		4.7[c]
Sheaffer		—		6.3[c]		6.4[c]
Scripto		—		7.4[d]		4.6[d]
Cigarettes	80		79		82	
R. J. Reynolds		7.1		4.7		4.3
American Tobacco		8.8		4.4		3.5
Liggett & Meyers		11.7		7.1		4.7
Philip Morris		8.7		6.8		6.7
Liquor	58		60		64	
Distillers-Seagrams		12.0		9.1		7.8
National Distillers		4.1		5.8		6.3
Schenley Industries		13.8		7.4		8.4
Hiram Walker		8.6		5.2		4.2

TABLE II (*contd.*)

Industry and firm	*Four-firm concentration Ratio 1963*	*Average annual percentage of advertising to sales revenue 1962–65: 7 Media*	*Four-firm concentration Ratio, 1958*	*Average annual percentage of advertising to sales revenue 1957–61: 7 Media*	*Four-firm concentration Ratio, 1964*	*Average annual percentage of advertising to sales revenue 1952–56: 7 Media*
Biscuits	59		65		71	
National Biscuit		6.1		3.3		2.0
Sunshine Biscuit		—		1.4[c]		1.4[c]
Canned Fruits & Vegetables	24		29		28	
California Packing		—		1.6		1.4
Libby-McNeil		—		1.2[c]		1.0[c]
Stokeley-VanCamp		—		1.5[c]		1.4[c]
Tires & Tubes	70		74		79	
Goodyear		1.8		0.8		0.8
B. F. Goodrich		1.9		0.8		0.7
Firestone		1.9		0.7		0.6
U.S. Rubber		2.2		0.6		0.5
Cereal	86		83		80	
Kellogg		12.2		8.0		5.4
Quaker Oats		5.4		4.4		3.5
Brewing	34		28		27	
Anheuser-Busch		8.4		4.0		2.8
Pabst Brewing		9.8		6.0		4.5
Falstaff Brewing		10.6		5.0		7.8
Schlitz		13.9		6.6[e]		5.5[e]
Soft Drinks[g]	62		55		53	
Coca Cola		7.2		4.2		4.2
Pepsi Cola		10.2		6.4		4.9
Canada Dry		—		4.8[c]		4.2[c]
Flour[h]	70		75		73	
General Mills		7.8		5.4		3.8
Pillsbury		7.0		4.7		2.8

TABLE II (*contd*).

Baking	23		22		20	
Continental Baking		2.7		3.5		1.8
Interstate Bakeries		—		2.0[c]		1.3[c]
Meat Packing	31		34		39	
Armour		1.0		0.7		0.4
Swift		0.6[f]		0.4		0.5
Wilson & Co.		—		0.3[c]		0.3[c]
John Morrell		—		0.3[c]		0.3[c]

[a] The years 1952 to 1954 include the advertising expenditure in 8 media, while the years 1955 to 1961 include only 7 media. The advertising data for the years 1962 to 1965 include 'unmeasured media' (expenditures on direct mail, net work and spot radio premiums, etc.), as well as expenditures traceable to major media.

[b] The sales revenue figures for the cigarette, liquor, and beer companies are net of excise taxes.

[c] Advertising data were available for the years 1952–59.

[d] Advertising data were available for the years 1952–57.

[e] Advertising data were available for the years 1956–61.

[f] Advertising data were unavailable for the year 1963.

[g] The four-digit class 'flavoring' was used rather than 'bottled soft drinks' because the former more closely represents the facts on actual concentration in the market. See Lester G. Telser, 'Advertising and Competition', *The Journal of Political Economy*, December 1964, p. 545.

[h] The four-digit class 'blended and prepared flour' was used rather than 'Flour Mills' because it is the former product which the flour companies principally advertise.

Sources:

Advertising Expenditures: *Printers' Ink, Advertisers' Guide to Marketing.*
Issues: *For 1963* (August 1963); *For 1960* (October 1959); *For 1959* (October 1958); and *For 1957* (August 1956).
Advertising Age.
Issues: August 26th, 1963
August 31st, 1964
August 30th, 1965
August 29th, 1966

Sales Revenue: *Moody's Industrials.*

Concentration Ratio: Subcommittee on Antitrust and Monopoly, U.S. Senate, *Concentration Ratios in Manufacturing Industry*, 1963, Washington, 1966.

REGULATION OF INTERNATIONAL LINER SHIPPING AND 'FREEDOM OF THE SEAS'*

by DANIEL MARX, JR.

DISSATISFACTION with the rates charged by ocean liners to carry cargo between nations has long been expressed in various parts of the world, but recently complainants have become increasingly articulate. Unless an internationally acceptable means of adjusting these complaints can be achieved, freedom of entry to many of the world's ports—an important aspect of 'freedom of the seas'—will be seriously threatened. Thirty-two developing nations recommended in 1964 that the United Nations establish appropriate international machinery on an inter-governmental level 'to tackle matters of maritime transport and ocean freight rates'.[1] They were supported by fifteen additional nations (three with reservations), and opposed by the leading industrial and maritime powers.[2] Although the United States was among the dissenters at the United Nations Conference on Trade and Development held at Geneva in 1964 (later referred to as UNCTAD) to the proposal to establish international machinery to 'tackle' maritime matters and ocean freight rates, the Congress of the United States is not pleased with cargo rates. The Joint Economic Committee of the Congress (subsequently referred to as JEC) has expressed its dismay at finding many freight rates on U.S. exports to be higher than those applicable to imports of the same commodity moving in the opposite direction, and that export rates from the U.S. are higher than the export rates from other industrial countries to a common foreign (e.g. Latin American) destination.[3] The JEC strongly recommends more rigorous enforcement of legislation authorizing the Federal Maritime Commission (FMC) to disapprove ocean freight rates that discriminate against the United States, more vigorous scrutiny of anti-competitive agreements, and suggests that consideration should be given to holding an international meeting of the major maritime nations to

* The author gratefully acknowledges a research grant from the Amos Tuck School of Business Administration, Dartmouth College.

[1] United Nations, Conference on Trade and Development (hereafter referred to as UNCTAD). *Final Act and Report* (Annex F, 'Report of the Third Committee,' Appendix II, Report of the Working Party on Shipping), (New York: United Nations, 1964), p. 223.

[2] Ibid., p. 229.

[3] U.S. Senate, Joint Economic Committee, Congress of the United States, *Discriminatory Ocean Freight Rates and the Balance of Payments*, 89th Congress, 1st session, S. Report, No. 1 (Washington: U.S. Government Printing Office, 1965), pp. 14–16; 18–19. Referred to hereafter as JEC.

seek a cooperative solution to the vexing problems of obtaining adequate information on anti-competitive agreements and on the cost and profitability of shipping companies.[4] A meeting limited to the maritime powers will not satisfy the developing nations, but is indicative of the difficulty the United States is encountering in its attempts to regulate unilaterally an industry whose participants and customers are very often nationals domiciled in other countries and subject to their jurisdictions.

Australia, New Zealand and the Union of South Africa, however, have managed to 'control' freight rates on some routes by instituting agreements under which shipping conferences on these routes have to negotiate the general level of freight rates with government-sponsored associations of shippers on the basis of formulae which include consideration of costs and the rate of return on capital employed. The lines submit audited voyage accounts to an accountant appointed by the shippers upon which an upward or downward revision of rates is negotiated.[5]

Traditionally, rates have been set by shipping conferences, cartel-like groups of liner shipping companies operating vessels on a given route, in order to minimize the dangers of cut-throat-rate wars and to maximize profits.[6] Some actual or potential price competition remains as tramps or vessels operating irregularly (in contrast to the more or less regularly advertised sailings to specified ports by the liner companies), and independent or non-conference liners may enter a service and charge rates below those quoted by the conference tariff. Various tying arrangements are offered shippers that remain loyal to the conference members in order to prevent, or at least minimize, competition from tramps and non-conference liner services. Deferred rebates to loyal shippers or lower rates to shippers who sign exclusive patronage contracts are the tying arrangements usually employed. (The deferred rebate is unlawful in the United States.) These conference arrangements have provided the member lines with varying degrees of monopoly power which, when great enough, may be abused. But the conferences have provided a procedure for reconciling the views of member carriers flying various national flags without directly involving their governments in the negotiations, thereby minimizing international friction and permitting commercial decisions to be taken somewhat more rapidly. Countries without a merchant marine, however, have no voice

[4] Ibid., pp. 3–6, 28–9.

[5] Arvid Frihagen, *Linjekonferanser Og Kartel—Lovgivning* (Shipping Conferences and Anti-Trust Laws). (Oslo: Scandinavian University Books, 1963), pp. 466–8, 470.

[6] For a description and evaluation of shipping conferences, see Daniel Marx, Jr., *International Shipping Cartels* (Princeton University Press, 1953).

in conference deliberations and even those who operate shipping sometimes feel that the conference-determined rates are inimical to their trading interests, especially if their shipping is privately owned. This has led to increased interest on the part of many hitherto non-maritime nations in establishing national-flag merchant fleets to operate on their major trade routes, or to threats to regulate ocean rates unilaterally or by an international agency that is to be created for this purpose.

Despite its shortcomings, the conference system is generally regarded as a necessity or at least as a lesser evil than the rate instability and possibly the rate wars which have often characterized liner shipping when a conference has broken down. A 'common measure of understanding' reached by the UNCTAD in 1964 at Geneva 'agreed that the Liner Conference system was necessary in order to secure stable rates and regular services'.[7] The Congress of the United States has studied the Conference system repeatedly over the past fifty years. The Shipping Act of 1916 followed a report made by the Alexander Committee of the House of Representatives and among other things exempted shipping conferences from U.S. antitrust laws provided the Conference agreement was approved by the Government's maritime regulatory agency.[8] More recently the House Merchant Marine and Fisheries Committee in 1961, the Antitrust Subcommittee of the House Judiciary Committee in 1962, and the Joint Economic Committee in 1965 all recognized the usefulness of the conference system, but all expressed dissatisfaction with various aspects of it and recommended stricter regulation.[9]

In 1961, the U.S. Congress gave the Federal Maritime Commision broader authority over all rates and conference practices. This legislation included a provision directing the FMC to disapprove rates that are detrimental to U.S. commerce.[10] Because of the jurisdictional conflicts inherent in the unilateral regulation of freight charges involving the trade of more than one country, the Commission did not immediately attempt to exercise this authority. In 1963, the Joint Economic Committee concerned with the importance of export expansion as a means of reducing the nation's balance of payments deficits turned its attention to ocean rates. Goaded by

[7] UNCTAD, op. cit., p. 228.

[8] 39 Stat. 733 (1917).

[9] U.S. Congress, House Committee of Merchant Marine and Fisheries, *Providing for the Operation of Steamship Conferences*, 87th Congress, 1st session, H. Report, #498, pp. 4, 7, 13. U.S. Congress, House Committee on the Judiciary, Antitrust Subcommittee, *The Ocean Freight Industry*, 87th Congress, 2nd session, pursuant to H. Resolution, #56, pp. 10–13; and JEC, op. cit., pp. 22–5.

[10] P. L. 87–346, October 3rd, 1961.

this Congressional pressure, the FMC began a series of studies of rates charged by conference and non-conference steamship lines sailing between this country and Europe and between the U.S. and Japan on some 100 commodities.[11] The Commission also started a program of pilot studies of some 40 additional commodities selected because of their importance or because of complaints by shippers. This action was resisted by the steamship industry, and by the principal maritime nations on the grounds that it was an infringement of their sovereignity. The United Kingdom went so far as to adopt legislation in July 1964, which made it unlawful for British steamship lines to obey the American demands for documents without the express approval of the Minister of Transport.[12]

This impasse was then discussed at subsequent sessions of the Organization for Economic Co-operation and Development (OECD), and in mid-December 1964, a compromise was reached under which 14 of the world's major maritime nations, including the U.S., agreed to employ their good offices to induce ship-owners to transmit the requested information to the OECD which would circulate it on a confidential basis among nations subscribing to the accord.[13]

Impatient with the time required by the FMC to obtain the information, the Joint Economic Committee reached conclusions based on hearings it had held and on a few samples of rate disparities inbound and outbound from the U.S. In January 1965, the JEC concluded that the international ocean freight rate structure is weighted against U.S. exports and that this country's exports bear most of the cost of vessel operation, even on routes where imports approximate exports in quantity and value. The Committee stressed that ocean freight rates are a significant factor in the cost of international trade. In 1962, they represented 12 per cent of the value of U.S. exports and 10 per cent of the value of U.S. imports, weightier in many cases than the U.S. Tariff which averaged 7 per cent of the value of imports in the same year.[14] The JEC also observed that evidence presented to it revealed that it costs more to ship U.S. exports to South America, Africa and India than it costs to ship comparable products to these destinations from Europe or Japan even after allowance for differences in mileage and loading and port costs.[15] The Committee suspected these disparities to be

[11] Federal Maritime Commission, *Third Annual Report*, 1964, p. 11.
[12] JEC, op. cit., p. 32.
[13] Edward A. Morrow, 'U.S. Obtains Pact on Freight Rates', *New York Times*, December 16th, 1965.
[14] JEC, op. cit., p. 9.
[15] Ibid., p. 13.

caused in part by the fact that foreign lines, many of whom also operate from Europe or Japan, outnumber U.S. flag lines in many shipping conferences serving the U.S., and also in part to American cargo preference legislation that reserves to U.S. vessels most government-owned or financed shipments.[16]

The effect of these observations on the developing countries can be easily imagined, and their concern will certainly not be lessened by the rejection of the European Maritime Powers in July 1965, of a demand by the United States that information about trans-Atlantic freight rate disparities, collected by the OECD, be made public.[17]

Latin-American countries have long questioned the system of liner rate making and at an Inter-American Maritime Conference in 1940 the U.S. government went to great pains to convince the representatives of the other American republics of the dangers and difficulties of regulating international ocean cargo rates. The Latin-American nations were not wholly convinced, or at least didn't remain so, as they joined other developing countries at the UNCTAD in 1964 in recommending international surveillance of maritime matters. The developing countries stressed the importance of shipping to their economies resulting from their heavy dependence on sea communications with the world's major trading centers and the burden of shipping services on their balances of payments. They suggested *inter alia* that freight rates on their traditional export cargoes should be fixed at fair and reasonable rates, that freight rates on new items of exports from developing nations should be granted low, promotional rates, and that tying arrangements and other conference practices should be regulated. They also maintained the solution of their ocean transport problems may often require the establishment of their own merchant fleets.[18] The reply of the industrial maritime nations drafted by Sweden, contained much economic sense, but the statement that 'free competition between shipowners' is the way to ensure efficient transport at lowest possible cost[19] could hardly be considered a valid description of the conference system of rate making, tying arrangements and the like, nor could it be considered persuasive or reassuring by the complainants.

The Shipping Committee of UNCTAD again raised the question of investigating freight rates at its November 1965 meeting, but in

[16] Ibid., pp. 20, 35.
[17] Edward A. Morrow, 'Congress Report stirs Dispute', *New York Times,* August 11th, 1965.
[18] UNCTAD, op. cit., p. 222.
[19] Ibid., p. 226.

order to avoid an open split with the maritime countries decided to postpone action until July 1966, pending a report by the United Nations' Staff describing the approach and methods such a rate investigation should take.

In all these hearings, investigations and discussions, the questions 'who pays the freight?' and 'how much difference do freight costs make?' are rarely, if ever, raised. The convention generally employed by balance of payments statisticians is that the importing nation pays, and while this no doubt is frequently the case, the incidence of freight charges, like the final resting place of taxes, is often indeterminate as it depends on the market structure of the commodity being shipped. The seller may in some cases absorb the freight cost. Too little is known of these market structures, but they are not necessarily the same for all countries exporting the same commodity and they differ in time as well as place. It is interesting to note that the Joint Economic Committee, the developing nations as well as Australia, New Zealand and South Africa, appear to be primarily concerned with export rates, although the latter did make reference to the importance to them of imported industrial goods, especially those required for development purposes. And, in a recent investigation of U.K.-Canada conferences, the Canadian Restrictive Trade Practices Commission observed 'The cost of ocean transportation significantly affects the placing of Canadian goods in foreign markets in competition with foreign producers. Also, ocean freights costs enter into the cost of imported goods, some of which are necessary components in articles further processed in Canada.'[20] The emphasis in these occasional references to import rates on industrial components and industrial goods required for development reinforce the general impression that little concern is felt over import rates in general and that high rates may, in fact, be welcomed as a form of protection for domestic import-competing industries. This is explicitly recognized by the Union of South Africa whose customs regulations permit an increase in the tariff on goods imported at especially low rates if the import causes injury to domestic producers of the same goods.[21]

The importance of freight rates is often substantial, but their significance can easily be exaggerated. Many factors affect an export sale, and ocean freight costs are frequently of minor importance. Foreign import duties, prohibitions against imports, currency restrictions, national habits and preferences, lower costs of

[20] Canada, Department of Justice, Restrictive Trade Practices Commission, *Shipping Conference Arrangements and Practices* (Ottawa: Queen's Printer, 1965), p. 99.
[21] Frihagen, op. cit., p. 467.

production abroad, credit terms, promptness of delivery, and the uniqueness of the exported product are among the other variables. And to these should be added the cost of inland transportation in the importing country. Some years ago a study showed that it often cost more to haul a shipment from San Juan, Puerto Rico, to the interior of this small island, than the ocean freight cost of carrying it from New York to San Juan, and, in at least one case it actually cost more to haul goods from uptown San Juan to the docks, than to carry it from San Juan to New York.[22] In short, ocean transport costs are often important and at times may be critical, but a great deal of research will be required to determine their actual significance and to ascertain who, in the final analysis, actually pays the freight.

If rates are to be consciously regulated, it would not only be highly desirable to have answers to the foregoing questions in order to possess some knowledge of the economic business implications of regulations but it is also important to have an understanding of the competing theories of rate determination. Should rates merely cover or slightly exceed out-of-pocket costs, should they cover such costs by an amount sufficient to cover each shipment's proportionate share of the supplementary capital and overhead expenses, or should they be based essentially on demand, i.e. on what the traffic will bear. When there is unused capacity a strong case can be made for marginal costs or out-of-pocket pricing, but when unused capacity is prevalent, as is often the case in liner shipping, such a pricing policy would drive out of business vessels that may be needed in other seasons of the year or in years when the volume of traffic is heavier. By the same token, however, this method would help eliminate chronic excess capacity. To charge each unit of cargo its proportionate share of capital and overhead costs will help maintain carrying capacity needed at other times, and so may charging what the traffic will bear. Charging each unit its proportional share of the supplementary costs has an aspect of equity, but it might well require rates too high for some commodities, thereby preventing their movement, and leave the capital and overhead expenses to be shared by a smaller volume of business. However, if rates are based on what the traffic will bear, there is no assurance that too many ships will not be operated. Rates based largely on demand usually cover out-of-pocket costs and as much more as the traffic will bear and competition permits. This allows some commodities to move that might not otherwise and helps spread the supplementary costs over a larger volume of traffic. The determination of 'what the

[22] Samuel E. Eastman and Daniel Marx, Jr., *Ships and Sugar* (Baltimore: University of Puerto Rico Press, 1953), pp. 129–30 and Chap. IX.

traffic will bear', however, is a highly contentious subject. It is this controversy that underlies much of the agitation for rate regulation. Such differential pricing requires a fairly high degree of monopoly power and this is precisely what the conference system provides. It is inevitable that not everyone will be satisfied with the decisions of those in a position to exercise the power to so differentiate or discriminate in favor of one commodity, by charging it less than its full share of the supplementary costs, and to discriminate against another commodity by charging it more. To complicate matters further, it is not always possible to allocate supplementary costs in a manner that does not seem capriciously arbitrary.

A vessel, like a sheep, produces simultaneously or jointly more than one product, and it is quite as arbitrary to assign so much overhead and capital expense to a vessel's lifting capacity and so much to the space it has available as it would be to say one-third or one-tenth or any other fraction of raising a sheep represented the cost of growing wool and the remainder the cost of mutton, hide, etc. Much the same can be said of cost allocation between the outbound and inbound portions of a voyage. Efficient operation of vessels requires a certain balance between bulky cargo and heavy cargo and between inbound and outbound loads. To obtain the optimum balance it is frequently necessary to charge rates that will attract the types of cargo required for maximum operating efficiency and this results in differentiating in the rates per unit of shipment.[23] Such price discrimination is not uncommon in either industrial or transport pricing. It is frowned on, however, by courts and regulatory agencies in the United States when it is determined to be unfairly or unduly discriminatory, a determination which, needless to say, is often very difficult to make.

Objective consideration of these disputable matters is difficult at best, and the difficulty is exacerbated when conflicting national interests are added to competing commercial interests. The close identification of many countries with their merchant marines

[23] The recent development of 'container shipping', which provides for the packing of goods in large containers that are then loaded directly onto a vessel from road or rail facilities and vice versa, may restrict the ability of ocean carriers to differentiate in the rates charged for transporting certain commodities when different goods are packed in the same container and when 'freight all kinds' or 'box' rates are quoted. 'Containerization' is progressing rapidly in shipping between the industrialized nations, especially on the North Atlantic route, but it may spread. A meeting, under United Nations auspices, to be held in London in May, 1968, to aid developing countries in planning transport programs will explore their use of containers. The future importance of 'box' rates is, however, not yet clear. If 'containerization' *and* 'box' rates were to become the customary methods of shipping most commodities, rate regulation would become somewhat less difficult. It is even conceivable that the need for conferences might decline and that competition might become an acceptable market structure for liner shipping. At present, this appears to be a long way off.

further aggravates the problem. The number of state-owned fleets has increased substantially since the Second World War as a result of the spread of socialism and the difficulties of financing private companies in developing countries. At least half of the twenty new national flag lines organized since 1949 were initially financed and are still largely controlled by governments.[24] Mixed ownership situations are also common—the merchant fleets of France, Italy, India and Spain are partially government-owned. The United States, in view of the size of the Military Sea Transport Service and the government-owned reserve fleet, might also be considered among the major maritime nations that have a partially government-owned merchant fleet.

In addition, the United States, along with many other nations, subsidizes the operation of its privately owned merchant marine. Whether or not government participation is justified on strategic or commercial grounds or both, the involvement of governments with their merchant shipping is both intimate and delicate.

Government support is, with increasing frequency, taking the form of cargo preference requirements or inducements to favor national flag ships. In addition to operating subsidies, which now cost the U.S. taxpayers approximately $200 million per year, the United States requires that 50 per cent or more of all its government-owned or financed cargoes must be shipped on U.S. flag vessels. The result is that more than 55 per cent of export tonnage and over 5 per cent of the imports carried by U.S. flag liners stemmed from this country's cargo preference laws. (Preference cargoes constituted more than 95 per cent of the exports and 57 per cent of the imports carried on U.S. flag tramp vessels).[25]

The increase in the number of independent nations has almost been matched by the increase in the number of national flag merchant marines. Whereas there were 46 maritime nations in 1949, there were at least 66 in 1963.[26] Developing countries, dissatisfied with their heavy dependence on the ships of developed maritime nations and their consequent lack of voice in ship operating and freight rate decisions, have inaugurated services under their own flags. The difficulty of operating these new fleets remuneratively is often great and aggravated by the refusal of conferences to admit newcomers to membership. Consequently, the precedent of U.S.

[24] Samuel A. Lawrence, *United States Merchant Shipping Policies and Politics* (Washington: The Brookings Institution, 1966), p. 100.

[25] U.S. Department of Commerce, Maritime Administration, *Contribution of Federal Aid Programs to the Oceanborne Foreign Trade of the United States 1959–1962* (Washington, 1964).

[26] Samuel A. Lawrence, op. cit., p. 98.

cargo preference laws has been siezed upon to apply cargo preference requirements to shipments to and from several developing countries. United States' objections to the application of flag preference to strictly commercial cargoes in which the government has no ownership or financial interest has, for the most part, seemed to be a distinction without a difference to the developing countries. In part, this may have been due to a voluntary deafness, but since the governments of such countries often have a stake in the marketing of primary products, in social overhead investments in roads, railways, utilities, etc., as well as in industrial development projects, the difference as well as the distinction often becomes increasingly blurred if not wholly invalid.

The economic advisability of developing countries using their scarce capital and foreign exchange to buy sufficient merchant vessels to carry a significant share of their commerce can be questioned, as can the justification of many of their suspicions concerning their being disadvantaged by dependence on the shipping of other nations. But the sovereign right to have ships under their own flag cannot be denied. If such vessels have a difficult time operating profitably in an industry chronically characterized by long periods of overcapacity, the incentive to enact cargo preference requirements becomes great, and the pooling of cargoes or revenues with other carriers a likely result. This may not improve either the rate structure for the developing country's shipments or its balance of payments, but it does make it a party to decisions affecting its foreign trade.

When nations, both of whom are supporting their merchant fleets, trade with each other, the solution has sometimes taken the form of bilateral treaties or of pooling arrangements. U.S. flag lines have entered several pools, especially with Latin-American lines, in which they have agreed to the number of sailings each may make, or have divided tonnage or revenues on the basis of some agreed formula.[27]

The more direct the participation of governments in these matters the greater is the tendency to bilateral solutions that may exclude efficient low-cost carriers operated by other nations, and the greater is the opportunity for international friction. The conference system, as previously mentioned helps to avoid national confrontations, and by stressing commercial considerations narrows the area of dispute to more amenable differences than when political problems are also involved. The conference system when faced with the appropriate amount of actual or potential competition not only mutes national

[27] See for example FMC (and its predecessors) Agreements 7796–7; 7797–5; 8505 and 9040.

differences but also provides a reasonably satisfactory economic solution. But when such competition is excessive or when it is inadequate the system leaves much to be desired. The fear or existence of inadequate competition is the more prevalent complaint, and has produced the agitation previously noted to supervise or regulate the practices of shipping conferences.

The complexity of the problem and the opportunities thus provided for reasonable persons, not to mention unreasonable parties, to disagree are, as already noted, enormous. Let us therefore examine briefly the more likely forces regulation can assume. The present system depends primarily upon self-regulation by the conferences. That there have only been a few attempts to date to regulate ocean freight rates unilaterally is largely due to the fear of internationally inconsistent decisions, and consequently the conference system has been widely condoned. Service competition among the conference member lines and actual or potential rate competition from independent carriers remains the most effective force now operating to keep ocean freight rates at a reasonable level. Dissatisfaction with conference self-regulation *cum* competition arises when competition is too strong and when it is insufficient. When competition is too vigorous the conference control will tend to break down and rate instability, rebating, and other palpably discriminatory practices and charges are likely to ensue. This has led to the employment by some conferences of an outside agency to supervise observance of the conference agreement and rates by all member lines, but such a neutral body has, of course, no control over any non-member lines that may be active. When outside competition is absent, however, dissatisfaction with the conference system is even more apt to arise because in this situation only self-restraint and internal competition among the member lines can prevent the conference from taking advantage of its monopoly power. It should be noted in passing that competition from overseas airlines is beginning to be felt. Besides reducing shipping's share of the United States overseas passenger market to 14 per cent, air transport has cut significantly into liner freight revenues by attracting premium cargoes.

The monopoly power of conferences, it is suggested, can also be moderated or completely neutralized by the countervailing power of associations of shippers. Such associations were organized with government assistance in Australia and New Zealand as early as 1929. More recently, in response to the growing threat of government regulation, European shipowners have encouraged the formation of national associations of shippers. Negotiations between a conference and individual shippers or trade associations are as old as conferences, but since 1955 Shipper's Councils have been formed in at least eleven Western European countries.[28] In 1964, a 'Note of Understanding' was concluded between European conference lines and Shippers Councils.[29] This 'Understanding' provides procedures for consultation between the conferences trading in and out of Europe and the importers and exporters of those countries. If shippers and shipowners cannot agree, the matter is to be referred to the appropriate Shippers' Council or Councils. In those cases where the conference and the Council cannot reach a mutually satisfactory understanding, the dispute can be referred to an independent panel of three nominees of the shipowners and three nominees of the Councils which would seek an equitable solution. This panel may co-opt an independent chairman if it feels that he would help it resolve the matter. All contractual relationships between the two parties are covered by the 'Understanding' except individual rates. Both parties are agreed that some freight rate matters of general principle may be discussed, but individual freight rates must continue to be determined by direct negotiation between the conference and the individual shipper or trade organization.

The shipowners have expressed the hope that this pattern for settling disputes could be extended beyond Europe. An extension would at least reduce and perhaps eliminate the pressure for governmental regulation, but it is doubtful that this procedure would be universally acceptable. It requires an atmosphere of mutual confidence between shippers and shipowners and an approximate balance of their economic power. It is far from clear that governments would be completely excluded from the deliberations in countries where important tonnage is owned or financed by governments or governmental agencies, where governments are large shippers, or where cargo preference laws prevail. Finally, the exclusion of individual rate questions is likely to prove unacceptable to many developing countries as they are often deeply interested in the export of one or two commodities, nor is this arrangement apt to appeal to the United States Congress which is steeped in a tradition of domestic regulation that is concerned with individual rates as well as rate levels. However, if the Councils prove to be an effective moderator of the countervailing powers of shipper and shipowner, this procedure may find acceptance in some additional countries.

[28] United Kingdom, Belgium, France, Italy, Netherlands, Norway, Sweden, Federal Republic of Germany, Switzerland, Denmark and Greece. *Shippers' Councils in Europe: Their Origin and Practice*, a pamphlet issued by the Committee of European Shipowners in consultation with representatives of the European Shippers' Councils (London, 1965).

[29] Ibid.

If neither self-regulation nor Shippers' Councils satisfy the critics, then external regulation is indicated. External regulation may be unilateral, bilateral, or multi-national. Australia, New Zealand and the Union of South Africa, as previously described, do, in fact, practice a form of unilateral rate regulation. The U.S. has, time and again, explicitly recognized the dangers and difficulties of unilateral regulation of an industry that is subject to another jurisdiction that may impose conflicting regulations, and yet Congress by statute and through pressure exerted by some of its committees has goaded the Federal Maritime Commission to more rigorous application of U.S. regulation of shipping practices and charges.

U.S. regulation of conferences is based on the necessity of conference agreements and practices receiving the approval of the FMC in order for them to be exempt from the application of antitrust legislation. And the reach of U.S. antitrust laws has been held, in the Aluminium Company of America case[30] to apply not only to conspiracies between American and foreign companies, but even to certain acts by foreign combinations alone for conduct outside the borders of the U.S. that have reprehensible consequences within its borders. Therefore, conferences in U.S. trades cannot operate legally without FMC approval and even their practices abroad may be held subject to U.S. jurisdiction regardless of their legality in the place they are conducted. The FMC in rare instances has threatened to cancel its approval of a conference agreement if the conference did not change a specific rate found to be so unreasonably high as to be detrimental to this nation's commerce.[31] In fact, all inbound and outbound rates charged by either conference or non-conference liners are legally subject to FMC control. Although this authority has been sparingly used, the Commission has been under considerable pressure from Congress to activate it, and in December 1965, formally began an investigation of rates in the U.S.-U.K. trade.[32] The law also provides that any carrier offering a deferred rebate, employing a 'fighting' ship to throttle competition, retaliating against a shipper or engaging in certain other unfair or unjustly discriminatory practices may be barred entry to U.S. ports.[33] Though this 'ultimate' sanction has not been used, its ominous threat to freedom of entry to U.S. ports remains. The FMC has ordered conferences based outside as well as inside the U.S. to use a loyalty patronage contract it has drafted in their agreements with both

[30] U.S. v. *Aluminium Co. of America*, 148 F. 2d. 416 (1945).
[31] JEC, op. cit., p. 27.
[32] Robert J. Morison, 'FMC Starts Wide Ship Rate Probe,' *The Journal of Commerce*, December 13th, 1965.
[33] 39 Stat. 728 (1917).

domestic and foreign shippers engaged in trade with this country.[34] The FMC has also asked shipping lines engaged in trade to and from the U.S. for details of the revenue tons of cargo carried, total gross freight revenues earned, as well as for the same information for certain commodities. Despite the view long held by the British Government that any port has jurisdiction over its trade and can impose whatever conditions it chooses,[35] the major maritime nations protested the FMC's request for information from their flag lines in 1964, and the British passed legislation making it unlawful for her carriers to comply with the request.[36] A voluntary agreement, as indicated in the foregoing, was reached to supply some of this information to the OECD on a confidential basis; but in 1965 a dispute broke out between the FMC and the United Kingdom over the proper dissemination of data concerning ocean freight rates.

If these differences concerning patronage contracts, requests for data, and possibly rates themselves cannot be resolved, the final sanction would either be to rescind the exemption from U.S. antitrust laws now provided conferences, or to close U.S. ports to the offending ships. The former would basically alter in the U.S. trades the structure under which liner shipping has operated throughout the world for almost a century. Whether or not liner shipping could adjust to a 'non-collusive' type of oligopoly, as have some industries in which there are also a small number of sellers, is not known. Past experience, however, has convinced governments throughout the world that the conference system is necessary. The second alternative, the closing of ports, would drastically alter freedom of entry, as provided in current treaties of friendship, commerce and navigation, and would make shipping subject to bilateral entry agreements as is the case for aircraft. Since one nation's exports are another nation's imports, a unilateral attempt at regulation is very apt to become bilateral regulation. Bilateralism will involve negotiations by governments and will often tend to subordinate economic considerations to political factors. The insistence of many developing countries that a merchant marine of their own is essential for their economic growth is already providing an impetus towards bilateral arrangements, especially where cargo preference for national flag vessels is required.[37]

[34] FMC, *Annual Report*, fiscal year ended June 30th, 1963, pp. 4–5.

[35] JEC, op. cit., pp. 32–3. Cases cited: *The Consul Corfitzon* (1917), App. Cas. 550; *Steamship 'Antilla' and other Vessels*, 7 Lloyd's Prize Cases, 401; *The Baron Stjernblad* (1918), App. Cas. 173, 178. *The Kronprinzessin Victoria* (1919), App. Cas. 261; *Inre Von Kantzow's Patent* (1944), ch. 318, 321.

[36] JEC, op. cit., p. 32.

[37] Consider, for example, a recent study that recommends a Latin-American Free Trade Association Maritime Commission empowered to review conference tariffs and

Another possibility is for a bilateral regulation and control of entry to operate along with a multinational body to negotiate rates which are, in turn, subject to approval by the two nations whose trade is involved. This is essentially the procedure employed by the international aviation industry. Rates are negotiated at the regional traffic conferences of the International Air Transport Association. These rates are then subject to approval by the nations involved who can deny landing rights to carriers charging rates that have not received government approval. The difficulties that have been encountered by the U.S. Civil Aeronautics Board in its attempts to reduce passenger fares across the Atlantic and the political problems involved in the negotiation of landing rights are well known and consequently need not be reiterated.

It is not astonishing, therefore, that the Joint Economic Committee has proposed an international meeting of the major maritime nations to seek a cooperative solution to shipping problems.[38] It is not all assured that such a gathering could reach a mutually acceptable solution, though it might succeed in narrowing the range of disagreement between the United States and the other maritime powers; but a conclave restricted to the major maritime nations would certainly not allay the suspicions of the developing countries.

When the Inter-governmental Maritime Consultative Organization (IMCO), an autonomous affiliate of the United Nations, was formed after World War II, there was vigorous disagreement concerning whether or not it should have any jurisdiction over rates and other commercial matters. Even though this organization can act only in a consultative and advisory capacity, it took almost ten years for its convention to be ratified by a sufficient number of nations.[39] IMCO can consider technical and safety matters, discriminatory practices of governments, and unfairly restrictive practices of shipping concerns. Its membership consists of most major maritime nations and many others. All members are represented in its Assembly, while its Council consists of: six governments of nations with the largest interest in providing shipping services, six governments of other nations with the largest interest in seaborne trade and four governments selected by the Assembly of which two are important shipping nations and the other two are significant

[38] JEC, op. cit., pp. 6–7.

[39] David J. Padwa, 'The Curriculum of IMCO'. *International Organization*, XIV, 1960, p. 537.

---

services and to license both LAFTA and foreign liner operations. Robert T. Brown, *Transport and Economic Integration of South America* (Washington: The Brookings Institution, 1966), p. 220.

traders. There is, of course, much overlapping in that many important trading nations are also important ship-operating nations, so that maritime countries dominate the Council.[40]

While IMCO may consider unfair restrictive practices of the shipping concerns, the complainant has the burden of proving that the shipping practice is not only restrictive but also unfair. Furthermore, the organization must be satisfied that the matter is incapable of settlement by commercial negotiations or by negotiation of the member governments concerned.[41] Though IMCO has only consultative and advisory authority, some countries believe that its powers over commercial matters are too broad, whereas other nations contend that it cannot offer adequate protection against abusive practices.

Many of the practices of liners that are resented are symptoms of that very frequent maritime ailment—excess tonnage—caused by a combination of economic and political factors. It is unlikely, therefore, that complaints will disappear or that IMCO as presently constituted can do much to remedy them. However, if multinational regulation were to evolve, it would seem logical to remodel IMCO by giving it a mandate to consider complaints without placing as much of the burden of proof on the complainants as it does now. Even so the developing nations are not likely to be satisfied with an organization dominated by ship-operating countries, and the latter have shown no inclination to subject their shipping to even a consultative and advisory body. Unless many of the leading maritime powers become more amenable to some form of multinational regulation of commercial matters, resort to one or more of the procedures previously discussed appears likely. Indeed, unilateral or bilateral regulation, at least by some countries, would appear probable, and such developments may very well lead to a revision of treaty arrangements that provide for freedom of entry.

Dissatisfaction with the conference system has produced agitation in many countries throughout the world to regulate the practices of shipping conferences and the rates they charge. Unless the conference can operate in such a manner as to remove at least all reasonable complaints and suspicions concerning them, some supplementary means of regulation will be created. Some believe that the secrecy with which conferences conduct their business is the cause of much unnecessary suspicion, whereas the conferences,

[40] An annex to IMCO's charter stipulated that the first Council was to be composed of Greece, the Netherlands, Norway, Sweden, the United Kingdom, and the United States as 'shipowners'; and of Argentina, Australia, Belgium, Canada, France and India as 'ship-users', Padwa, op. cit. p. 532.

[41] Padwa, op. cit., p. 535.

most of their members, and many foreign governments consider conference deliberations as confidential business decisions, the knowledge of which would only assist active and potential competitors.[42] It is unlikely, therefore, that all reasonable dissatisfaction will soon disappear. Consequently, some outside regulation appears increasingly likely. Whether it will be achieved by shippers' councils or applied unilaterally, bilaterally, or multinationally remains to be seen. Each has its own advantages, shortcomings and difficulties. Shippers' Councils or multinational regulation, if either can be made acceptable to the great majority of the economically more important industrialized and developing nations, have the great advantage of preserving freedom of entry for merchant shipping and the attendant advantage of helping preserve competition from the most efficient operators regardless of the nationality of the carrier. Unilateral or bilateral regulation, on the other hand, is very apt to seriously impair this aspect of 'freedom of the seas', which would be directly contrary to current efforts to liberalize world trade. It would indeed be ironical if commodity trade were to be liberalized while national restrictions were imposed on the ocean carriers of these goods.

DARTMOUTH COLLEGE

[42] It is possible that if conferences throughout the world published their tariffs, agreed to adequate advance notice of rate increases, and were willing to let an international organization (e.g. IMCO) regulate conference practices such as patronage contracts, membership eligibility, etc., the pressure for unilateral regulation might be reduced. The success of such concessions, were they to be made, is far from certain, but they warrant careful consideration by the industry and the maritime powers lest developments, far less to their liking, occur.

THE NEED FOR PRODUCT MARKET ANALYSIS

A CASE STUDY OF THE FEASIBILITY OF IMPORT SUBSTITUTION IN NIGERIA

by Philip C. Packard

1. *Feasibility Studies*

In recent years, economists and planners have referred repeatedly to the need for systematic evaluation of industrial (and other) projects in the poor countries. Indeed, the demand has become so great that one is apt to forget that feasibility studies (or industry studies or project evaluations) are a rather sophisticated form of supply and demand analysis. This is especially so for those poor countries (the majority) which have mixed economies, meaning that they have under-developed market systems, a dependence on foreign trade, and inadequate government controls even though we may speak optimistically of planning. Sophisticated project proposals may well miss the characteristics of these poor countries.

Studies of proposed industrial projects are usually fairly well detailed on the supply side: technology and costs are well understood, though understanding is based on industrial experience in the advanced nations. Cost data are usually *not* presented in comparative terms, showing alternative plant sizes; and adjustments are for the most part inadequate to take account of differences in economic climates between the poor and industrialized nations.

On the whole, market analyses of the demand for products either for intermediate or final uses are sadly lacking in the poor countries. One need only recall the dictum of Adam Smith on the size of the market to question the indiscriminate commitment of scarce resources to industrial projects. It therefore follows that product-market estimation has key importance in feasibility studies. The relevance (or lack of it) of cost data can then become clear and refinements to the supply and demand analysis ('economic' feasibility) can be built up to answer whether the project is feasible or not.

Our concern is with the difficulties that arise when an enterprise is established without adequate market estimations. The lessons, I think, are clear.

2. *The Modern Shoe Industry*

Data have been gathered on the Modern Shoe Industry in Owerri,

Eastern Nigeria.[1] They cover for the most part the calendar year 1965 and rest upon the conditions prevailing in Nigeria at that time. The shoe factory was opened in Owerri the latter part of 1964. Public discussion at the time attributed the location to the severe unemployment in this province and the attendant pressures on the government to establish industries. Owerri lies between the port city of Port Harcourt (the import point and a major market) and the market town of Onitsha. The siting of the factory involves no special penalties in costs of production or distribution though the decision to invest was certainly a political one. Sources of equity capital are twofold: £96,000 from the Eastern Region Government and £24,000 from a European concern. The initial agreement provides for technical and administrative supervision from this European firm and a contract to supply the factory with capital equipment. The total equity of £120,000 is less than the net assets of the shoe factory (listed below) since the machinery costs are to be borne by the supplier with a repayment schedule of five years. The control of the enterprise (though not its everyday operation) is in the hands of a board reflecting the public and private ownership of equity.

3. *Costing*

The methods of production in the Owerri plant conform to those of modern plants in industrialized countries. The labour force is associated directly with machine processes so that most tasks in the plant are of a mechanical and routinized nature. Moreover, plant capacity is flexible in that more than one type of product (a pair of shoes) of varying design and quality can be produced in a given work period. In other words, the shoe factory's products are not the handicrafts which make up a large (but unknown) portion of the conglomerate shoe market in Nigeria. Multi-product production indeed is carried on. In such a situation it is possible to analyse each type of product for its direct variable unit costs. Overhead costs are certainly more difficult to estimate, but if we assume, for example, that overhead costs vary in the same proportion as unit variable cost per product, total unit costs of each product can be obtained. Estimates of total unit costs would be necessary in a proposed plant contemplating initial production and for changes in on-going production. However, the problem I wish to pose is one of 'the'

[1] I owe much to data made available to me by J. N. Afuba when we were formerly associated in the University of Nigeria. The responsibility for the accuracy and presentation of these data rests with me and not with Afuba. I wish also to thank the officials of the Modern Shoe Industry for their co-operation, which does not imply any concurrence with my expressed views.

product market and its effects upon the plant *in toto*. This market problem will be found to be so severe that it is possible for us to speak of the costing of the 'representative' pair of shoes. These variable costs are based on an array of shoes at present in production of qualitatively different designs. A different composition of production would alter unit variable cost but not so much as to upset the arguments which follow.

Table I summarizes the actual value of fixed assets and the

TABLE I

TOTAL CAPITAL REQUIREMENTS

Fixed Assets		
Land		No Cost
Buildings		25,000
Office Equipment		1,500
Leather Machines		85,000
Rubber Machines		32,830
Electrical Installations		2,377
Total Fixed Assets		£146,707
Working Capital*		
	Days	
Raw Materials	30	39,600
Indirect Labour	30	1,050
Administrative Costs	30	3,000
Sales Costs	30	120
Total Working Capital		£43,770
Total Capital Requirements		£190,477

* It is assumed that the capital locked up in total working capital turns over every thirty days. This is an estimate made by the factory.

estimated working capital to give the total capital requirements for the factory. It will be noticed that working capital for *Sales Costs* is low. We shall return to this question later. The overhead costs are expressed as estimates in Table II.

Table II incorporates a number of assumptions, namely: useful (economic) lives of fixed assets; the interest rate; and, of course, the size of staff (sales staff is reckoned to be extremely low). If, as is usually the case, these assumptions prove optimistic in the light of the economic conditions in poor countries, overhead costs may rise, let us say, by 15 to 25 per cent per annum. Both Tables I and II admit of no alternative technology. The 'size' of the plant is fixed.

Variable costs per pair of shoes are, as indicated earlier, estimated averages of these costs over all the various types of products manufactured. Therefore, each type of cost in Table III is averaged and

TABLE II

ESTIMATED OVERHEAD COSTS PER ANNUM

Depreciation	*Cost*	*Years of Economic Life*	*Amount*
Buildings	£25,000	30	£833
Machines	117,830	10	11,783
Electrical Installations	2,377	20	119
Office Equipment	1,500	20	75
	Total Depreciation per annum		£12,810
Interest			
Fixed Assets (£146,707) at 6% per annum			£4,401
Working Capital (£43,770) at 6% per annum			2,626
		Total Interest	£7,027
Other Estimated Overhead Costs			
Supplies and Maintenance			£138
Indirect Labour			9,625
Sales Staff			1,110
Administration			27,500
	Total Other Estimated Overhead Costs		£38,363
	Total Overhead Costs per annum (estimated)		£58,200

TABLE III

VARIABLE COSTS PER 'REPRESENTATIVE' PAIR OF SHOES

	Pence		*Per Cent*
Electricity and Water	26.22		
Excise Taxes	36.00		
Direct Labour	12.00		
Raw Materials	190.64		
Total Variable Cost per Unit	264.86	(approx. 22/-)	
Raw Materials			
Local	23.66		12.4
Imports	166.98		87.6
(of which leather)	(113.00)		(59.3)
Total	190.64		100.0

summed to give total variable costs per unit of product (our 'representative' pair of shoes). Furthermore, variable costs are taken as proportionate to output, which is a very useful assumption, and does little violence to the cost data. Raw materials are of greatest importance to variable cost and imports constitute the bulk of these by value. Leather imports make up 60 per cent of total variable unit costs and would certainly affect the estimates in raw material costs if shoe sizes varied greatly. In practice, the only sharp distinction in raw material costs would be between leather shoes on the one hand and rubber boots and canvas shoes on the other. (Rubber boots and canvas shoes are not of importance for the shoe factory, small as its total production is at the moment.)

The shoe factory has a rated capacity of 330,000 pairs of shoes per annum, based on two work shifts of eight hours each. If we take no account of 'running-in' problems both with respect to machinery and the labour force, total unit costs of production can be reckoned in the following manner:

TABLE IV

TOTAL UNIT COSTS PER 'REPRESENTATIVE' PAIR OF SHOES

Overhead Costs per annum (estimated)	£58,200
Variable Cost per unit	264.86d.
Output per annum (pairs of shoes)	£330,000

$$\text{Total Unit Cost} = \frac{£58{,}200}{330{,}000} + 264.86\text{d.}$$
$$= 307.19\text{d.}$$
$$= 25/7$$

The overhead costs of £58,200 include interest on capital in fixed assets and estimated working capital (see Table II). The figure of 25/7 is then the cost of our representative pair of shoes if per annum production is at rated capacity.

4. *The Market for Manufactured Shoes*

The hope for the Owerri plant rests on replacing imports of manufactured shoes into Nigeria. One can infer from the import data (with great scepticism) that home production could be substituted. The ten-fold growth in imports constituted the strongest basis for any supposition about the market, for, from imports of about 380,000 pairs of shoes in 1950 the market grew to over 3,000,000 pairs by 1960. Expectations were in 1964 that some 30 per cent of the imports were consumed in Eastern Nigeria. If this is the case, well over 500,000 pairs of shoes per annum might be sold by the Owerri plant.

The question is, of course, what shoes at what prices? There are no estimates of particular kinds of shoes imported either by the

Federal Government's customs or by the Owerri enterprise. Price estimates are rough, but can be obtained in the following way. The *average* C.I.F. import price per pair of shoes varies between 13/– and 15/–. Import duties run about 3/– a pair. Most leather shoes sold at retail in urban markets vary between 30/– and 40/–, so that if we take 35/– as the average (an informed guess!), the residual for mark-ups and distribution together amounts to 17/– to 19/– a pair. Obviously, mark-ups and final retail prices depend upon methods of distribution as well as consumers.

The market in recent years has been supplied with a growing (by how much?) home production carried on in seven factories (this excludes untold numbers of handicraft producers). Only Bata in Ikeja is considered large enough to supply a significant output to compete with the Owerri plant. Declines in imports from 3.46 million pairs in 1960 to 2.35 million in 1963 have been attributed to Bata, but it does not have the capacity to supply the entire market. The distribution of shoes is in the hands of a wholesaling and retailing network built up on the importation of shoes. Large foreign firms have virtually controlled this import trade, either passing along the commodities to Nigerian dealers who are their agents, or selling direct to the large expatriate retail outlets. Costs of distribution have been borne by the dealers who are at liberty to fix retail prices. Only Bata has developed extensive retail outlets and advertised throughout the Federation.

The market, therefore, with the exception of Bata as the major home producer, is an import market. The marketing channels for this trade can be considered to be well developed but in the hands of distributors, not manufacturers. The difficulties of marketing which a new factory will certainly face can only be eased by either establishing a distribution system itself (a most difficult task) or integrating its production into the established network of distribution. These difficulties *are* price difficulties such as the estimates of demand elasticities and their relations to product quality differences. But the institutional complexities of wholesaling and retailing are also at issue.

I should stress that this summary of the market, sketchy as it is, constitutes the sum of information available to the Owerri enterprise.

The Owerri factory has chosen not to retail its products itself. Dealers have been contacted in the major market towns of the region. However, no advertising campaign has been mounted and sales activity by the enterprise is virtually nil (as the cost figures demonstrate). The conclusion is inescapable: the enterprise has no firm estimates of the kinds of products it could sell at a range of prices.

There is no integration of production and distribution activities by the firm.

5. *Break-Even Analysis*

Figure 1 compares the costs of production and sales prices with different production runs. Total costs for any output are reckoned by adding the total of constant variable costs per unit of 22/– for the output concerned to the estimated overhead costs of £58,200. Total capacity of 330,000 per annum is indicated in Fig. 1. *Weighted average* selling prices for the representative pair of shoes must be £1.28 in order to break even at capacity production. Present average price is £1.20 which does not allow break-even at all. However, it can be seen from the figure that present production of about 43,000 pairs per annum would only produce break-even at £2.46 per pair. This average price is above the 30/– to 40/– referred to earlier. I have been informed by traders in the Enugu market[2] that an average price above 40/– is quite unrealistic. Therefore, no realistic selling price exists for the Owerri enterprise for break-even. Losses are inevitable.

If one were to ask whether the Owerri plant should have been built, my answer would be no! A few points of interest remain, before I conclude.

6. *Odds and Ends*

The appropriateness of the size of the plant cannot be judged until the product market is estimated. Let us look at overhead costs. The buildings and machinery do fix the physical capacity of production per annum and therefore depreciation and interest costs. Since a fair degree of product flexibility exists, the decision about plant scale very probably was reached after calculations by the designers on the lowest attainable unit costs. This assumes away the marketing problem. We can ask whether smaller plant size—presumably more labour using—would have sufficed. The answer is no, for the organizational experience needed as a requisite for controlling a large direct labour force per unit of product in the environment of a poor country is not to be had from an industrialized country habituated to progressive labour-saving technology. It goes without saying that qualified entrepreneurs are in short supply in Nigeria. Moreover, total capacity should be broken down into components allocated for specific products. We have here a joint-cost problem and the added one of required specialized equipment

[2] This is somewhat casual empirical information, but it is the kind which should be given great weight in price analysis.

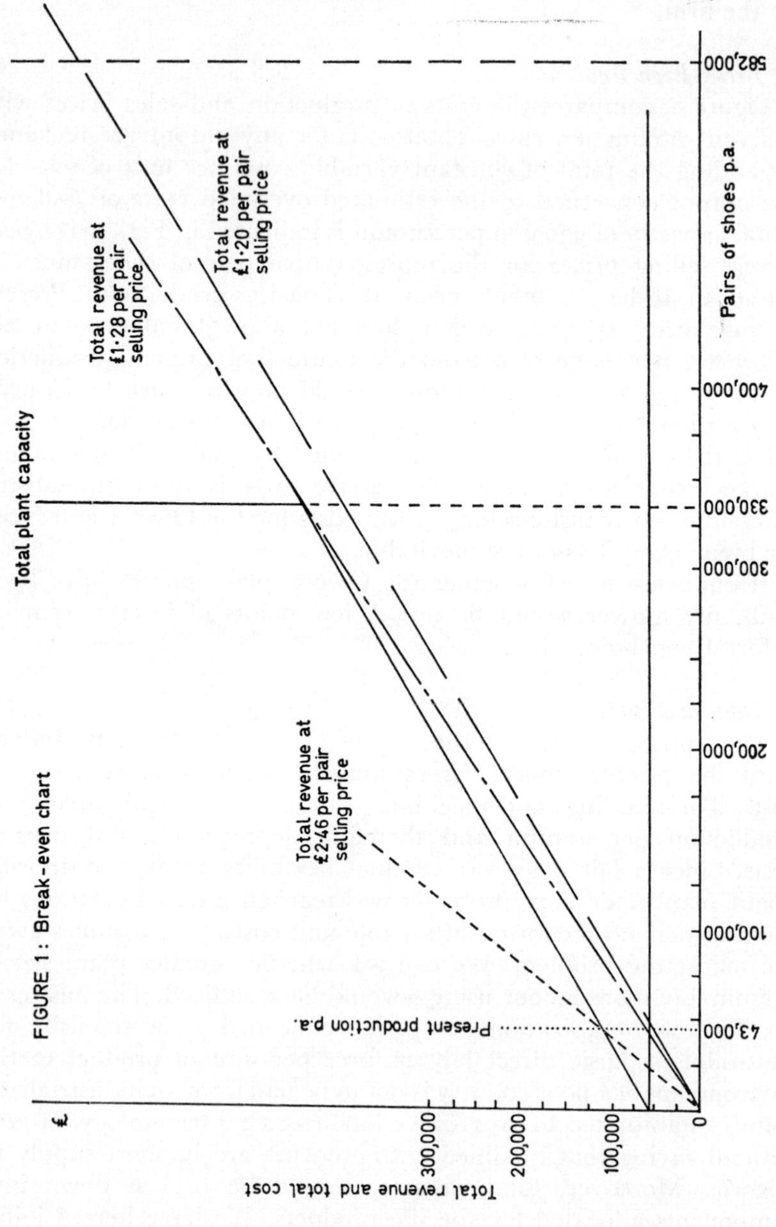

FIGURE 1: Break-even chart

also. The market for shoes enters directly into the choice of plant equipment.

Sales promotion can be considered to involve a reduction in the value of gross sales or an increase in costs of production (and distribution). Since the latter form is chosen for the Owerri plant, the size of the plant is affected by market considerations. In our case a much needed increase in promotional activity would raise both overhead costs and the sale of output needed to break even at any price (see Fig. 1).

Working capital is at best an estimate. In the present case it is underestimated precisely because the market is not known. Inventory policy with respect to inputs and the final products have plagued the Owerri plant. The resulting overhead costs tend to be higher than those estimated in Table I.

7. *Conclusion*

I should like to conclude by asking two not wholly unrelated questions: why should such a plant be built; and how does one develop a reasonable approach to analysing a proposed industrial project?

As indicated earlier, political pressures no doubt had great influence on the investment decisions at Owerri. It would be fruitless to speculate further, but one other piece of evidence is worth discussing: equity ownership of the Owerri enterprise. Eighty per cent ownership by government indicates not only financial interest but longer run financial responsibility by government. *If*, at least for a period of time, losses are to be sustained, government will bear this burden. An added intangible consideration is that in an atmosphere of *economic development* (desired but not fulfilled), government must stand ready to support faltering enterprise by guaranteeing reasonable returns to private *and* foreign equity holders. I ask myself whether the normal pressures of a market system to weigh investments carefully are operative in such a situation. Put bluntly, why have a feasibility study at all unless government insists? (There are, of course, engineering considerations, but these do not necessarily involve a full-blown feasibility study.)

Let me stress once again the role of the market. There is neither widespread nor sustained nor coherent economic planning in Nigeria. In such an atmosphere one must begin with the product market. The size and character of the market sets the framework for alternative estimates of unit costs, production and therefore probable plant scales. These interrelated cost and demand estimates have to precede more detailed estimations of the project's economic desirability as opposed to (perhaps different) financial estimations. One (and I mean government in this case) gets into unmanageable difficulties if discussions about investments are diverted to government policy questions such as import duty and excise tax levels to gain relief, before some reasonable assessments of costs and demand are made.

Surely, adjustments of the economic environment facing the firm can be considered *if* and once analysis has shown some ground for optimism for future success of the enterprise. In other words, government policy should be viewed as a series of *marginal* adjustments and not as major changes in the structure of the economic environment. This, I believe, conforms to the present capacity of governments of the poor countries to effect change.[3]

It follows, therefore, that if an enterprise is to succeed, it must have major self-sustaining qualities. These have to be assessed *prior* to investment, and, since as a general rule, government will be found as the prime mover in industrialization, the task of assessment falls on government. It is no doubt uncomfortable for civil servants to think as businessmen, but the exigencies of development cry out for it.

INSTITUTE OF SOCIAL STUDIES, THE HAGUE

[3] The reader should remember that we are talking about industrial projects and not social-overhead investments. *Government* ability to invest in the long run does indeed depend upon a general positive rate of return on investments in the economy.

CONCENTRATION AND PRICE-COST MARGINS: A COMMENT

HASKEL BENISHAY

IN the July 1966 issue of this journal, N. R. Collins and L. E. Preston report on a multiple regression analysis of a cross section of 32 food manufacturing industries, where the profit margin is determined by four variables: the concentration ratio, extent of market, capital-output ratio and rate of growth.

They report a net positive association of price-cost margins with the concentration ratio and consequently suggest a positive relation between monopoly and profit. They note at the outset that 'prices are higher and price-cost margins wider under conditions of monopoly than under conditions of competition', and conclude that the analysis 'strongly supports the hypothesis that there is a positive relationship between price-cost margins and concentration'. Other statements, as well as a striking scatter diagram, convey the notion that concentration brings about higher monopoly profits.

But the price-cost margin or profit margin on sales *is not the relevant rate of profit.* Long and costly processes are associated with low sales-to-assets (output-to-capital) ratios and with high profit-to-sales ratios (profit margins). *Ceteris paribus*, the firm with the higher sales-to-assets ratio will tend to have a lower profit-to-sales ratio. Competitive forces tend to equalize rates of return on equity or on assets not profit margins on sales, for investment will flow from poorer to better returns on investment. The use of a sales profit margin to represent a rate of return on assets or on equity is simply inappropriate.

The inclusion of a capital-output ratio (assets-to-sales ratio) in the regression may make good the shortcomings of the price-cost margin if the right capital-output ratio is employed. For this result, one should employ the capital-output ratios of the four-digit industries in the sample. But the authors use the capital output-ratios of the wider groupings known as three-digit industries each of which includes a varying number of four-digit industries. (For example, Industry 202, Dairy Products, includes 2021, Creamery Butter 2022, Cheese, etc.) Consequently, there is little assurance that their three-digit capital-output ratios supply the missing link needed to convert an irrelevant profit-to-sales ratio to a relevant profit-to-assets ratio. If industries of higher concentration also have lower sales-to-assets ratios and high profit-to-sales ratios, a spurious association is generated between concentration and price-cost margins (sales' profit margins).

If the regression is run with the assets-to-sales, or capital-output ratio, of the respective four-digit industries, and the results are similar, the authors' claim for positive association between concentration and rates of return will become plausible. If they substitute the ratio of profits to assets for their ratio of profits to sales, re-run their regressions, and still get a positive association with concentration, theirs will be a strong result indeed.

If, on the other hand, no association emerges after incorporating these suggestions, nothing is lost. The absence of association between concentration and profits is no less significant a finding than is its presence.

NORTHWESTERN UNIVERSITY

A NOTE ON 'MEASURING SHOPPING COSTS'[1]

by Robert Bacon

In his article on measuring shopping costs Professor Brief advances a method of estimating the ratio of shopping costs to purchase price. The purpose of this note is neither to take issue with the importance of this exercise nor with the basic approach to obtaining this ratio, but rather with the details of Brief's method.

The objections raised are of two types: one is with the formulation of the price equation and the other rather lesser objections are with the algebra. In particular it is shown how, using what seems to be the correct algebra, the two approaches, Brief's and the one put forward in this note, can be used to obtain the relevant estimates.

Brief argues that shopping costs consist of (a) the price paid to the shopkeeper and (b) the marginal cost of buying the goods. This distinction is a useful one in all location economics and is not a controvertible issue. However, in passing from this to the algebraic formulation Brief continues: let π = total price, p = price of the good and s = unit cost of shopping.

$$\therefore \pi = p.s.$$

This multiplication of two costs to produce a total cost seems debatable and the more usual formulation would be to set π equal to the *sum* of the two costs (this is the formulation used as an alternative in this note). An example may help to clarify the issue: if a good were to have zero price (some kind of free offer) but the consumer had to collect it, then on Brief's model this would involve the consumer in zero total cost despite any transport cost that might be involved. If the alternative suggestion were used, then the total cost would be the transport cost involved in collecting this particular good.

The next step in the argument is to write the demand function for any particular good:

$$Y = f(\pi, x)$$

where Y is the quantity demanded and x stands for all other factors apart from the total price that enter the demand function. The elasticities of demand with respect to these three prices are:

$$e_\pi = \frac{df}{d\pi} \cdot \frac{\pi}{Y}\ \ e_p = \frac{df}{dp} \cdot \frac{p}{Y},\ \ e_s = \frac{df}{ds} \cdot \frac{s}{Y}$$

$$\left(\frac{df}{d\pi} \text{ is exactly equivalent to } \frac{dY}{d\pi}\right).$$

[1] 'Measuring shopping costs' by Richard P. Brief in *The Journal of Industrial Economics*, May 1967.

Brief states that for his formulation:

$$\frac{df}{d\pi} = \frac{df}{dp} = \frac{df}{ds}.$$

This is in fact incorrect for the formulation by Brief, although as is shown below it turns out to be correct for the alternative formulation. In his case df/dp is obtained by the 'function of a function' rule of calculus, and hence

$$\frac{df}{dp} = \frac{df}{d\pi} \cdot \frac{d\pi}{dp} = \frac{df}{d\pi}.s$$

Similarly

$$\frac{df}{ds} = \frac{df}{d\pi} \cdot p.$$

Hence

$$e_\pi = \frac{df}{d\pi} \cdot \frac{\pi}{Y}, e_p = \frac{df}{d\pi} \cdot \frac{p}{Y}.s = \frac{df}{d\pi} \cdot \frac{\pi}{Y}, \text{and } e_s = \frac{df}{d\pi} \cdot \frac{\pi}{Y}.$$

Thus using Brief's formulation $e_\pi = e_p = e_s$, rather than the results given in his article:

$$\frac{e_\pi}{e_p} = \frac{\pi}{p} \text{ and } \frac{e_\pi}{e_s} = \frac{\pi}{s}.$$

If the alternative formulation ($\pi = p+s$) is adopted then the results are as given for Brief's article:

$$\frac{e_\pi}{e_s} = \frac{\pi}{s} \text{ and } \frac{e_\pi}{e_p} = \frac{\pi}{p}.$$

In the actual estimation of the demand function Brief arrives at the following:

$$Y = a.(p.s)^b.x^h.z^g \quad (1)$$

where x is all other demand factors and z is the nuisance variables (a, b, h and g are constants to be estimated). Since s cannot be observed Brief, from considerations of spatial economics, makes the substitution $s = D^{-n}$, where D is the density of population and n is another constant to be estimated. Hence the equation:

$$Y = a.(p)^b.D^{b'}.x^h.z^g \quad \text{where } b' = b.n \quad (2)$$

This equation is estimated for liquor sales in New York State using each county as one observation. The price of liquor is fixed and thus in this case does not enter into the calculations. This equation gives an estimate of b', and this is apparently treated by Brief as an estimate of b. This is valid only if n is known to be equal to one. This estimate of the elasticity of demand with respect to shopping costs is compared by Brief to a separate estimate of the elasticity of demand with respect to price. According to his algebra the ratio of the two is equal to the ratio of shopping costs to price. It has been shown that for two reasons this is not going to be the case: firstly even on his assumptions the algebra would give the two elasticities, correctly estimated, as being the same.[2] Secondly by forgetting that b' includes n it is not correct (unless there is separate information that n is equal to one) to use b' instead of b. This latter problem can be circumvented even without knowledge of n, if a good is chosen where there is some variation in price. This would mean that price entered the equation and a separate estimate of b would be obtained. This would gain nothing except a check that the two elasticities were roughly equal.

How can this dilemma be avoided? It seems that if the alternative price hypothesis is used then a useful relation between the elasticities and the actual costs is obtained. To use this information and the known value of the elasticity of demand with respect to price it would seem to be necessary to rewrite the demand equation in a 'linear' form:

$$Y = a+b.(p+s)+h.x+g.z.$$

Then it would be necessary for simple estimation to assume a simpler relation between s and D (unless n were known from separate studies): one possibility would be to assume that s was equal to n/D.

$$\therefore\ Y = a+b.p+\frac{b.n}{D}+h.x+g.z.$$

This formulation loses one substantial advantage relative to the formulation in Brief's paper: as is well known a linear demand function has an infinite number of values of the elasticity of demand, each one corresponding to the values of price and the other factors which are used. However, for the range of prices and other variables of interest there will be a range of elasticities of demand with respect to the shopping cost. This, taken with the known elasticity of demand with respect to price, will give a range of values of the

[2] The estimate of the elasticity of demand with respect to purchase price is 0.840, while the estimated value of the elasticity of demand with respect to shopping costs is 0.094: these are very different, and it must be assumed that this is because of the joint effect of the value of n not being equal to unity, and the unsatisfactory nature of the price formation equation.

ratio of shopping cost to purchase price. As Professor Brief remarks: 'It seems to me that for certain products, geographical areas and/or periods of history, shopping costs may be an important element of price.'

CONCLUSIONS

Although the details of Professor Brief's algebra used to derive an estimate of the ratio of shopping costs to purchase price are wrong in places, this paper has shown that by making what may be a more satisfactory assumption about the composition of total cost to the consumer it is possible to derive a range of values for the ratio of shopping costs to purchase price of a given good.

NUFFIELD COLLEGE
OXFORD

PUBLICATIONS RECEIVED

An Approach to the Welfare Analysis of Intertemporal Resource Allocation, by Jerome Rothenberg, Lecture Series 22, Center of Planning and Economic Research, Athens, 1967.

The Biology of Work, by O. G. Edholm, World University Library, Weidenfeld & Nicolson, 1967, 14s.

The Construction and Use of Economic Models, by A. R. Bergstrom, The English Universities Press Ltd., 1967, 40s.

Contemporary Economics, edited by Reuben E. Slesinger, Mark Perlman and Asher Isaacs, Selected Readings, Second Edition, Allyn & Bacon, Inc., Boston, 1967.

Demografía y Economía, No. 1, El Colegio de México, 1967, Extranjero Dls. 2.50.

A Fiscal Program for a Balanced Federalism, a Statement by the Research and Policy Committee of the Committee for Economic Development, 1967, $1.00.

Geographical Distribution of Federal Funds for Research and Development, Fiscal Year 1965, Surveys of Science Resources Series, National Science Foundation, 1967, copies from the Superintendent of Documents, U.S. Government Printing Office, Washington, D.C. 20402, at $1.00.

The German Economy: 1870 to the Present, by Gustav Stolper, Weidenfeld & Nicolson, 1967, 50s.

The History of the Indian Tea Industry, by Sir Percival Griffiths, Weidenfeld & Nicolson, 1967, 8 gns.

Industria e Commercio in Liguria nell' età del Risorgmento (1700–1861), by Luigi Bulferetti and Claudio Costantini, Studi e Recherche di Storia Economica Italianonell' età de Risorgimento, Banca Commerciale Italiano, Milano, 1966.

Industrial Retardation in Britain 1880–1914, by A. L. Levine, Weidenfeld & Nicolson, 1967, 42s.

The Inter-Industry Structure of Missouri 1958, by Floyd K. Harmston and Claude E. Monroe, No. 10 of a series defining the problems and prospects for Missouri's economy, Research Center, School of Business and Public Administration, University of Missouri, 1967, $2.00.

18 Lectures on Industrial Society, by Raymond Aron, translated by M. K. Bottomore, Weidenfeld & Nicolson, 1967, paperback 18s., hardback 42s.

Measuring Job Vacancies, by John G. Myers and Daniel Creamer, a Feasibility Study in the Rochester, N.Y. Area, Studies in Business Economics No. 97, National Industrial Conference Board, Inc., The Conference Board in Economics, 1967, NICB Associates and Government agencies $3.50, students and teachers $3.50, others $17.50.

Modello di Sviluppo di un Settore in Rapida Crescita, by Romano Prodi, L'Industria della Ceramica per l'Edilizia, Collana d'Economia, Ricercher di Economia Applicata No. 1, Franco Angeli Editor—Milan, 1966, L.2.000.

Monetary Planning, by Xenophon Zolotas, Bank of Greece Papers and Lectures 22, Athens, 1967.

National Patterns of R&D Resources, Funds and Manpower in the United States, National Science Foundation, 1967, copies of the report may be ordered from the Superintendent of Documents, U.S. Government Printing Office, Washington, D.C. 20402, at $30 a copy.

New Prospects for the International Finance of Development, by N. T. Wang, Essays in International Finance No. 59, April 1967, International Finance Section, Department of Economics, Princeton University Press, $3.00.

Notes on Telephone Development, a Decade of Telecommunication Development, Post Office Engineering Union, 1967.

Particles and Accelerators, by Robert Gouiran, translated by W. F. G. Crozier, World University Library, Weidenfeld & Nicolson, 1967, paperback 14s., hardback 25s.

The Political Economy of South Africa, by Ralph Horwitz, Weidenfeld & Nicolson, 1967, 63s.

Problems of Stocks and Storage, edited by A. J. H. Morrell, Mathematical and Statistical Techniques for Industry, Monograph No. 4, published by Oliver & Boyd for I.C.I., 25s.

Il Progresso Tecnico-Organizzativo nel Settore Marittimo-Portuale, by Sergio Vaccà, Instituto di Tecnica Economica, Università degli Studi di Genova, Serie Monografie N. 1, G. Giappichelli, Editore, Torino, 1967, L.2800.

The Rate of Exchange and the Terms of Trade, by S. A. Ozga, Weidenfeld & Nicolson, 1967, 21s.

Regulation of Transport Innovation, by Paul W. MacAvoy and James Sloss, the ICC and Unit Coal Trains to the East Coast, Random House Series in Industrial Economics, Random House, Inc., 1967, $2.50.

A Report on the Seminar on the Current Economic Problems of Pakistan, held January 28–30 1967, Pakistan Institute of Development Economics, inland Rs.5.00, foreign $2.00.

Scientists and Engineers from Abroad 1962–64, Surveys of Science Resources Series, National Science Foundation, 1967, copies from the Superintendent of Documents, U.S. Government Printing Office, Washington, D.C. 20402, at $0.45.

Socio-Economic Data and Parameters of Venezuela 1950–1965, English translation, Inter-American Development Bank, Socio-Economic Development Division, 1967.

Studies in the Recovery of Capital, from Aspects of Accounting Relating to the Recovery of Capital, by Shinkichi Minemura, Tsushin Co. Ltd., Tokyo, $3.00 and ¥800.

Theoretical Issues in International Economics, by M. O. Clement, Richard L. Pfister and Kenneth J. Rothwell, Constable, 1967, 60s.

Trade Union Growth and Recognition, by George Sayers Bain, Research Papers 6, Royal Commission on Trade Unions and Employers' Associations, H.M.S.O., 1967, 10s. 6d.

Worker-Owned Plywood Companies, by Katrina V. Berman, an Economic Analysis, Economic and Business Studies Bulletin No. 42, College of Economics and Business, Washington State University, and Bureau of Economic and Business Research, Washington State University Press, 1967, $7.50.

DYNAMIC PROGRAMMING EXTENSIONS TO THE THEORY OF THE FIRM

by T. M. Whitin[1]

I

In spite of the existence of many conceptual and empirical difficulties, the theory of the firm, as set forth for most economics students of today, has remained essentially unaltered from what it was thirty years ago. It is not the intent of this article to dwell on these difficulties which are, for the most part, well known, but rather to show how a considerable number of them can be avoided through the use of probabilistic dynamic programming models. The typical static, one-period marginalist model can be shown to be a special case of the models developed which are far richer in content because of the wide variety of more realistic assumptions which can be accommodated.

As evidence that other authors are not entirely satisfied with the present state of the theory, the following quotations are cited:

> In the absence of any empirical restraint, the temptation is to continue the deductive process, refining, extending and amplifying the body of analysis. Ultimately it becomes apparent, even without systematic comparison in the scientific sense, that its conclusions do not meet the required test of interpreting reality. Equilibrium price analysis has been developed to a stage at which it is no longer theory; it has become a protracted exercise in logic. . . . It is the business of price theory (or so this paper has already stated) to explain price determination. As yet there is no theory, there are only a few tentative hypotheses.[2]

> But I must register my belief that the ending of marginalist static equilibrium at the level of the firm as the seat of a sovereign *general* theory would free us to use our economists' tools on change and chance in the real world in a way that our supposed 'legacy' has denied to us. I count it as a real obstacle to dynamic thinking that this particular static theory has encouraged us to make *a priori* generalizations about the behaviour of businesses without any feeling that it was part of

[1] Wesleyan University. This article was written while the author was on a U.S. National Science Foundation Fellowship at the Netherlands School of Economics, Econometric Institute.

[2] Romney Robinson, 'The Economics of Disequilibrium Price', *Quarterly Journal of Economics*, 1961, p. 229.

> the job of the theorist to get near the apparently muddy and confused world of business management.[3]
>
> Unfortunately there are many facts and facets of an economy which need to be explained, but which cannot be explained using this model.
>
> . . . There is need for an adequate economic theory to serve as a basis for analysis, prediction and as an aid in policy evaluation.[4]

As an example of some of the problems in static, marginal analysis consider the theory of monopoly. The profit-maximizing monopolist is assumed to produce an output such that the marginal cost of producing that output is equal to the marginal revenue resulting from its sale. It is implicitly assumed that the monopolist produces and sells identical quantities, that he knows the (certain) demand function for his product, that discounting (interest) considerations do not affect his price and output decision, and that the marginal cost and marginal revenue functions are independent of each other. In addition, if the monopolist is to stay in business in the long-run and in the short-run, it is necessary that his short-run and long-run average revenues be not less than his short-run and long-run average costs, respectively.

If one were to confess that the monopolist did not know the demand function with certainty (and no one seriously contends that he has such knowledge), most of the analytical structure crumbles. No longer is there any reason to suppose that the quantity produced is the same as the quantity sold, nor that the quantity produced corresponds to the expected sales quantity.[5] Once the possibility of stocks is introduced several complications arise. First of all, the monopolist must formulate an optimal 'production policy' and 'price policy' rather than an optimal output and price. This optimal policy must indicate what amount should be produced for each possible level of initial inventory and what price should be set. Furthermore, the existence of stocks destroys the independence of supply and demand functions for at least two distinct reasons.

Firstly, the size of stock can influence demand through its effect on the actual desires of the consumer, and secondly, when the quantity demanded is subject to probabilistic variations, *expected*

[3] P. W. S. Andrews, *On Competition in Economic Theory*, London, 1964, p. 92.

[4] Martin Shubik, 'Objective Functions and Models of Corporate Optimization', *Quarterly Journal of Economics*, 1961, p. 345.

[5] Without introducing risk, the quantities a monopolist produces and sells are not necessarily equal. See for example, A. Smithies, 'The Maximization of Profits Over Time with Changing Cost and Demand Functions', *Econometrica*, October 1939, pp. 312–18, or F. and V. Lutz, *The Theory of Investment of the Firm*, Princeton University Press, 1951.

marginal revenue cannot be discussed meaningfully except with respect to a particular stock situation and particular production and price decisions.

Finally, once stocks are permitted to enter the analysis, the level of the discount rate can exert an influence on the optimal level of production. With respect to this last consideration, it should be pointed out that some of the most widely used textbooks on intermediate price theory contain no analysis of discounting.[6] The level of the discount rate will, in general, affect both price and production policy.

II

In the dynamic programming approach to be developed here, the monopolist is assumed to know, for each of a discrete number of prices, the probability distribution for the quantity demanded.[7] He is assumed to be interested in maximizing the discounted value of expected profits over an infinite time horizon at a known discount rate and he is assumed (for simplicity only) to know his cost function with certainty. Time is divided into a number of discrete periods with the same demand distribution and cost function in each period. The monopolist has a discrete number of possible production, and hence, inventory levels. For each possible level of incoming inventory the monopolist's optimal price and production policy will be determined. An interesting aspect of the model is that the optimality of any given policy can be ascertained extremely simply. In the event that an initial policy is not optimal a technique of improving the policy until optimality is obtained is specified.[8]

For each possible level of incoming inventory, $i = 0, 1, 2, \ldots$, various pairs (x, p) of discrete production levels x_k, $k = 0, 1, 2, \ldots$[9] and price levels p_m, $m = 0, 1, 2, \ldots$ will be considered. For any given (x_k, p_m), the monopolist knows the probability distribution of demand and hence the probability of ending the period with inventory $j = 0, 1, 2, \ldots$. The symbol ρ_{ij} is used to designate the probability of starting with inventory i and ending with inventory j. For each ρ_{ij}, for any price and output combination, the profits associated with initial inventory i and ending inventory j are known, and will be denoted by π_{ij}. These profit levels are known since for initial

6 For example, R. Leftwich, *The Price System and Resource Allocation*, Holt, Rinehart, and Winston, third edition, 1966.

7 The probability distribution of demand can be a function of the number of units of inventory without complicating the analysis. Also the cost function can depend on the stock level.

8 This technique is due to Ronald Howard, *Dynamic Programming and Markov Processes*, Wiley, 1960. The ensuing model employs Howard's technique.

9 For simplicity, production will be considered as instantaneous.

inventory i, ending inventory j, price p_m, and output x_k, sales revenues are p_m times the sales quantity $i + x_k - j$, while total cost consists of the cost of producing x_k units and the inventory costs associated with initial inventory i, production x_k, and final inventory j.[10] The expected profits for a single period for a specified initial inventory, price, and production level is obtained by multiplying each π_{ij} by the corresponding ρ_{ij} and summing over j, the possible ending inventory states corresponding to each possible demand. For each price-output policy, for each initial inventory level i the values

$$(1) \qquad q_i(p_m, x_k) = \sum_{\text{all } j} \rho_{ij}\pi_{ij}$$

are calculated. These give the expected single-period profits for each possible initial inventory level and price-output combination. For each initial inventory, select one price-output combination. Let q_i represent the expected single-period profits for the selected combination.

Let v_i represent the expected value of discounted profits resulting when the monopolist starts with initial inventory i and has selected a price-output combination for each initial inventory. The probabilities of ending the period with inventory j are known. The expected value of discounted profits, starting in state i, can be viewed as the immediate profits q_i plus the expected value of discounted profits for all remaining periods discounted by β, the discount factor for one period,[11] i.e.

$$(2) \qquad v_i = q_i + \beta \sum_{\text{all } j} \rho_{ij} v_j \qquad i = 1, 2, \ldots$$

There is an equation for each initial inventory. It can be shown that there exists a solution to equations (2) as long as β is less than unity.[12] Designate the solution to equations (2) by v_i^0 ($i = 1, 2, \ldots$). The v_i^0 values can next be utilized to ascertain whether or not the optimal price-output combination was selected for each incoming inventory level. Consider some particular level of incoming inventory, say i. Suppose a different price-output combination is used for the first period and the price-output combinations that resulted in equations (2) are used for all subsequent periods. Designate the values of q_i and ρ_{ij} appropriate under the new policy by q_i^1 and ρ_{ij}^1. Then for each price-output combination the 'test quantity'

$$(3) \qquad q_i^1 + \beta \sum_{\text{all } j} \rho_{ij}^1 v_j^0$$

[10] Frequently it is more convenient to assign the inventory costs only to ending inventory j. To simplify the exposition, this assumption will be used in the subsequent analysis.

[11] $\beta = \frac{1}{1+e}$ where e is the appropriate one-period interest rate.

[12] See G. Hadley, *Nonlinear and Dynamic Programming*, Addison-Wesley, 1963, p. 457.

gives the expected discounted profits resulting from *selecting a new price-output combination for the first period and the previously selected price-output combinations for all subsequent periods*. If any 'test quantity' is higher than v_i^0, profits can be increased by selecting the corresponding price-output combination.

For each incoming inventory, select the price-output combination with the highest test quantity (3). Then set up a new system of equations (2) for the resulting price-output combinations. Calculate new test quantities based on the solution to these equations, say v_i^1. If the maximum of these new test quantities, for each initial inventory, occurs for the price-output combination used in calculating v_i^1, the optimal combinations have been found. If not, again select the price-output combinations corresponding to the maximum test quantities and solve equations (2) again. The process converges quite rapidly on the optimal price-quantity combinations, and the procedure must result in the discovery of the optimal price and quantity policy.[13] A convenient initial starting-point is to select, for each level of incoming inventory, the price-output combination with the highest expected single-period profits.

It should be noted that the model can accommodate a wide variety of assumptions concerning the cost and demand function. If the interest rate is zero (i.e., $\beta = 1$), the expected profits are infinite. However, a slight modification of the above technique can solve these cases.[14]

Also, it should be observed that the various difficulties in the theory of the firm mentioned in the previous section have been eliminated. Specifically, probabilistic demands have been incorporated in the model as well as inventories of the product. Any known effect of stocks on sales can be included in the model through the probabilities ρ_{ij}. The effect of stocks on expected revenues is automatically included in the model through the π_{ij}. It will be pointed out later that the model can be extended to handle other complications.

From the computational side, the model is quite simple, involving the solution of linear equations (2). With the aid of electronic computers a large number of discrete price-output policies can be tested with little difficulty. The discrete nature of the alternative courses of action is not a very serious limitation to the usefulness of the model.

It was mentioned above that the classical monopoly model is a trivial special case of the above model. If one assumes that there

[13] See R. A. Howard, op. cit., for illustrative examples.
[14] Ibid., chs. 1–6.

are no inventories and that the quantity demanded is a known function of price, then only one level of initial and final inventory is possible, namely zero. The probability of ending with o inventory is unity. For each possible output there is a unique price at which the whole output can be sold. The π_{00} values corresponding to various output levels can be calculated. The single period profit is equal to π_{00} since ρ_{00} is unity. Select the x_k with the q_0 value that maximizes one-period profits. The same x_k can be selected in all subsequent periods to maximize discounted expected profits since the profits of any period are independent of all other periods. The 'test quantity' procedure can be used to verify this intuitively obvious result. Start by selecting the x_k that maximizes single-period profits q_0. Then, we have:

$$v_0 = q_0 + \beta v_0, \text{ or}$$

$$v_0 = \frac{q_0}{1-\beta}$$

Obviously no test quantity can result in a higher value than $q_0 + \beta v_0$. Hence the optimum production level has been obtained. An alternative way of looking at v_0 is to consider it as the discounted sum of a profit stream of q_0 per period starting immediately and going on infinitely many periods, i.e.:

$$v_0 = q_0 + \beta q_0 + \beta^2 q_0 + \dots$$

$$= \frac{q_0}{1-\beta}$$

Naturally, q_0 is maximized by selecting the highest output for which marginal revenue exceeds marginal cost.

III

For simplicity of exposition, the following illustrative example only allows a few possible inventory states. Initially it is assumed that the price is given and the problem is then reduced to one of ascertaining the optimal output for each level of incoming inventory. Later a second price and the accompanying probability demand distribution is introduced. The cost function assumed is also extremely simple. It should be clear that complication of the demand and cost functions changes the amount of computations but does not affect the validity of the approach.

The entrepreneur in question produces a product that he plans to sell at a price of \$8 per unit. At this price it has been estimated that, in a single period, he can sell no units with probability 1/10; exactly one unit with probability 3/10; exactly 2 units with probability ½; and exactly 3 units with probability 1/10. His production costs are assumed to be $1 for the first unit, $2 for the second unit, $3 for the third unit, etc. Total inventory costs per period are assigned to units of ending inventory as follows: one unit, $.20; two units, $.60; and three units, $1.20. A discount factor, β, of .9 is used. It is known that it is never desirable to start a period with more than a total of three units of combined production and inventory. Under these assumptions, the following table results. In the body of the table, the left-hand figure in each cell represents the ρ_{ij},

Payoff Table

Initial inventory	*Production*	Ending Inventory (j)								
		0		1		2		3		q_i
i	x_k									
0	0	1	0						0	0
	1	.9	7	.1	−1.2					6.18
	2	.6	13	.3	4.8	.1	−3.6			8.88
	3	.1	18	.5	9.8	.3	1.4	.1	−7.2	6.4
1	0	.9	8	.1	−.2					7.18
	1	.6	15	.3	6.8	.1	−1.6			10.88
	2	.1	21	.5	12.8	.3	4.4	.1	−4.2	9.4
2	0	.6	16	.3	7.8	.1	−.6			11.88
	1	.1	23	.5	14.8	.3	6.4	.1	−2.2	11.4
3	0	.1	24	.5	15.8	.3	7.4	.1	−1.2	12.4

probability of starting with inventory i and ending with inventory j, given that x_k units are produced. The right-hand figure in each cell gives the π_{ij} the profits that result when initial inventory is i, production x_k, and final inventory j, that is, the profits that result when $i+x_k-j$ units are demanded.

On the left-hand side of the table the first column represents the level of initial inventory, the second column the number of units of production. On the top border of the table are the various possible states of ending inventory. The column on the right-hand edge gives the expected values of single-period profits for each production policy. For a detailed analysis of the numbers within the cells, examine the cell corresponding to one unit of initial inventory, two units of production, and 2 units of ending inventory. Starting with one unit of inventory and 2 units of production, one can end with 2 units of inventory only when exactly one unit is demanded. The probability of one unit being demanded is .3, the left-hand entry in the cell. The concomitant profits in this event are $8 revenue less $3 production cost and $.60 inventory cost, i.e. $4.40. The q value in the last column corresponding to 2 units of production and 1 unit of initial inventory is obtained by summing the products of the two numbers in each cell in the row, i.e.

$$.1 \times 21 + .5 \times 12.8 + .3 \times 4.4 + .1 + (-4.2) = 9.40.$$

To start the computations of the v_i, it is only necessary to select a production level for each level of initial inventory. Following the suggestion above, the production of 2 units when initial inventory is zero, one unit of production when initial inventory one, and zero units of production for initial inventory of 2 or 3 units maximizes single-period profits. Equations (2) are then:

$$\begin{aligned} v_0 &= 8.88 + .9(.6v_0 + .3v_1 + .1v_2) \\ v_1 &= 10.88 + .9(.6v_0 + .3v_1 + .1v_2) \\ v_2 &= 11.88 + .9(.6v_0 + .3v_1 + .1v_2) \\ v_3 &= 12.4 \ + .9(.1v_0 + .5v_1 + .3v_2 + .1v_3) \end{aligned}$$

When it is noted that $v_1 = v_0 + 2$ and $v_2 = v_0 + 3$, the equations can easily be solved to give $v_0 = 96.90$; $v_1 = 98.90$; $v_2 = 99.90$; and $v_3 = 101.76$.

Using these values, the test quantities (3) are calculated. The table below gives all of the test quantities.

Test Quantity Calculations

Initial inventory	*Production*	$q_i^1 + \beta\Sigma_j p_{ij}^1 v_j^0$	*Test quantity*
0	0	0 +.9[96.9]	= 87.21
	1	6.18+.9[.9(96.9)+.1(98.9)]	= 93.57
	2	8.88+.9[.6(96.9)+.3(98.9)+.1(99.9)]	= 96.90
	3	6.4 +.9[.1(96.9)+.5(98.9)+.3(99.9)+.1(101.76)]	= 95.76
1	0	7.18+.9[.9(96.9)+.1(98.9)]	= 94.57
	1	10.88+.9[.6(96.9)+.3(98.9)+.1(99.9)]	= 98.90
	2	9.4 +.9[.1(96.9)+.5(98.9)+.3(99.9)+.1(101.76)]	= 98.76
2	0	11.88+.9[.6(96.9)+.3(98.9)+.1(99.9)]	= 99.90
	1	11.4 +.9[.1(96.9)+.5(98.9)+.3(99.9)+.1(101.76)]	= 100.76
3	0	12.4 +.9[.1(96.9)+.5(98.9)+.3(99.9)+.1(101.76)]	= 101.76

The highest test quantities occur for initial inventory 0, produce 2; for inventory 1, produce 1; for inventory 2, produce 1, and for inventory 3, produce 0. This policy yields a new set of equations (2):

$$v_0 = 8.88+.9[.6v_0+.3v_1+.1v_2]$$
$$v_1 = 10.88+.9[.6v_0+.3v_1+.1v_2]$$
$$v_2 = 11.4 +.9[.1v_0+.5v_1+.3v_2+.1v_3]$$
$$v_3 = 12.4 +.9[.1v_0+.5v_1+.3v_2+.1v_3]$$

The solution is $v_0 = 97.89$; $v_1 = 99.89$, $v_2 = 101.98$; and $v_3 = 102.98$. Using these values to calculate test quantities (3) gives for each level of initial inventory and production, designated (i, x_k) the following table:

(i, x_k)	*Test quantity*
(0, 0)	88.10
(0, 1)	94.46
(0, 2)	97.89 ←
(0, 3)	96.98
(1, 0)	95.46
(1, 1)	99.89
(1, 2)	99.98 ←
(2, 0)	100.89
(2, 1)	101.98 ←
(3, 0)	102.98 ←

The arrows designate the maximum test quantity for each initial inventory. Using the production policy indicated by the arrows, a final set of equations (2) is obtained:

$$v_0 = 8.88+.9(.6v_0+.3v_1+.1v_2)$$
$$v_1 = 9.4 +.9(.1v_0+.5v_1+.3v_2+.1v_3)$$
$$v_2 = 11.4 +.9(.1v_0+.5v_1+.3v_2+.1v_3)$$
$$v_3 = 12.4 +.9(.1v_0+.5v_1+.3v_2+.1v_3)$$

The solution is $v_0 = 98.09$; $v_1 = 100.18$; $v_2 = 102.18$; and $v_3 = 103.18$. The corresponding test quantities are:

(i, x_k)	(0, 0)	(0, 1)	(0, 2)	(0, 3)	(1, 0)	(1, 1)	(1, 2)	(2, 0)	(2, 1)	(3, 0)
Test quantity	88.28	94.65	98.09	97.18	95.65	100.09	100.18	101.09	102.18	103.18

The maximum test quantity occurs for the same production policy as at the previous round, indicating that the optimal policy, namely (0, 2), (1, 2), (2, 1), and (3, 0), has been found.

It is perhaps intuitively clear that lowering β, i.e. raising the interest rate can alter optimal policy toward that with the highest single-period profits. This is obviously the case for $\beta = 0$, when only single-period profits exist. The reader can easily verify that for $\beta = .8$, optimal policy includes (1, 1) rather than (1, 2). Here the expected values of discounted profits are $v_0 = 48.34$; $v_1 = 50.34$; $v_2 = 52.19$, and $v_3 = 53.19$.

Now consider the original example ($\beta = .9$ again) with the possibility of setting the price at \$9.30 as well as at \$8.00. It has been estimated that at a price of \$9.30, the entrepreneur has a probability of .2 of demand 0, a .35 probability of one unit demand, a .4 probability of exactly two units demand, and a .05 probability of exactly 3 units demand. At the price of \$9.30 the following table results:

Payoff Table

		Ending Inventory (j)									
Initial inventory i	*Production* x_k	0		1		2		3		q	*Test quantities*
0	0	1	0							0	88.28
	1	.8	8.3	.2	−1.2					6.40	95.78
	2	.45	15.6	.35	6.1	.2	−3.6			8.43	98.10
	3	.05	21.9	.4	12.4	.35	2.7	.2	−7.2	5.56	96.80
1	0	.8	9.3	.2	−.2					7.40	96.78
	1	.45	17.6	.35	8.1	.2	−1.6			10.43	100.10
	2	.05	24.9	.4	15.4	.35	5.7	.2	−4.2	8.56	99.80
2	0	.45	18.6	.35	9.1	.2	−.6			11.43	101.10
	1	.05	26.9	.4	17.4	.35	7.7	.2	−2.2	10.56	101.80
3	0	.05	27.9	.4	18.4	.35	8.7	.2	−1.2	11.56	102.80

The test quantities in the last column are based on the final set of v_i in the problem with only the \$8 price, namely $v_0 = 98.09$; $v_1 = 100.18$; $v_2 = 102.18$; and $v_3 = 103.18$. In only one instance does the test quantity exceed the v_i of the policy with the \$8 price, namely for initial inventory 0, the maximum test quantity is 98.10 for an output of 2 units. Thus, when initial inventory is 0 gains can be made by changing the price to \$9.30 and producing 2 units rather than leaving the price at \$8. A new set of equations (2) is constructed with this policy:

$$
\begin{aligned}
v_0 &= 8.43 + .9[.45v_0 + .35v_1 + .2v_2] \\
v_1 &= 9.4 + .9[.1v_0 + .5v_1 + .3v_2 + .1v_3] \\
v_2 &= 11.4 + .9[.1v_0 + .5v_1 + .3v_2 + .1v_3] \\
v_3 &= 12.4 + .9[.1v_0 + .5v_1 + .3v_2 + .1v_3]
\end{aligned}
$$

The solution is $v_0 = 98.17$; $v_1 = 100.24$; $v_2 = 102.24$; and $v_3 = 103.24$. With these values a new set of test quantities is computed for each initial inventory and each price-output policy. The following table gives the test quantities for each (i, p_m, x_k)

(i, p_m, x_k)	Test quantity
0, 8, 0	88.35
0, 8, 1	94.72
0, 8, 2	98.16
0, 8, 3	97.24
0, 9.3, 0	88.35
0, 9.3, 1	95.13
0, 9.3, 2	98.17 *
0, 9.3, 3	96.85
1, 8, 0	95.72
1, 8, 1	100.16
1, 8, 2	100.24 *
1, 9.3, 0	96.13
1, 9.3, 1	100.17
1, 9.3, 2	99.85
2, 8, 0	101.16
2, 8, 1	102.24 *
2, 9.3, 0	101.17
2, 9.3, 1	101.85
3, 8, 0	103.24 *
3, 9.3, 0	102.85

Since the maximum test quantity for each level of initial inventory (indicated by the asterisk) occurs for the same price-output combinations just used in calculating the v_i, the optimum solution has been obtained.

There are several considerations which lead to a reduction in the amount of computation. For any given price, all policies with a common value of initial inventory plus production have identical expected revenues and inventory costs. These policies only differ because different quantities are produced and hence different production costs. These production cost differentials remain constant from iteration to iteration, and are reflected in test quantity differentials *independent of the values of the* v_i. Thus, one has only to calculate test quantities for $i = 0$ and adjust all others by the appropriate production cost differential. For example, $(i, x_k) = (0, 3)$ differs from $(2, 1)$ by an amount equal to the cost of production of the second and third units, or \$5. Furthermore, an initial set of v_i can be obtained by selecting policies with a common price and a common value of initial inventory plus production. The differences between v_i values will then be known production cost differentials, making it possible to substitute in terms of one v_i and solve *a single equation in one unknown*. Even at later iterations the number of equations to be solved will be very small compared with the total number of possible values of initial inventory.

Incremental analysis can be used to determine the policy with the maximum test quantity for each initial inventory state, from the test quantities in the zero initial inventory case. Let $v_0(y, p_m)$ represent the test quantity for initial inventory 0 when y units are produced and the price is p_m. The letter y is used to designate the value of production plus initial inventory, i.e. $y = x_k + i$.

For $i = 0$

$$v_0(y, p_m) = v_0(y, p_m)$$

For $i > 0$,

$$v_i(y, p_m) = v_0(y, p_m) + k^1(y) + \ldots + k^1(y-i+1)$$

where $k^1(y)$ represents the marginal production cost of the yth unit of production. Let

$$\begin{aligned} \Delta v_i(y, p_m) &= v_0(y, p_m) - v_o(y-1, p_m) \\ &= v_0(y, p_m) - v_0(y-1, p_m) + k^1(y) - k^1(y-i) \end{aligned} \tag{4}$$

Select, for any $i > 0$, the highest y such that $\Delta v_i(y, p_m) > 0$. The corresponding value of x is equal to $y - i$. For any $i > 0$, this x maximizes the test quantity for the price under consideration. In the event that marginal production costs are constant, it is clear that the $k^1(y) - k^1(y-1)$ term is zero, indicating that the same price and production policy (produce up to y) will be optimal for all levels of initial inventory.[15]

Note that in the constant marginal production cost case the optimal price is the same for all levels of initial inventory, and the production policy involves the same total of initial inventory plus

[15] This assumes that the profit function is concave toward the origin. If a set-up cost is assumed which is incurred only for production levels greater than zero, the above remarks can be applied to an sS policy, i.e. (if initial inventory $< s$, produce up to total stock of S).

production. Thus, the optimal solution can be found very simply by maximizing $v_0(y, p_m)$ at the first iteration. Here

$$v_0(y, p_m) = \frac{1}{1-\beta} q_0(y, p_m) + \frac{\beta c}{1-\beta} \sum_{j=1}^{y} j\rho_{0j},$$

where c represents the marginal cost of producing one unit. The optimum can be found directly or with aid of incremental equations to find the optimum y for each price.

In the event that both unit production costs (c) and unit carrying charges on inventory (c_i) are constant, for any price p_m, it can be shown that

(5)

$$\Delta v_0(y, p_m) = \frac{1}{1-\beta}[p_m \rho_{00}(y, p_m) - c_i(\ -\rho_{00}(y, p_m)) - c + \beta c(1-\rho_{00}(y, p_m))]$$

The yth unit adds to expected discounted profits when equation (5) is positive. This is the case whenever

(6)
$$\rho_{00}(y, p_m) > \frac{c + c_i - \beta c}{p + c_i - \beta c}$$

Thus, for any price the highest y should be selected such that (6) is satisfied. There is a relatively simple intuitive interpretation of (6) when it is written:

(7)
$$p_m \rho_{00}(y, p_m) > c - \beta c[1-\rho_{00}(y, p_m)] + c_i[1-\rho_{00}(y, p_m)]$$

The left-hand side gives the expected marginal revenue and the right-hand side the expected marginal cost. The latter is the unit cost, c, reduced by the expected discounted value of the unit cost saving resulting from lower production the next period, and increased by expected inventory charge increases.

IV

The above model can be extended to include other real-world phenomena such as advertising, seasonal demand variations, and other types of changes in demand and cost functions. The inclusion of advertising would be straightforward, merely increasing the number of policy variables with respect to which the entrepreneur maximizes. For each initial inventory, the entrepreneur must select an optimal price, production and advertising policy. The difficulties, of course, would lie in estimating what are the effects of advertising policies on the probability distribution of demand.

The extension of the probabilistic dynamic programming model to include seasonal factors has been carried out already.[16] The capability of including this important element of reality is a substantial advantage of the programming approach. In the economic literature a discussion of seasonal factors is almost non-existent while in business they constitute one of the principal factors underlying demand determination. A method of handling seasonal demand fluctuations in the case of certainly known demand has already been successfully applied.[17]

When changes in demand and/or cost conditions are anticipated, a multi-period dynamic programming model can be employed with the relevant demand and cost characteristics. Rather than the above model with an infinite horizon, a model with a finite horizon can be employed. In the probabilistic case it will be necessary to use a 'backward' solution, starting at the final period. For each level of initial inventory an optimal policy is ascertained. Next, for each level of initial inventory in the next to last period the policy which, combined with optimal last period policy, optimizes profits over the two periods is calculated, etc., until one finally calculates optimal policy for the present period.

The area of optimal equipment replacement policy is another place where dynamic programming models appear to be of much use. Interesting calculations for automobile replacement with the automobiles being subject to probabilities of not surviving without incurring prohibitively expensive repairs were exhibited by Ronald Howard.[18] Given data on the cost of buying cars of various ages and on the trade-in values and operating costs, the optimal policies were calculated by the technique illustrated in the previous section. The state of the system, described by the age of the car in three-month periods ran from 1 to 40. For each state the decision was made as to keep the car or trade it in for a car of various ages. Although the total number of possible policies was 41^{40}, Howard's iterative technique converged on the optimal policy in 7 steps.

V

The model described in sections II and III has extended the conventional theory of the firm to allow for the effects of probabilistic demand, inventories and explicit inclusion of the interest rate. The classical results of marginal revenue equals marginal cost occur only in a trivial special case. It remains to explore further some implications of the model for industrial equilibrium and for the conven-

[16] Jens Ove Riis, 'Discounted Markov Programming in a Periodic Process', *Operations Research*, Nov.–Dec., 1965, pp. 920–9.

[17] H. M. Wagner and T. M. Whitin, 'Dynamic Version of the Economic Lot Size Model', *Management Science*, October 1958, pp. 89–96.

[18] Op. cit., pp. 54–9.

tional theory of the firm. With respect to the latter, it will be shown that, once probabilistic elements are permitted, neither the concept of marginal revenue nor even expected marginal revenue is useful in any but the simplest cases. Also the concepts of *output* and *price* must be replaced by *output and price policies*. Finally, the marginal revenue is not analytically independent of the cost function.

As far as the individual firm is concerned, the model of section II is an equilibrium model under stationary demand and cost conditions.[19] The amount produced under optimal policy is equal to the amount demanded minus the amount of unfilled demand due to stockouts. If such was not the case, stocks of goods would rise without limit if supply exceeded demand over the infinite horizon assumed.

However, the problem of equilibrium of the industry has not been discussed. It is the belief of the author that analysis of disequilibrium situations is highly relevant. It should be noted that the dynamic programming approach can be used under stationary or changing conditions and is by no means wedded to an equilibrium concept. The suggestion that development of an adequate economic theory of the firm has been hindered by its stress on equilibrium has been made forcefully by others.[20] Nevertheless, equilibriumists may gain some slight consolation from some equilibrating tendencies that can be observed in the dynamic programming model. When stocks of goods are low, the optimal price policy may involve an increase in price. In the numerical illustration, a zero initial inventory level made a price increase desirable. Also, when initial stocks are high, a typical characteristic of the model is that production levels and price are lower.

Another case of interest is that of a firm in an industry where there is an administered price.[21] If the entrepreneur can estimate the probability distribution of demand, his level of output will be determinate. In R. Robinson's article the precise nature of sales and production was not specified, as 'Sales simply approximate *AB* . . . output levels *such as AB*'.[22] It would seem as though demand is either subject to probabilistic influences or something similar and that the level of demand in one period would influence the level of production in the subsequent period or periods, as in the above dynamic programming model.

Turning next to the relevance of the present paper for conventional marginal analysis, several different cases will be distinguished

[19] A non-stationary, non-equilibrium model, however, is also possible, as indicated in the previous section.

[20] P. W. S. Andrews, op. cit., p. 71, 90 ff.; R. Robinson, op. cit., p. 233.

[21] R. Robinson, op. cit., pp. 204–8.

[22] Ibid., pp. 205–6, italics mine.

all involving probabilistic demands. The three cases to be analyzed are a single period case with a fixed price, a single period case with demand a function of price, and an infinite horizon case. The marginal revenue function is useful and relevant only in the first of these situations. In the second, marginal revenue is a function of cost, and in the third marginal revenue is a function of cost as well as of optimal price-output policy.

For the single period model with a fixed price, assume for simplicity that the commodity in question is worthless at the end of the period and that it is produced or bought at the start of the period in accordance with a known cost function. Marginal revenue here is the change in expected total revenue resulting from an increase in production. Production increases are profitable as long as expected marginal revenue exceeds marginal cost. Expected marginal revenue is merely the probability of selling the marginal output multiplied by the price. A graphical solution is shown in Figure 1. *OA* is the price;

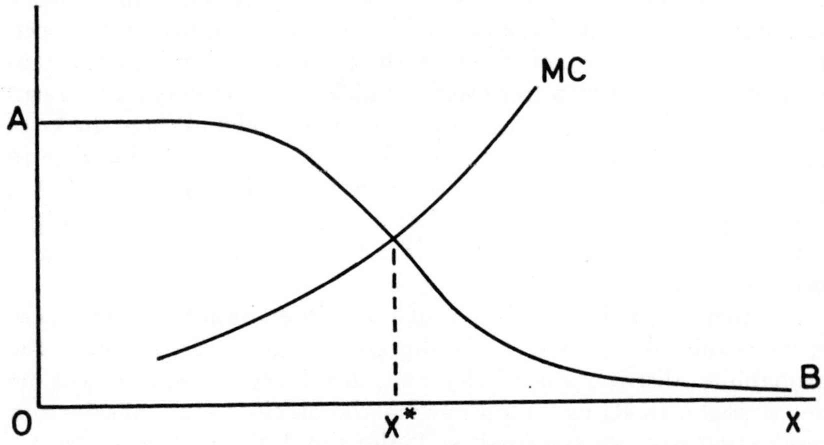

Figure 1

AB, the expected marginal revenue curve is the price multiplied by the probability of selling out for each possible output level, *X*; and *MC* is the marginal cost. The left-hand portion of *AB* is parallel to the *X*-axis as long as it is certain that demand will exceed *X*. As selling production increments becomes less likely the curve drops downward toward the *X*-axis. Here X^* is the optimal production level.[23] This example is straightforward and involves only inserting

[23] Analytically X^* can be determined by the equation $\int_{X^*}^{\infty} q(X)dx = \frac{MC}{p}$, where $q(X)$ is the probability density function of demand, *MC* is the marginal cost, and p the price.

the modifier 'expected' before marginal revenue. Note that the classical perfect competition solution MC = price results only when marginal cost intersects expected marginal revenue on its horizontal section. However, when the probability distribution of demand is a function of price, the situation is altered. Expected marginal revenue is defined as the change in expected total revenue resulting from a unit increase in production, or in the case of divisible units as the derivative of the expected total revenue function. Note that there is no longer a unique price corresponding to each output level. There is, however, only one *relevant* price for each output, namely the price corresponding to intersection of an expected marginal revenue curve for some fixed price and the marginal cost curve, i.e. such as the price OA for output X^* in Figure 1.[24] Expected total revenue is the area under curves such as AB between the price-axis and the dotted line at X^*. Marginal revenue is the corresponding change in or derivative of expected total revenue. Expected marginal revenue cannot be determined without reference to the intersection of curves such as AB and the marginal cost curve. Thus, marginal revenue is a function of marginal cost. Indeed it is possible to construct an analytical expression for marginal revenue in which marginal cost occurs explicitly. It appears, then, that when probabilistic demands are considered there occurs a complete destruction of 'the analytical independence of cost and demand functions, which marginal equilibrium theorists take for granted, and which, indeed, is essential for the formal validity of their work'.[25]

In the infinite horizon case, the above problems with respect to marginal revenue occur. In addition, the meaning of marginal revenue is further clouded in that it cannot be calculated except with respect to a complete specification of price and output policy for each possible level of incoming inventory. Thus, even when there is a fixed price, a simple expected marginal revenue concept is no longer possible, for expected discounted revenues are a function of production policy for each initial inventory level.[26] Since one must calculate optimal policies in order to ascertain expected discounted marginal revenue, the usefulness of the procedure would seem to be questionable.

In summary, the basic model developed in this paper indicates a way of extending the theory of the firm to incorporate a number of

[24] It does not seem unreasonable to assume that there is only one such intersection for each output. However, if such is not the case the result is merely to complicate the MR concept further.

[25] P. W. S. Andrews, op. cit., p. 60.

[26] In the case of fixed price and constant unit production costs expected marginal revenue can be calculated simply, since optimal policies for each initial inventory state involve a constant level of initial inventory plus production.

additional considerations, the most important of which is probabilistic demand functions. The conventional marginal analysis results constitute a special case of the model. In addition it is shown that the conventional marginal concepts cannot in general be extended to the stochastic demand cases without introducing interdependency between cost and demand functions. The approach requires few restrictions on the nature of demand or cost functions and, unlike the conventional theory, incorporates discounting in a manner which affects price and output behavior, thus making it an integral part of the theory.

WESLEYAN UNIVERSITY, MIDDLETOWN, CONNECTICUT

A NOTE ON MERGERS AND THE BUSINESS CYCLE[1]

By C. J. Maule

Two writers, whose work has been published under the auspices of the National Bureau of Economic Research, have reported conflicting views about the relationship between merger activity and the business cycle in the United States. It is the purpose of this note to examine the source of the conflict and to evaluate the accuracy of each view.

In a survey article on mergers Professor Markham concludes that

> These data do not give strong support to the thesis that merger cycles are timed closely with business cycles. The correlation between mergers and general business activity for the 1919–39 period is only a little better than that which would be expected of two time series moving at random.[2]

National Bureau of Economic Research reference cycles are used by Markham as indicators of the business cycle.

In the course of a detailed examination of mergers in the United States R. L. Nelson has expressed the following view

> The merger activity of the past six decades has exhibited high, though not perfect, conformity to changes in general business conditions. The National Bureau of Economic Research has recorded fourteen cycles in general business activity between 1897 and 1954. The series of merger disappearances exhibited twelve cycles of activity. Eleven of the twelve cycles showed a definite timing relationship to the turning points of the reference cycles.[3]

These conclusions are derived from the examination of time periods which are not exactly similar. However, there are a sufficient number of years common to both studies to permit a comparison to be made.

As will be shown below the divergent opinions for the same time periods are due to differences in the source of the data, in the form in

[1] Parts of this note appeared in the author's Ph.D. thesis for the University of London which was written under the supervision of Professor B. S. Yamey.

[2] J. W. Markham, 'Survey of the Evidence and Findings on Mergers', in *Business Concentration and Price Policy*, N.B.E.R., Princeton University Press, Princeton, 1955, pp. 151–2.

[3] R. L. Nelson, *Merger Movements in American Industry*, N.B.E.R., Princeton University Press, Princeton, 1959, pp. 108 and 111.

which the data are used and in the evaluation of the data made by each writer.

Markham's study examines the years 1887 to 1904 and 1919 to 1939, while Nelson's conclusions are based on data from 1895 to 1954. The years treated by both writers are therefore 1895 to 1904 and 1919 to 1939. These periods will be examined first.

1895–1904

DATA ON MERGERS

Markham measures merger activity by the annual number of mergers. His series is derived from the lists of Conant, Watkins, Moody and the Bureau of the Census.[4] The number of mergers selected each year is the highest number shown in any of these lists.[5] Markham is careful to note that the data are incomplete and subject to errors so that spurious cycles may occur.[6]

Nelson represents merger activity by the number of firms which disappear due to mergers each quarter. His basic sources are the columns of the *Commercial and Financial Chronicle* and the writers consulted by Markham. Any merger reported in any of these sources was subjected to a rigorous verification procedure before it was included in the final list.[7]

DATA ON THE BUSINESS CYCLE

Both Markham and Nelson use National Bureau of Economic Research reference cycle dates but Markham uses them in their annual and Nelson in their quarterly form (Table I). This is a basic difference. Markham's view appears to be that it is difficult to use quarterly data in the case of mergers because exact dates of some mergers are not known.[8]

RELATIONSHIP BETWEEN MERGERS AND THE BUSINESS CYCLE

The two writers use different techniques to measure the association between the two variables. Markham employs the Fechner–

[4] Luther Conant, Jr., 'Industrial Consolidations in the United States', *American Statistical Associations Publications*, vol. 7, March 1901; Myron W. Watkins, *Industrial Combinations and Public Policy*, Houghton, Mifflin, 1927; *Twelfth Census of the United States*, Bureau of the Census, vol. VII, part 1, pp. XXV ff.; John Moody, *The Truth about the Trusts*, Moody Publishing Co., 1904.

[5] Markham, op. cit., pp. 149 and 151.

[6] Ibid., p. 150.

[7] Nelson, op. cit., pp. 13–16.

[8] Markham, op. cit., p. 150, footnote to Table 1.

TABLE I

DATES OF BUSINESS CYCLE AND MERGER TURNING POINTS

MARKHAM AND NELSON

Year	Markham Turning points (annual)		Nelson Turning points (quarterly)		Merger leads (−) and lags (+) in quarters
	Business cycles	Mergers	Business cycles	Mergers	
1895	P				
1896	T			T3	−3
1897			T2		
1898					
1899	P	P	P3	P3	0
1900	T	T	T4	T2	−2
1901				P4	−4
1902		P	P4		
1903	P				
1904	T		T3	T3	0
1919	T		T2		
1920	P	P	P1	P2	+1
1921	T		T3		
1922		T			
1923	P		P2	T3	−4
1924	T		T3		
1925					
1926	P		P3	P1	−2
1927	T		T4	T1	−3
1928					
1929	P	P	P2	P1	−1
1930					
1931					
1932	T				
1933			T1	T4	+3
1934		T			
1935		P			
1936				P1	−5
1937	P		P2		
1938	T		T2		
1939		T		T3	−5

SOURCE: Markham, op. cit., pp. 149–51.
Nelson, op. cit., p. 109.

Note: P = peak and T = trough

Markham states that his data reveal that there are two and a half merger cycles and six turning points from 1919 to 1939, although he does not identify their dates. The turning points shown in this table have therefore been deduced from the statistics which Markham presents. Four turning points are easily identified, peaks in 1920 and 1929 and troughs in 1922 and 1934. The other two turning points are presumably 1935, a peak but which hardly deserves to be so-called, and the final year 1939, a trough. The only other reasonable possibility is that 1919, the initial year, was taken as a trough in place of 1939, but this seems to be ruled out by a later statement that only two out of the six turning points coincide with business cycle turning points. If 1919 had been a turning point this statement would have been false. Markham, op. cit., p. 151.

Weber[9] index of directional correlation while Nelson compares the timing of the turning points of both sets of data. Both methods will be used on each writer's data.

Between 1887 and 1904 Markham calculates the Fechner–Weber index equal to 0.65;[10] for the shorter period 1895 to 1904, which is examined here, the index equals 0.80. A similar calculation applied to Nelson's data (1895 to 1904) results in a value of 0.55.

Nelson indicates that there are 5 merger cycle and 5 business cycle turning points. In two instances the turning points coincide, and in three other instances merger turning points lead business cycle turning points by from two to four quarters. A similar comparison made with Markham's data, in which there are three merger cycle turning points and six business cycle turning points, reveals that coincidence occurs in two cases and the third merger turning point leads the business cycle turning point by one year.[11]

In commenting on this period Markham notes that the high value of the Fechner–Weber index is due to the almost unique era of merger activity in the United States while the 'two business cycles of 1897–1900 and 1900–04 were relatively insignificant'.[12] An index of directional correlation such as the one used here does not distinguish between the strength of changes, but merely takes cognizance of the direction of change.

Nelson's summary of this period is that

> It was apparent, however, that the business cycle was important in the timing of the first merger movement.[13]

It is doubtful, therefore, whether Markham, using his own technique of correlation on Nelson's data would have arrived at Nelson's conclusion. Nor probably would Nelson, using his technique on Markham's data, have arrived at the summary quoted above.

Speculation on probable views in hypothetical cases is unimportant. The point is that in this period different conclusions were

[9] The Fechner–Weber index is: $I = (C-D)/(C+D)$, where C is the total number of years or months in which the directional movement of the two series coincides, and D is the total in which they move in opposite directions. The index for two time series moving at random should equal zero. The index measures directional correlation and does not account for the amplitude of the changes in the series that are being correlated. Conclusions based on the index must therefore be treated with caution. See Markham, op. cit., p. 150 n.

[10] Ibid., p. 150.

[11] Markham states that between 1887 and 1904 there were three merger cycles and six turning points but he does not say in which years these turning points occurred. The three turning points for the period 1895 to 1904 have therefore had to be selected from the data which Markham presents. Ibid., p. 150.

[12] Ibid., p. 152.

[13] Nelson, op. cit., p. 106.

reached on the basis of differences in the source of data, in the form in which the data were used and in each writer's evaluation of the data.

1919–1939

DATA ON MERGERS AND THE BUSINESS CYCLE

In this period both writers use the same merger data, the number of disappearing firms as recorded by Thorp and Crowder.[14] However, the annual totals of the quarterly data used by Nelson and of the annual data used by Markham tend to vary, Markham covering a larger number; for example in 1929 Markham records 1245 and Nelson 1207 disappearing firms. The reason for this is that the original data appear in annual and quarterly form, but the annual totals exceed the quarterly totals since lack of information prevented some mergers from being allocated to a particular quarter. Nelson uses the sum of the quarterly data while Markham uses the annual totals. Furthermore Nelson seasonally adjusts his data which lead to further discrepancies, sometimes positive and sometimes negative, between the annual totals of the quarterly data in their adjusted and unadjusted form. In each case the source of business cycle data is as described for the earlier period.

RELATIONSHIP BETWEEN MERGERS AND THE BUSINESS CYCLE

Markham calculates the Fechner–Weber index equal to 0.20; a similar calculation applied to Nelson's data results in a value of 0.31. These are both low values for this index, and lower than the comparable values for the earlier period.

Markham's data reveal eleven business cycle and six merger cycle turning points. The merger turning points coincide twice, lag three times and lead once business cycle turning points. On this basis Markham concludes that, 'these data do not give strong support to the thesis that merger cycles are timed closely with business cycles'.[15]

Nelson indicates that there are eleven business cycle and eight merger cycle turning points. Mergers lead the business cycle in five cases (from one to five quarters) and lag the business cycle in three cases (from one to five quarters).

Nelson recognizes two additional merger cycle turning points, in 1926 and 1927. The reason for this appears to be that in their annual

[14] See Willard Thorp and Walter F. Crowder, *The Structure of Industry*, Temporary National Economic Committee Monograph 27, 1941, p. 233.

[15] Markham, op. cit., p. 151.

form the data for these years appear as a point of inflexion in the series, while in quarterly form two turning points can be located.

The total impression given by these findings is that there is neither a close nor a consistent relationship between mergers and the business cycle over the course of the years 1895 to 1904 and 1919 to 1939.

However, before a more definite judgment can be made one further aspect of the data requires attention. Nelson's conclusions are based on an examination of the whole period from 1895 to 1954, and so it is fair to ask whether the inclusion of data from 1905 to 1918 and from 1948 to 1954 would serve to strengthen his view.

For the whole period 1895 to 1954 Nelson finds that merger cycles most frequently lead business cycles both at the peak and trough.[16] However, an examination of his data reveals that although leads are more frequent than lags the variation in both is considerable. At the trough the timing of merger cycle turning points varies from a lead of three-quarters in some cases to a lag of five quarters in others; at the peak the variation is from a lead of ten quarters to a lag of one quarter. This highlights one of the problems in trying to derive leads and lags between time series. The method tends to be arbitrary since the decision as to whether a turning point leads or lags another depends upon the choice, and usually the *a priori* disposition, of the individual. For example why should the merger trough in 1927 (1st quarter) be said to lead the business cycle trough in 1927 (3rd quarter) rather than lag the peak in 1926 (3rd quarter)?

In summary it would seem that the available evidence supports Professor Markham's view that merger cycles are not timed closely with business cycles. The differing view of Nelson occurs due to differences in the source and form of the data used, and in his evaluation of the data.

In a recent article Nelson, again without reference to Markham's work, has repeated his contention concerning the 1895–1956 period that

> . . . mergers responded positively and with high consistency to the business cycle. . . . Merger peaks were found to precede by an appreciable interval the peaks in the reference cycle; the average merger peak led the average reference cycle peak by about ten months.[17]

[16] Nelson, op. cit., pp. 108–12.

[17] R. L. Nelson, 'Business Cycle Factors in the Choice between Internal and External Growth' in *The Corporate Merger*, Eds. W. W. Alberts and J. E. Segall, University of Chicago Press, Chicago, 1966, pp. 52–70.

In this article the time series of mergers has been extended to 1962 and comparisons are made from 1919 to 1961 between the turning points in the merger series and those in the reference cycle series. The same conclusion of a lead relationship is derived. It is, however, questionable whether the data warrant such a finding for the following reasons.[18]

(*a*) The merger series is presented on a monthly basis necessitating the conversion of the quarterly data from 1919 to 1954. This is done arbitrarily 'by taking the "center month" of the turning point of the quarterly series as the monthly turning point'. The outcome is that, except for two unexplained cases, merger turning points always occur in February, May, August and November. Comparisons are then made with monthly reference cycle turning points.

(*b*) The merger turning points have been aligned with the reference cycle points such that the former most frequently lead the latter e.g. a merger trough in November 1918 is matched with a reference cycle trough in April 1919 to show a lead; however, a merger peak occurs in May 1920 and if this had been matched with the reference cycle trough it would have revealed a lagged relationship. The reason for the choice of matching dates is not given but presumably it reflects again the *a priori* notions of the writer. The dates are thus presented so as to be consistent with the hypothesis tested.

Nelson's procedure becomes all the more dubious when merger turning points occur and reference cycle turning points do not and vice versa. In these cases no comparisons can be made and it is merely assumed that either one or the other series missed a cycle.

(*c*) The average duration of the lead is shown to be 9.38 months at the peaks and 1.22 months at the troughs. Six out of eight observations at the peak and six out of nine (not out of seven as shown) observations at the trough reveal a lead relationship. However, the dispersion of observations from which the averages are calculated is from a lead of 30 to a lag of 4 months at the peak, and from a lead of 11 to a lag of 14 at the trough.

For these reasons it is difficult to remain convinced that the data support the hypothesis that mergers are closely timed with the business cycle and that merger turning points tend to lead business cycle turning points.

MCMASTER UNIVERSITY, HAMILTON, ONTARIO

[18] The following discussion relates to Table 1, ibid., p. 57.

CYCLICAL BEHAVIOR OF MANUFACTURING PLANTS

by T. Y. Shen*

In recent years several investigators have demonstrated a relationship between labor productivity changes and output changes for manufacturing industries using monthly or quarterly data. Their analyses have implied quite different views of decision making by the firm during a cycle. In one extreme, Hultgren employed the cyclical phase as a catch-all for dynamic factors such as time lag, shift in technology, expectation and uncertainty.[1] In this approach the firm strives to adapt to the cycle and its behavior is largely determined by its ability at each point of time to ascertain the course of the cycle. The willingness and the capacity of the firm to adapt is taken for granted so that amplitude and duration of the cycle are disregarded. The implied assumption of foresight on the part of decision makers is clearly unrealistic. Many authors have therefore introduced lagged response,[2] expectation formation,[3] and devices such as buffer stock in their analyses. Nevertheless the underlying assumption remains that the firm modifies its 'desired' labor force in continuous response to cyclical sales and output fluctuations.

A quite different approach is exemplified by Wilson and Eckstein.[4] They explained labor productivity fluctuations within the framework of a neo-classical equilibrium-minded firm which establishes a 'planned output' based on its fixed plant and equipment. The firm attempts to maintain its labor force at this chosen level. By utilizing a unique short run cost curve in the analysis, the approach implies that the firm makes its calculations from assumed equilibrium conditions. The impact of dynamic factors on the cost curve and on demand is not stressed since these factors are regarded as temporary and random.

The relative merits of the two approaches from the point of view

* I would like to thank Richard Day and Harold Watts for their helpful suggestions, the National Science Foundation for financial support, and the University of California (Davis) computer center for machine time allowance.

[1] Thor Hultgren, *Changes in Labor Costs During Cycles in Production and in Business* (NBER Occasional Paper, No. 74, 1960).

[2] Edwin Kuh, 'Cyclical and Secular Labor Productivity in U.S. Manufacturing', *Review of Economics and Statistics* (Vol. XLVII, 1965), and F. P. R. Brechling, 'The Relationship Between Output and Employment in British Manufacturing Industries,' *Review of Economic Studies* (Vol. XXXII, 1965).

[3] Charles Holt, Franco Modigliani, John Muth and Herbert Simon, *Planning Production, Inventories, and Work Force* (Prentice-Hall, 1960).

[4] Thomas Wilson and Otto Eckstein, 'Short-run Productivity Behavior in U.S. Manufacturing', *Review of Economics and Statistics* (Vol. XLVI, 1964).

of the producer depend largely upon the regularity, duration and severity of the cyclical fluctuations to which his sales and output are subjected. These characteristics determine both the degree of foresight which a producer could possess and the costs of continuous adaptation. The principal findings of the present paper are: 1. that the 'cycles' for manufacturing plants are much shorter in duration and wider in amplitude than industry cycles and appear to be quite irregular; and 2. that, as follows from 1, the plants appear to establish 'equilibrium' outputs and then attempt to maintain their labor force at levels corresponding to these outputs despite sales and output fluctuations. In addition, the role of the different cyclical parameters is found to be negligible in determining the labor input response to output changes. The Wilson-Eckstein approach therefore appears to be more relevant in describing the cyclical behavior of manufacturing plants. The equilibrium cost function hence represents a better starting point in the short run analysis. Of course, systematic and predictable deviations from the equilibrium position do take place frequently for many firms. In such cases the study of adaptation behavior and 'adjustment functions' are needed to supplement the equilibrium analysis.

I. BASIC HYPOTHESIS

Our basic hypothesis is concerned with the relationship between the independent variable, changes in output, and the dependent variable, changes in production worker manhours. For an individual plant, the two principal factors determining this relationship (and hence labor productivity) are friction costs and stretching costs. Friction costs are incurred when labor input is altered in response to output changes. They include such items as overtime and severance pay, loss of younger workers and trained workers, training costs of new workers, and the value attached by workers to a steady job in their choice of employment. Stretching costs are incurred when labor is held constant while output changes. They result directly from straining of inputs or from idle capacity, and indirectly from the foregone gains due to capital-labor substitution.[5] The actual labor adjustment management makes to any output change depends on weighing the two costs.

[5] Directly, stretching costs include the higher wage rate of overtime man hours and monetary inducements required for the more intensive utilization of labor. Indirectly, if capital and labor may be freely substituted for each other, idle capital may be utilized in place of labor during a downswing, and over-stretched capital may be relieved by additional labor during an upswing—if capital is assumed to be given in the short run. In either case it would be more costly to keep labor input constant.

Our hypothesis may be formulated in elasticity terms and illustrated by the LL-curve in Fig. 1. Starting from some 'origin'—its definition will be discussed in the next section—the shape of the LL-curve follows from a consideration of the nature of friction costs and stretching costs. Friction costs depend on changes in labor input.

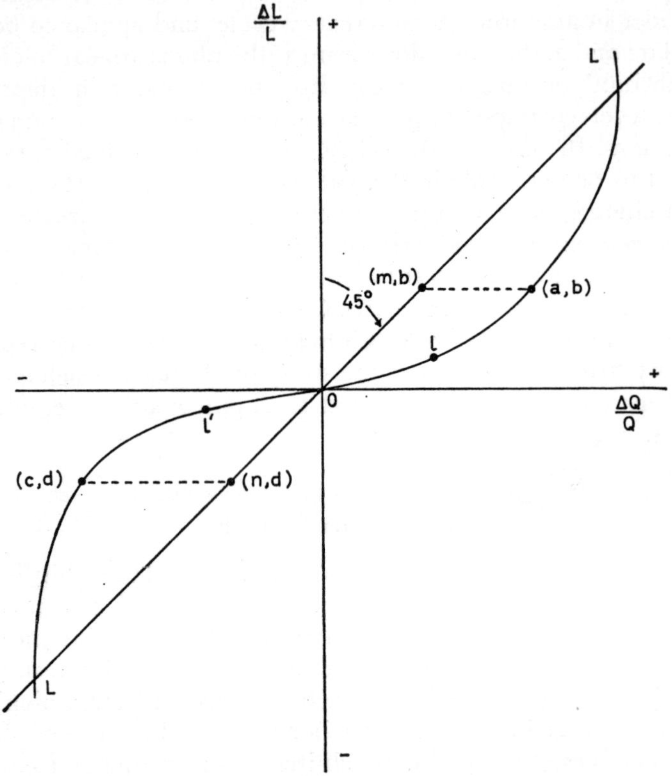

Fig. 1

Stretching costs depend on changes in output, and are reduced only if some adjustment is made in labor input. Consequently for small changes in output, stretching costs are low and the producer may refrain from hiring (including the assignment of overtime work) or layoff to avoid friction costs. For large changes in output, however, stretching costs rise and the producer would seek relief by altering the labor input.[6] Since capital stock is assumed to be given in the short

[6] It is probably reasonable to assume that friction costs is approximately a linear function of labor employed or laid off, while the stretching costs tend to rise more and more rapidly as output increases or decreases from the 'origin,' even when relief is sought by an alteration of the labor input.

run, eventually stretching costs become so high that friction costs would be relatively unimportant. The producer will alter his labor input freely and the picture will then be completely dominated by diminishing returns.[7] When that happens, marginal productivity of labor increases with any reduction of labor input and decreases with any addition of labor input. Labor output elasticity—proportionate change in labor input relative to proportionate change in output—consequently increases steadily as output moves farther and farther away from the origin.

The LL-curve may be given either a cross-section or a time series interpretation. In the cross-section interpretation, the curve describes the various labour input adjustments a producer makes in response to the postulated changes in output from the output level at the origin. With a fixed origin and a series of (approximately) monotonic changes in output, the same curve would also describe the time path of a producer's labor input and output changes. More specifically, the producer resists changes in labor input during the first few time periods when output change from the origin is still small. As output change continues, he makes more and more complete labor adjustments. The LL-curve thus describes the time path of labor and output changes during upswings and downswings, although its parameters will probably depend in part on such factors as rate of change of output and the degree of validity of the monotonicity assumption.[8]

II. THE CHOICE OF AN ORIGIN

One concept of origin from which labor output elasticity may be measured is the 'equilibrium output'. In the short run this output is ordinarily determined by the given plant and equipment and corresponds to the lowest point on the short run cost curve under the usual pure competition assumptions. However, if some built-in stretchability in inputs exists, the producer may wish to keep the inputs nearly constant at that equilibrium level within some range of output. Then labor productivity would rise if output were increased beyond the equilibrium and would fall if output were reduced below the equilibrium. This equilibrium may therefore be portrayed by the origin on the LL-curve.

In the context of cyclical fluctuations a second concept of origin is possible. If the cycle is systematic and predictable it may be more

[7] Ultimately, of course, the producer may have to add to or liquidate his capital stock.

[8] This two-fold interpretation of the LL-curve justifies the pooling of successive cross-sections of plant data in the empirical testing below.

profitable for the producer to take his cue from the market and adapt to the cycle. If he follows this strategy, the origin of the LL-curve would be the peak or trough of the business cycle. The peak or trough labor input would be more or less maintained until a clear course of downswing or upswing is established, and then a more complete adjustment of labor input would be made. The adjustment process continues until the course of the cycle is reversed and a new origin is established at the new turning point. In this case labor productivity would be directly related to the phase of a cycle.

Using the first concept of the origin, the equilibrium output level may be approximated by the geometric average of outputs during a period sufficiently brief so that plant and equipment may be taken as given, yet still long enough so that the average is not biased by the predominance of a specific place of a cycle.[9] The average minimizes the proportionate variations and therefore the need for input stretching and input idling. The equilibrium labor input may then be defined as the labor input required to produce the equilibrium output without stretching and may be approximated by the actual labor input at the equilibrium output. This definition closely resembles the use of 'planned output' in the Wilson-Eckstein model.

Applying the equilibrium concept of origin to a plant subject to cyclical fluctuations, the equilibrium output lies between peaks and troughs and divides a trough-to-trough cycle into four phases: recovery, prosperity, recession and depression. During recovery, the producer is anxious to increase his labor force back to the equilibrium level; labor productivity falls and then rises. During prosperity the producer at first hesitates to increase his labor force, but then overcomes his hesitancy and revises his 'planned output' in response to rising demand. Labor productivity first rises and then falls. Recession is analogous to recovery; labor productivity first rises and then falls. Depression is analogous to prosperity; labor productivity first declines and then rises. It is possible, of course, that during the course of a cycle the producer does not revise his plans and thus fails to reach the points (a, b) or (c, d) on the LL-curve. Then labor productivity rises continually as output rises from a trough to a peak and declines continually as output declines from a peak to a trough. We will refer to the first productivity sequence as Wilson-Eckstein Hypothesis One ('WE–1'), and the second, more abbreviated productivity sequence as Wilson-Eckstein Hypothesis Two ('WE–2').

In its simple form the second concept of origin is implied in Hultgren's work. The labor productivity sequence based on this

[9] In the empirical analysis below, the equilibrium output is approximated by the trend value of output after a trend has been computed for each plant.

concept is quite different. As Hultgren asserted, 'widespread increases in production in various industries in the early stages of a general business expansion are associated with widespread increases in output per manhour, and that the prevalence of such increases, both in output and output per manhour, tends to diminish as the expansion nears its end. . . . When a recession begins, reductions in output become typical and so, to a lesser extent, do reductions in output per manhour. . . . When the reductions in output finally became prevalent, increases in output per manhour again became the rule,'[10] This sequence will be referred to as the Hultgren Hypothesis ('H').

Of course, plants may well differ in their desire and capacity to plan ahead or to adapt to a cycle, and cycles have differed widely from each other in the last forty years. It is not surprising, therefore, that only a minority of industries have followed the sequence asserted by the Hultgren Hypothesis:[11]

Hypothesis	*Labor productivity sequence from one turning point to another*	*Number of expansions or contractions*	
		Expansions	*Contractions*
WE–1	Fall, rise, fall	0	
WE–2	Rise	43	
H	Rise, fall	27	
	Other sequences	20	
WE–1	Rise, fall, rise		4
WE–2	Fall		27
H	Fall, rise		25
	Other sequences		43

These results would suggest that WE–2 and H are complementary hypotheses. When they are taken together they provide a rather good explanation of productivity behavior during the course of a cycle. But such mixed results are of little use unless it can be known in advance whether the productivity sequence during a specific cycle will be described by WE–2 or by H. Furthermore, Hultgren's data include a large number of annual time series, are subject to aggregation errors, and cover the severe Great Depression as well as the mild post-war cycles. The need for clarification obviously exists.

[10] Hultgren, op. cit., p. xiv.
[11] Based on Hultgren, op. cit., p. 24.

III. DATA

The behavior of manufacturing plants during a cycle may be approached directly. Are the cyclical fluctuations regular enough for most of the plants to make successful forecasts? Are the fluctuations of sufficient duration and severity to justify adaptation of the labor force? At present we know very little about the answers to these questions. Because of timing differences, the industry output series are almost certainly misleading. Individual manufacturing plants have been studied and many investigators have shown that sales forecast and production planning may be carried out successfully.[12] But such depth studies are still rare and shed only limited light on the actual behavior of the plants.

In the present paper we can only try to provide an impressionistic picture of the fluctuations confronted by a 'random' collection of manufacturing plants in Massachusetts.[13] In all, by personal interviews conducted in 1961, we have collected data for 116 plants—mostly for the six year span from January 1955 to December 1960. From the information taken from the production records, we have compiled monthly time series of labor input (production worker manhours) and output (value of output in constant dollars).

The output data for each plant were visually inspected for turning points. Although this procedure is arbitrary, well-defined patterns of cyclical upswing and downswing were discerned in most instances. It was found that, of the 88 plants for which data are available for 60 months or more, seasonal fluctuations are the predominant source of short-term fluctuation in 12 plants. For the remaining plants, one to three turning points are evident in the output series of 23 plants, four to seven turning points in 34 plants, eight to eleven turning points in 13 plants and more than twelve turning points in 6 plants. During the same period, there were just three turning points for the industry in the aggregate: peaks in 1956 and 1959 and trough in 1958. Clearly plants are subject to more frequent fluctuations than industries.

The synchronization of turning points for individual plants is only fair. For non-durable goods industries in New England, a peak was registered in January 1956 and a trough in June 1958. For durable goods industries a peak was registered in March 1957 and a trough in July 1958.[14] If we take the seven months centered around these peak

[12] Holt *et al.*, op. cit.

[13] A random sample with respect to size and location was initially prepared for each two-digit industry. However, the actual sample was determined largely by the willingness of the plant managements to cooperate.

[14] Based on employment series. Individual industries reached the peak in 1956–57 at very different times, but the timing of their troughs was close together in 1958. See Frank Gery, 'Post War Fluctuations in New England Employment' (Federal Reserve Bank of Boston).

and trough months, the number of seasonally adjusted peaks and troughs registered by individual plants is:

	Number of plants with a peak	*Number of plants with a trough*	*Number of plants with a peak and a trough*	*Number of plants with no peak or trough*
During the seven months around the 1956–57 peak:				
Non-durable Goods Industries	11	2	4	12
Durable Goods Industries	23	3	3	20
During the seven months around the 1958 trough:				
Non-durable Goods Industries	2	18	2	9
Durable Goods Industries	6	26	4	12

These figures indicate that only slightly more than one-half of the plants reach a peak or a trough within the seven months' interval surrounding the industry turning points.[15] Furthermore, since individual plants have considerably more turning points than industries some of the peaks and troughs within the seven months' interval may be unrelated to the general industry turning points.

The fluctuation of individual plant output also has greater amplitude than that of industry output. This can be seen from Table I. The industry ratio of trough output to peak output was compiled

TABLE I

AMPLITUDE OF INDUSTRY AND PLANT OUTPUT FLUCTUATIONS

Ratio of trough month output to peak month output	*Expansion of production*		*Contraction of production*	
	Number of industry expansions	*Number of plant expansions*	*Number of industry contractions*	*Number of plant contractions*
90.0–99.9	4	9	5	8
80.0–89.9	12	17	22	17
70.0–79.9	12	29	12	32
60.0–69.9	11	56	8	58
50.0–59.9	3	61	2	54
40.0–49.9	7	63	5	57
30.0–39.9	3	50	2	56
20.0–29.9	2	38	0	28
10.0–19.9	1	17	1	12
0.1– 9.9	0	10	0	12

[15] We do not have sufficient data to compare the individual plant turning point with the corresponding two-digit SIC industry turning point.

by Hultgren.[16] The plant ratios are calculated from the seasonally adjusted output of our sample plants.[17] It is evident that the amplitude of output fluctuation of a typical plant is nearly twice that of the industry.[18] Furthermore, the amplitude of plant output fluctuation is approximately four times as great as the amplitude implied by the Federal Reserve manufacturing production index. It must therefore be concluded that individual plants are subject to more violent and frequent fluctuations in output than that indicated by industry figures, and the timing of their output fluctuations is only poorly predicted by the timing of the general business cycles.

IV. EMPIRICAL RESULTS: WILSON-ECKSTEIN HYPOTHESIS VERSUS HULTGREN HYPOTHESIS

We have argued that the short-run cyclical productivity behavior of manufacturing plants may be summarized by the LL-curve:

$$Y = f(X) \tag{1}$$

Under the Wilson-Eckstein Hypothesis Y is the percentage deviation of current month manhour input from the equilibrium level manhour input, and X is the percentage deviation of current month output from the equilibrium level output.[19] Since we do not wish to take symmetry and reversibility for granted, the LL-curve is estimated separately for the revival, prosperity, recession and depression phases of the cycle. This means that we estimate both the LL-curve to the right of the origin and the LL-curve to the left of the origin twice: Once for the upswing and once for the downswing. If WE–1 holds then equation (1) may be approximated by a quadratic function; if WE–2 holds then equation (1) may be approximated by a linear function.

The results support the WE–2 hypothesis and indicate a remarkable 'stretchability' of labor. There is considerable evidence for this conclusion. First, in all cases a quadratic function provides only a

[16] Only those industries for which monthly output data were used are included. The industries are: meat, cotton, wool, hosiery, paper, tires, shoes, cement, steel and railroads. See Hultgren, op. cit., pp. 18–19.

[17] Seasonal adjustment reduces the amplitude of fluctuations.

[18] The amplitude of plant output fluctuations depends on the selection of turning points. By omitting milder cycles, the number of turning points is reduced but the amplitude is increased. Since for the period under consideration we have identified a much larger number of turning points for individual plants than industry turning points, the amplitude of plant fluctuations may only contain a downward bias. The removal of this bias would not affect our conclusions.

[19] The percentage declines from the origin are adjusted so that their numerical values are symmetrical to the percentage increases. Thus a 50 per cent decline is adjusted to 100 per cent. This procedure enables us to compare the regression coefficients estimated from the declines with those from the increases.

slightly better explanation of labor input changes than a linear function, indicating that—despite the great amplitude of output fluctuations—there has been no need to accelerate hiring or layoff. Second, as the WE–2 results presented in Table II show, there is no significant correlation between changes in output and changes in labor input for the plants in nearly half of the industries, and there is only a fair correlation in the rest of the cases. Obviously many plants have not been induced by the output change to alter their labor input. Third, the intercept coefficients are generally between 0 and −.10 and the slope coefficients between .60 and .80. This means that hardly any meaningful labor adjustment is made until the output has deviated by 10 to 15 per cent from the equilibrium level, and even then the 'marginal' adjustment is still significantly less than proportional.

The most interesting result, however, is the higher slope coefficients for the revival and recession phases. This is a direct implication of the Wilson-Eckstein Hypothesis: a producer is hesitant to alter his labor force away from the equilibrium level and eager to move back to the equilibrium level once it is justified by the prospect of demand. In terms of productivity sequence, productivity rises continually during an upswing although the rate of increase is reduced once the equilibrium level is passed, and it falls continually during a downswing although the rate of decline is reduced once the equilibrium level is passed. This sequence is a direct contradiction of the Hultgren Hypothesis.

The Hultgren Hypothesis, of course, may be tested directly. Again referring to equation (1), Y must now be interpreted as the percentage change of labor input from the turning point month to the current month, and X as the percentage change of output from the turning point month to the current month. Testing for the upswing and the downswing separately, the Hultgren Hypothesis implies a quadratic relationship between X and Y with the regression coefficient for the quadratic term positive. Table III shows that there are almost twice as many negative b_3's as positive ones.

There are some plausible explanations of why some industry-wide productivity series have followed the Hultgren sequence even though the individual plants have not. Towards the end of an industry upswing, output and therefore productivity increases might have slowed down significantly for many plants and even reversed for some others. This offsets the productivity increases of some of the plants that are still increasing their output; the data would then show the characteristic Hultgren sequence of a rise and fall of industry productivity during an upswing. The same is also true at the

Table II

WILSON-ECKSTEIN HYPOTHESIS

Industry	(1) Revival $(-y) = a_1 + a_2(-x)$						(2) Prosperity $y = a_1 + a_2(x)$					
	$\overline{X}$	$\overline{Y}$	*No. of obser-vations*	a_1	a_2	R^2	$\overline{X}$	$\overline{Y}$	*No. of obser-vations*	a_1	a_2	R^2
Food					(1)	.05					(1)	.00
Textiles	.76	.60	133	.12	.63 (±.02)	.85**					(1)	.08
Apparels					(1)	.04					(1)	.08
Lumber Products					(1)	.15	.38	.11	64	.01	.24 (±.04)	.33**
Furniture and Fixtures			(2)						(2)			
Paper Products	.07	.03	72	−.01	.62 (±.13)	.22*					(1)	.00
Printing and Publishing			(2)								(1)	.02
Chemicals					(1)	.16					(1)	.24
Petroleum and Coal			(2)								(1)	.01
Rubber Products	.14	.08	102	−.01	.72 (±.11)	.29**	.26	.20	123	.03	.63 (±.06)	.48**
Leather Products					(1)	.08					(1)	.13
Stone, Clay and Glass	.31	.26	53	.03	.69 (±.08)	.60**	.33	.10	39	−.14	.72 (±.07)	.72**
Primary Metals	.61	.47	152	−.12	.98 (±.03)	.86**	.61	.39	143	−.05	.72 (±.02)	.89**
Fabricated Metals	.27	.37	155	−.16	2.02 (±.13)	.63**	.30	.21	165	.01	.63 (±.08)	.28**
Non-electric Machinery	.22	.15	205	.04	.49 (±.07)	.19**					(1)	.02
Electric Machinery	.35	.12	116	−.02	.39 (±.08)	.18*	.44	.22	187	−.01	.51 (±.05)	.35**
Transportation Equipment	.33	.35	90	−.07	1.27 (±.08)	.70**	.42	.24	108	−.04	.68 (±.09)	.34**
Instruments					(1)	.24	.28	.11	100	−.03	.50 (±.05)	.52**
Miscellaneous					(1)	.01	.23	.07	40	−.04	.51 (±.11)	.38*

TABLE II *continued*

	(3) Recession $y = a_1 + a_2(x)$						(4) Depression $(-y) = a_1 + a_2(-x)$					
Industry	$\overline{X}$	$\overline{Y}$	*No. of observations*	a_1	a_2	R	$\overline{X}$	$\overline{Y}$	*No. of observations*	a_1	a_2	R^2
Food					(1)	.14					(1)	.15
Textiles					(1)	.24	2.47	1.54	104	.06	.60 (±.00)	1.00**
Apparels					(1)	.09					(1)	.05
Lumber Products			(2)								(1)	.02
Furniture and Fixtures			(2)						(2)			
Paper Products	.09	.08	77	−.03	1.55 (±.14)	.49**	.14	.08	115	−.01	.68 (±.08)	.40**
Printing and Publishing	.04	−.01	47	−.04	.77 (±.18)	.28**			(2)			
Chemicals					(1)	.34					(1)	.14
Petroleum and Coal			(2)								(1)	.38
Rubber Products	.15	.09	77	−.01	.72 (±.11)	.37**	.21	.17	75	.03	.07 (±.09)	.48**
Leather Products	.11	.08	45	−.07	1.34 (±.21)	.49**					(1)	.19
Stone, Clay and Glass					(1)	.05	.29	.07	38	−.10	.57 (±.12)	.39**
Primary Metals					(1)	.26	.36	.18	112	−.01	.55 (±.05)	.54**
Fabricated Metals	.19	.09	114	−.16	1.26 (±.14)	.39**	.30	.16	183	−.06	.77 (±.08)	.33**
Non-electric Machinery	.17	.06	89	−.06	.74 (±.12)	.30**					(1)	.00
Electric Machinery					(1)	.04	.31	.22	86	.09	.42 (±.06)	.38**
Transportation Equipment	.17	.03	19	−.08	.70 (±.14)	.60**	.30	.14	92	−.08	.75 (±.08)	.53**
Instruments					(1)	.06	.42	.37	64	.05	.75 (±.08)	.60**
Miscellaneous					(1)	.36					(1)	.23

Notes: * = R^2 significant at 5% level.
** = R^2 significant at 1% level.
(1) = R^2 not significant.
(2) = Less than 15 observations in the sample.

TABLE III

HULTGREN HYPOTHESIS

Industry	(1) Upswing $y = b_1 + b_2(x) + b_3(x^2)$					(2) Downswing $(-y) = b_1 + b_2(-x) + b_3(-x)^2$				
	No. of observations	b_1	b_2	b_3	R^2	*No. of observations*	b_1	b_2	b_3	R^2
Food	161	.08	.26 (±.07)	−.09 (±.03)	.10	205	.06	.45 (±.08)	−.11 (±.03)	.15
Textiles	269	.12	.54 (±.08)	−.02 (±.01)	.44**	252	−.24	.67 (±.03)	.00 (±.00)	.95**
Apparels	90	.05	.33 (±.15)	−.19 (±.07)	.09	196	.10	.08 (±.07)	−.02 (±.02)	.16
Lumber Products	76	.19	−.02 (±.12)	.06 (±.04)	.29*	120	.01	.46 (±.09)	−.11 (±.03)	.18
Furniture and Fixtures	18	−.01	.86 (±.41)	−.34 (±.23)	.38	(1)				
Paper Products	273	.02	.00 (±.14)	.25 (±.08)	.33**	217	.08	−.07 (±.20)	.99 (±.23)	.32**
Printing and Publishing	156	.06	−.27 (±.22)	−.29 (±.36)	.16	89	−.02	.25 (±.43)	−.52 (±1.09)	.00
Chemicals	91	.05	−.01 (±.10)	.11 (±.05)	.29*	138	.04	.50 (±.10)	−.18 (±.07)	.33**
Petroleum and Coal	72	−.10	.63 (±.27)	.08 (±.15)	.56**	61	1.09	−9.36 (±1.24)	.14 (±.10)	.88**
Rubber Products	210	−.01	.72 (±.08)	−.04 (±.03)	.59**	212	−.06	.96 (±.11)	−.13 (±.07)	.56**
Leather Products	127	−.01	.61 (±.17)	−.20 (±.14)	.26*	127	.03	.51 (±.15)	−.15 (±.12)	.22*
Stone, Clay and Glass	87	−.05	.40 (±.13)	.01 (±.05)	.47**	100	.16	.16 (±.15)	.09 (±.05)	.37**
Primary Metals	200	−.12	.53 (±.06)	.04 (±.01)	.92**	282	.05	.36 (±.03)	.02 (±.00)	.78**
Fabricated Metals	343	−.32	1.29 (±.22)	−.12 (±.06)	.28**	387	.16	.02 (±.05)	.23 (±.01)	.90**
Non-electric Machinery	401	.13	.17 (±.05)	−.02 (±.01)	.04	498	.17	.18 (±.03)	−.01 (±.00)	.08
Electric Machinery	274	−.03	.48 (±.05)	−.03 (±.01)	.53**	210	.08	.51 (±.05)	−.03 (±.01)	.53**
Transportation Equipment	147	−.07	.43 (±.18)	.06 (±.04)	.43**	246	−.15	.89 (±.05)	.03 (±.00)	.59**
Instruments	162	−.11	.41 (±.08)	.00 (±.02)	.44**	134	−.06	.71 (±.13)	−.06 (±.05)	.59**
Miscellaneous	59	.14	.01 (±.28)	.22 (±.18)	.29	67	.02	.63 (±.20)	−.39 (±.17)	.18

Notes: * R^2 significant at 5% level.
** R^2 significant at 1% level.
(1) Less than 15 observations in the sample.

end of a downswing. Another explanation is that Hultgren's data include figures for the Great Depression. Plants might well have abandoned their planned equilibrium output during that severe cycle; it would certainly be reasonable to expect them to conform to the Hultgren Hypothesis in their behavior.

V. EMPIRICAL RESULTS: THE ROLE OF CYCLICAL FACTORS

The empirical results reported in the last section are based on the simplifying assumption that different cycles experienced by the plants over the years are structurally alike, so that labor adjustments depend only on the deviation of output from some norm. In fact, of course, cyclical fluctuations differ widely in their amplitude, duration and the degree of certitude in passing from one phase to another. Plant behavior may be expected to vary with respect to these factors, and it is possible to attribute the negative results for the Hultgren Hypothesis to the neglect of inter-plant as well as the inter-temporal differences in plant cycles—in fact these differences are probably much greater than differences in industry cycles.

It is tempting to take these factors into consideration by stratifying the plant data according to the nature of the cycles. However, the nature of a cycle cannot be determined until the cycle has run its full course. It is therefore more reasonable to assume that the plant decision is made on the basis of information covering the period from the turning point month to the 'current month'. Such information may be summarized by four parameters, which more or less define what a plant can know about its position in its own cycle.

The first parameter is N, the number of months that have elapsed since a turning point. Referring to Figure 2,[20] the turning point is t_o and the 'current' period is t_n. N is simply the difference between t_o and t_n. A large N is expected to help in the formation of expectations. Despite the development of business guesstimates, the correct identification of a turning point at the time it occurs remains elusive. In the first few months after a turning point, therefore, the producer may harbour doubts concerning the course of the cycle and refrain from making labor input adjustments in response to changes in output. It is only with time that a producer ventures to formulate definite expectations.

The other parameters require some notations:

(1) Net change of output, NC, defined as:

$$NC = Q_o - Q_n$$

[20] The figure describes the situation after a peak. The situation after a trough is symmetrical.

where Q_o is turning point month output and Q_n the current month output.

(2) Total change of output, TC, defined as:

$$TC = \sum_{i=1}^{n} (Q_o - Q_i)$$

In Figure 2, TC is measured by the area that is shaded.

(3) Gross change of output, GC, defined as:

$$GC = \sum_{i=0}^{n-1} (Q_i - Q_{i+1}) \text{ for all i where } (Q_i - Q_{i+1}) > 0$$

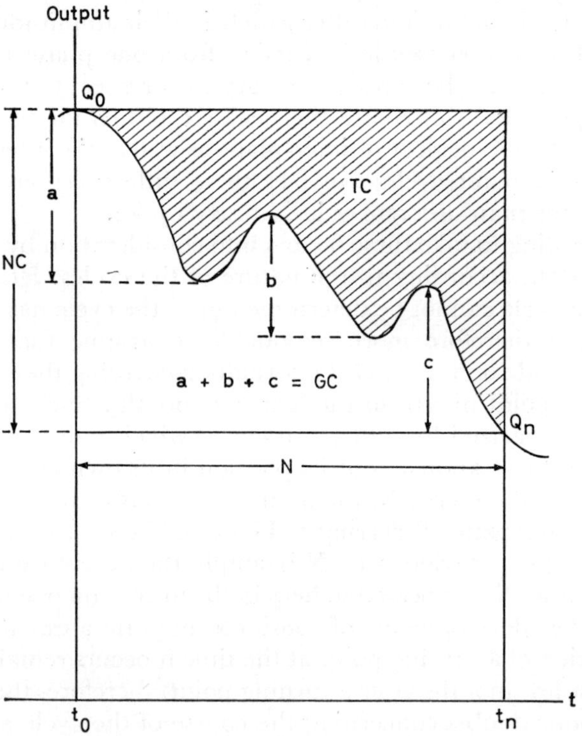

Fig. 2

In Fig. 2, GC is equal to the sum of the three separate output declines, a, b and c.

Three parameters may be computed from NC, TC and GC. The first parameter is α, measuring time lag:[21]

$$\alpha = \frac{1}{N} (TC/NC)$$

[21] Time lag is not computed for the cases where $N = 1$.

Evidently α would be large if a given change of output from the turning point takes place at an early time—a time close to the turning point. Other things being equal, a large labor output elasticity—both labor and output deviations measured from the turning point—for a large value of α would indicate the presence of time lag in labor adjustment.

The second parameter, β, measures uncertainty:

$$\beta = GC/NC$$

For given N and for a given net change of output, β is large if there have been frequent and wide fluctuations between t_o and t_n. These fluctuations presumably increase the uncertainty of the course of the cycle.

The third parameter, γ, measures urgency:

$$\gamma = \frac{1}{N}(NC/Q_o)$$

This is simply the relative rate of output change. A higher rate of output change is a conspicuous signal and increases the urgency for input adjustments.

Hultgren Hypothesis may now be re-formulated. Starting from a turning point, the labor adjustment to output changes depends on the producer's evaluation of the cycle. Again with Y representing the percentage change of labor input from the turning point month to the current month and X the similarly defined percentage change of output, then the relationship between Y and X may be expressed by:

$$Y = c_1 + c_2 X$$

The parameters in this equation are expected to depend on N, α, β and γ. More specifically, Hultgren Hypothesis states that a producer 'rides' with the cycle, making labor adjustments in response to output change if the cycle is well established and relatively free from uncertainties. In addition, he may also react differently to mild and sharp output changes and may react only after some time lag to a given output change.

Table IV presents the empirical results. The role of the cyclical factors—N, α, β and γ—is tested individually and the data, pooled without regard for industry or plant identity, have been stratified according to parameter values. The α, β and γ classes are defined so that a higher class designation corresponds to a higher parameter value. Only those observations with $N \geqslant 4$ were utilized in testing the role of α and those with $N \geqslant 5$ in testing the role of γ.

TABLE IV

THE ROLE OF CYCLICAL FACTORS IN HULTGREN HYPOTHESIS

A. *The role of* N

N	Upswing: *No. of observations*	c_1	c_2	R^2	Downswing: *No. of observations*	c_1	c_2	R^2
1	370	.08	.15±.02	.11	393	.13	.03±.01	.01
2,3	638	.04	.32±.02	.22	698	−.06	.56±.00	.96
4–6	722	−.04	.51±.03	.33	798	.06	.38±.05	.08
7–24	1388	−.05	.53±.01	.48	1565	.05	.45±.01	.67
over 24	98	−.12	.61±.04	.69	101	.60	.26±.04	.29

B. *The role of* α

α-class	Upswing: *No. of observations*	c_1	c_2	R^2	Downswing: *No. of observaations*	c_1	c_2	R^2
1	30	−.01	.26±.10	.19	39	.01	.37±.09	.29
2	193	−.05	.47±.03	.54	209	.18	.24±.02	.38
3	726	.05	.39±.02	.46	780	.16	.47±.01	.58
4	485	−.10	.62±.03	.40	504	.24	.15±.03	.60
5	692	−.11	.69±.02	.54	850	.12	.12±.02	.04

C. *The role of* β

N	*β-class*	Upswing: *No. of observations*	c_1	c_2	R^2	Downswing: *No. of observations*	c_1	c^2	R^2
8	1	35	.17	.31±.09	.25	35	.20	.26±.11	.13
	2	27	−.14	.69±.10	.66	23	−.01	.55±.10	.57
	3	27	−.17	.64±.07	.77	36	.08	.32±.13	.15
	4	30	−.11	.78±.11	.62	28	.14	.32±.20	.09
	5	15	.06	.62±.74	.05	11	.13	.29±.30	.09
	6	17	−.13	.62±.07	.82	36	.08	.20±.31	.01
10	1	25	.06	.34±.09	.38	29	.38	−.01±.09	.00
	2	21	−.32	1.28±.35	.41	31	.08	.42±.06	.61
	3	23	−.17	.75±.24	.33	19	.27	−.08±.18	.01
	4	16	−.10	.77±.19	.53	19	.08	.38±.19	.18
	5	10	−.03	.45±.05	.90	16	−.12	1.36±.27	.64
	6	16	.09	−.03±.12	.00	15	.00	.15±.24	.03

D. *The role of* γ

γ-class	Upswing: *No. of observations*	c_1	c_2	R^2	Downswing: *No. of observations*	c_1	c_2	R^2
1	375	−.06	.74±.06	.29	637	−.02	.85±.06	.27
2	446	−.02	.37±.05	.10	588	−.05	.72±.05	.30
3	482	.00	.43±.04	.18	455	−.09	.73±.38	.45
4	487	−.08	.55±.04	.34	383	.13	.31±.04	.16
5	138	.11	.53±.09	.19	85	−.15	.59±.17	.12

The results suggest that the cyclical factors enjoy only a very limited role in the determination of the producer behavior during the upswing. Labor adjustment does appear to be more complete (larger c_2) and more uniform (larger R^2) as the number of months from a turning point increases. To some extent c_2 also increases while α increases and decreases while β increases,[22] indicating the presence of a time lag and some impact of uncertainty. The role of γ is the most questionable; there appears to be little relationship between the sharpness of the fluctuations and the labor adjustment.

During the downswing, labor adjustments in response to output changes from a turning point are highly variable and can in no way be meaningfully accounted for by the difference in cyclical parameters.[23] Consequently, taking both upswing and downswing into consideration, there is little evidence that differences in plant cycle are important in explaining differences in producer behavior. Furthermore, since producer behavior does not seem to be systematically related to the values of the cyclical parameters, there can be little ground to expect that the labor productivity of a plant would vary systematically with the phase of the plant output cycle—except where the phase of a cycle is directly related to the level of output. This last case, of course, can best be explained by the non-cyclical Wilson-Eckstein Hypothesis.

VI. CONCLUSIONS

We have shown that 'cycles' for manufacturing plants are much shorter in duration and wider in amplitude than industry cycles. Assuming that changes in labor input are adjustments to change in output, we have discovered only a weak relationship between the two changes and the labor output elasticity tends to be considerably less than unity for the wide range of output changes. This stretchability of labor may be accounted for by built-in flexibility in production, strong union pressure against layoff during a downswing and technological change during an upswing. The stretching of labor serves to minimize friction costs, which are particularly high if cycles are short and violent.

The lack of labor adjustment in response to output changes results in rising productivity during a period of output expansion and falling

[22] It is curious that where β is very small (e.g., where output fluctuations since a turning point have been minimal relative to a net change of output), c_2 has a low value. Is it possible that a producer would 'over-adjust' if he is somewhat in the dark and not quite knowing where he is going, and 'under-adjust' if he is completely in the dark?

[23] This may be explained by the fact that during a downswing the downward adjustment of labor depends critically on management-labor relationship which varies from plant to plant and is quite independent of the cyclical parameters.

productivity during a period of output contraction. Two alternative hypotheses may be formulated, however, that could lead to different productivity sequences during the successive phases of a cycle. The first hypothesis postulates that labor adjustment is made from the turning point level of production, and leads to the productivity sequence described by Hultgren. The second hypothesis postulate that labor adjustment is made from a planned level of production. This hypothesis was proposed by Wilson and Eckstein and leads to a somewhat different productivity sequence in which cyclical factors do not enjoy an independent role. The empirical results appear to support the Wilson-Eckstein Hypothesis.

The implication of our finding is two-fold. For the cycle, labor stretching is an important stabilizer. Assuming constant wages, the greater the labor productivity increase during an upswing and the labor productivity decline during a downswing, the more the excess demand and the excess supply will be reduced. Our finding shows that production worker manhours do not vary in proportion to output change, and this reinforces the stabilizing effect of overheads in production. The potential of this stabilizer is considerable. There was little evidence that the plants in our sample had reached some limit of stretching and were forced to make more complete labor adjustments —even though their outputs were more than doubled or halved. In a somewhat more severe cycle than we have observed, therefore, further stretching may well be feasible. In addition, during a severe cycle plants are likely to experience greater synchronization in their output changes. This further strengthens the stabilizer effect. On the other hand, of course, stretching cannot be expected to last indefinitely. Consequently if a boom or a depression is not curtailed within a limited time period, the stabilizer may turn into a destabilizer.

Our finding also has some implication for the theory of the firm. The decision-maker of a plant chooses a planned output and a planned labor input. He resists any alteration of his labor input from this planned level, and once the alteration has been made, he is anxious to return to the planned level as soon as the trend of output deviation from the planned level is reversed. Thus there is one short run cost curve for the upswing and another short run cost curve for the downswing. Since upswings and downswings in the output of one plant are not independent of upswings and downswings in the output of other plants, the short run cost curves of individual plants are interdependent. A plant can no longer make price and output decisions from its short run cost curve alone. This is surely a good explanation of why firms in the real world engage in 'full cost' pricing, according to which producers set their prices solely on the basis of their *long run* cost of production. And, to make the circle complete, this can also explain why cyclical factors have been found to be largely irrelevant to producer decision-making—and why the Wilson-Eckstein Hypothesis has been found to be preferable to the Hultgren Hypothesis.

UNIVERSITY OF CALIFORNIA,
DAVIS.

THE REGIONAL SIGNIFICANCE OF I.C.F.C.[1]

by G. Davies

I. INTRODUCTION

The public pressures which gave rise to the Industrial and Commercial Finance Corporation came both from the City and from the Regions, in a common desire to prevent a recurrence of mass unemployment, which had extended with unbearable severity over Northern and Western Britain, through the establishment of a new kind of financial institution. In its formative discussions the regional pressures from the highest unemployment areas were the stronger; in the event, its whole life has been spent in an age of inflation and the bulk of its finances has flowed into the regions of full or overfull employment. Nevertheless, these dual initiating forces help to explain the retention by the Corporation of its two-fold functions, not only as a catalyst of growth for small and medium firms—by far its major feature—but also as an agency conscious of the part it can play in helping to solve the regional problem. It may well be that the predominance of its primary role obscures, or perhaps even inhibits, its contribution to the solution of regional difficulties. It is the purpose of this paper to analyse the regional significance of the Corporation by first tracing the emergence of the present regional pattern of its administration, then to examine thc main causal factors of the present regional distribution of its finances, and finally to consider the ways in which present trends may influence the future regional disposal of its funds with its important consequences for differential regional growth.

II. THE GROWTH OF I.C.F.C. AND THE DEVELOPMENT OF BRANCHES

The I.C.F.C. is often perturbed about its role in the regions. Its spiritual grandfather, the Macmillan Committee, was formed, according to its terms of reference, 'To inquire into banking, finance and credit . . . and to make recommendations to enable these agencies to promote the development of trade and commerce *and the employment of labour*'.[2]

The Fifth Report of the Commissioner for the Special Areas,

[1] The writer wishes to express his thanks to the General Manager and secretary and to the Regional Managers and their staffs for their assistance in providing detailed local statistics and for their patience in answering his many questions in interviews and correspondence.

[2] Cmd. 3897 of 1931, p. 1. Emphasis added.

gives a clearer picture of the Macmillan gap than does the original document and emphasizes that 'It is a loss to the country if there is a genuine demand for capital by men able to make good use of it, for that demand not to be supplied. . . . The question is important, therefore, not merely for the future of the Special Areas but also for the full exploitation of new invention and new opportunities of employment. *It is particularly important for the Special Areas, and indeed any area which is in need of a greater variety of employment.*'[3] Consequently the idea of such an Institution as having a strong bias towards unemployment areas was widely and strongly held. The Corporation's immediate instigator was, as Lord Piercy reminded us in the Memorandum which he submitted to the Radcliffe Committee, the 'Report of the Steering Committee on Post-War Employment'.[4] It came therefore as no surprise to read, in the Corporation's First Annual Report, that: 'It is our practice to give particular consideration, where we can, to proposals reaching us from development areas.'[5] The Corporation was born with a strong social conscience. Its careful collection and unique publication of regional statistics, its repeated expression in later Reports of its desire to do more work in such regions, and the enthusiastic welcome and careful treatment given to such applications by the Regional Managers, all these are confirmation of the continued presence of this social conscience.

However, as a City institution, which has to make a reasonable profit if it is to continue in existence, the Corporation has had also to develop what its first Chairman has called 'an institutional conscience'. In his own words: 'It is of the essence of good management of a financial institution that a high degree of conscience about the management of its funds shall permeate it from top to bottom This factor—the institutional conscience—is one reason why an institution may be a less comfortable sleeping partner than the private person.'[6] It is also the reason why it cannot allow itself to be ruled by its social conscience alone and why regional pressures may sometimes have to be resisted. This forms the basic philosophy influencing both the overall growth rate and the regional pattern of the Corporation's activities.

As shown in Table I, the life of I.C.F.C. is conveniently divided into three roughly equal stages each of about seven years. The first, from July 1945 until March 31st, 1952 is the time of its 'Establishment and Consolidation'; the second, from 1952 to 1959, a period of

[3] Cmd. 5896 of 1938, paras. 5 & 7. Emphasis added.
[4] Cmnd. 827 of 1959: Memoranda, Vol. III, p. 198.
[5] I.C.F.C.'s First Annual Report, 1946, p. 2.
[6] From an Address by Lord Piercy to the Birmingham Centre of the Institute of Industrial Administration, October 11th, 1950.

slackened growth, almost names itself—the 'Doldrums'; and the final stage of reorganization and vigorously renewed growth follows, from 1959 to the present, which, in view of the dramatic contrast with the previous stage, merits the title of the 'Soaring Sixties'. The figures appear to show that (apart from the second stage when special circumstances were at work to depress the Corporation's national rate of growth), there can be little criticism of the Corporation's overall growth rate—so long as the constraints of an unsubsidized private enterprise framework are maintained. Far from being merely 'a post-war reconstruction measure'[7] or a 'temporary concern'[8] the I.C.F.C. has carved out a permanent and prominent place for itself in the economy of Great Britain.

TABLE I

I.C.F.C. NEW BUSINESS TRANSACTED ANNUALLY 1945 TO 1966

£'000

Stage I		*Stage II*		*Stage III*	
1946	£1,239	1953	£2,952	1960	£6,374
1947	4,337	1954	4,003	1961	9,503
1948	4,920	1955	5,474	1962	9,147
1949	1,902	1956	5,028	1963	8,272
1950	3,270	1957	2,496	1964	11,955
1951	6,794	1958	3,834	1965	17,669
1952	6,102	1959	5,017	1966	19,468

Table II shows the regional pattern of the Corporation's Branch Offices. It commenced business on July 20th, 1945 in various makeshift city offices, until opening at Drapers Gardens on January 7th, 1946. On the expiry of its lease it moved into its present buildings, especially constructed for it, at Piercy House, on January 1st, 1963. Although operating from London alone for the first 6 years of its existence, in a sense it had (and still has) a wider range of offices and agencies than any similar organization outside the Post Office, for its parent banks operated as its ears and eyes throughout the country. However, as the business grew it became more and more essential to take the Corporation into the regions rather than expect businessmen in the provinces to travel up to London. Hence it has painstakingly built up its regional branches, in certain cases showing a considerable degree of faith in the future growth of demand for their facilities. Five were set up in the period 1950 to 1955; none in the latter part of the 'Doldrums'; and seven in the first six years of the successful

[7] Cmd. 827 (1959), *Report on the Working of the Monetary System*, Memoranda of Evidence, Vol. III, p. 201.
[8] Cmd. 827. Report, para. 945.

'Sixties'. It is interesting to note that the first branches were in areas of relatively full employment (Birmingham, Manchester, Edinburgh, Leicester and Leeds); not until the 1960s were centres set up in areas of unequivocally high unemployment, such as Glasgow and Newcastle. The pressure on the London Head Office, its most successful region, grew so intense that a policy of decentralization was begun in March 1965 when the Eastern Counties Branch was established at Cambridge, followed by the Western Counties Branch at Reading, June 1966.

TABLE II

THE REGIONAL ADMINISTRATION OF I.C.F.C. AS SHOWN BY THE ESTABLISHMENT OF BRANCH OFFICES

1	London	July 20th,	1945
2	Birmingham	April 1st,	1951
3	Manchester	March 17th,	1952
4	Edinburgh	May 1st,	1953
5	Leicester	January 1st,	1955
6	Leeds	June 1st,	1955
7	Cardiff	June 1st,	1960
8	Bristol	October 12th,	1960
9	Glasgow	February 1st,	1961
10	Cambridge	March 24th,	1965
11	Newcastle	May 3rd,	1965
12	Reading	June 15th,	1966

A regional breakdown of the number of applications (analogous to the pattern of demand), of withdrawals and approvals for the well-established branches is given in Table III. One of the strongest of the complaints made against the Corporation in its early years, and one that often recurs, concerned the high numbers of applications for assistance which were rejected. Thus of some 840 applications examined in its first year of operation, only some 133 were accepted. By 1950 the situation was even more gloomy, for only 47 cases were approved out of over 500 applications. For every ten firms seeking aid, eight or nine were sent away empty handed. In retrospect, however, those complaints which were made on the score that the reason for this situation lay in the ultra-conservative policy of the Corporation appear to have been considerably exaggerated. Obviously the lack of balance between applications and acceptances could arise equally from an excess of applications as from an exceedingly cautious examination process within I.C.F.C.—and given the immediate post-war climate of strongly excessive demand making for a very profitable sellers' market on the one hand, and the general rationing system with the tightness of Capital Issues Control and similar financial restrictions, any avenue appearing to offer a lucrative escape from such restrictions would be inundated with applications.

TABLE III

REGIONAL ANALYSIS OF NUMBERS OF APPLICATIONS, REJECTIONS, AND APPROVALS, YEAR TO MARCH 31st, 1965

Region	*Brought forward*		*New cases opened*		*Rejected*		*Withdrawn*		*Approved*		*Carried forward*	
	First	*Further*	*First*	*Further*	*First*	*Further*	*First*	*Further*	*First*	*Further*	*First*	*Further*
Head Office		1	6	8					6	9		
London & S.E.	21	8	165	73	21		47	6	80		38	17
Birmingham	13	4	53	25	9	2	17	4	30	20	10	3
Manchester	4	8	29	12	2		8	3	16	15	7	2
Edinburgh	2		20	8	1		4	2	13	6	4	
Leeds	8	1	36	23	6	2	6	4	22	15	10	3
Leicester	7	1	33	33			9	6	25	26	6	2
Wales	4		19	3	3		5		13	2	2	1
Bristol	10	3	33	11	10		12	1	17	13	4	
Glasgow	6		28	6	3		3	1	22	4	6	1
Total	75	26	422	202	55	4	111	27	244	168	87	29

FIRST applications refer to initial applications from firms which have not previously had loans from I.C.F.C.
FURTHER applications are from firms which have previously received such assistance.

Subsequently there has been a double educative process at work informing lender and borrower. Like all new institutions the Corporation had to feel its way: and the process of applying for its services was also new as far as the firms which came to it were concerned, for, almost by definition, they were not likely to have had previous access to the capital market, so that as a rule their staff were untrained in the required directions. The notion that here in I.C.F.C. was subsidized credit on tap, had to be dispelled. The investigation process, legal, technical and accounting, required for vetting the provision of permanent capital, was lengthier, more round-about and more detailed than was the practice with bank lending of the type its customers were normally associated with. Again, the distinction between an 'Equiry' and an 'Application' is not so clear-cut in practice as it might appear to be to the uninitiated. In order to be scrupulously fair to all comers, I.C.F.C. was probably rather too generous in its definition of 'applications' in its formative years: a more realistic definition would automatically increase the percentage of successful applicants and reduce the suspense of firms awaiting the result of their approach to the Corporation. Part of I.C.F.C.'s activities is concerned with new firms and with firms involved in the preparation of new processes or experimenting with new techniques, where there are no easy guide-lines of precedence to follow, and where the risks are exceptionally high. Consequently there was a limit to the amount of such activity that could be reasonably financed by the Corporation: its experiences in this direction helped the Radcliffe Committee to define this new 'gap', and the Corporation, among others, has been particularly active in setting up more specialized organizations to deal with this problem—but in the early years this problem could not be so clearly seen and these specialized institutions were not then in existence. Already, however, by the end of its first year, Lord Piercy was very conscious of these criticisms, and made a fair case in answer to them: 'It has been suggested that the Corporation has adopted an unduly conservative policy—outbanking the bankers, I think, was the phrase. . . . The fact is that we are trying to combine with prudence, a maximum of usefulness according to our lights.'[9]

The two-way educative process has been one of the principal causes which have led to dramatically changed results with regard to the percentage of applications accepted. Indeed the position is almost exactly the reverse recently compared with that which gave rise to so much adverse criticism in earlier years. A more realistic definition of what constitutes an application has been adopted and adhered to with a high degree of consistency from year to year and from place to place. The rise of some 1500 or more hire purchase and industrial banking companies; the syphoning off of tricky or highly risky innovating business on to specialist institutions like the Estate Duties Investment Trust, the Ship Mortgage Finance Company, and Technical Development Capital Ltd.; the change from a sellers' to a buyers' market; the more widely diffused knowledge among firms of the kind of proposals likely to stand a reasonable chance of acceptance—these are some of the features which have worked together to bring down the rejection ratio. Also contributing substantially to the same welcome result has been the increased favourable bias stemming from further applications from existing or previous customers with their built-in success record. The statistics as shown in Table III, clearly indicate the extent of the bias and the revolution in application/acceptance ratios. The one-in-ten extreme of some of the earlier years had been turned round to a nine-in-ten acceptance rate by 1965, when out of 624 cases opened only 59 were rejected. The probability that it was chiefly an excess demand

[9] I.C.F.C.'s First Annual Report, 1946, p. 4.

which contributed to the high number of rejections made in earlier years is indicated by comparing the 840 applications in the first year, which had to be dealt with by a handful of staff in difficult conditions in hastily improvised and changing offices in London, with the 624 new applications processed in 1965 by a much larger well-trained staff in nine well-established offices widely dispersed over much of the country.

III. THE NATURE AND CAUSES OF THE REGIONAL DISPOSAL OF I.C.F.C. FINANCES

If all the world were a uniformly fertile plain, the pattern of settlement, according to August Lösch,[10] would assume that of a series of regular hexagons, each with its own urban centre. Trade and credit flows would similarly be even and uniform throughout the human honeycomb. But the inequalities of natural endowment, and man's rebellious propensity to create from the most logical paradise a more earthly chaos, has landed us with our present conurbations, among which, in Britain, London is, of course, supreme. This situation is greeted by a mixture of feelings ranging from the joyous acceptance of writers like Peter Hall, through the probably realistic apathy of the non-writers, to the righteously rebellious like the authors of the famous Barlow Report of 1940 and Donald Read's 'The English Provinces' of 1964. Thus the Barlow Report concluded: 'The disadvantages in many, if not in most of the great industrial concentrations . . . constitute serious handicaps and even in some respects dangers to the nation's life and development.'[11] With particular reference to the London Region its opinion was that: 'The continued drift of the industrial population to London and the Home Counties constitutes a social, economic and strategical problem which demands immediate attention.'[12] It is Read's view that 'Life in the sprawling suburbs of the capital is as near to desert aridity as life in the provinces' in large part because of this drain to London. Peter Hall, on the contrary, presumably on the basis of some instinctive referendum, believes 'The fact remains that people prefer London.'[13] Be that as it may, the concentration of head offices, particularly in the field of finance with the culmination of the amalgamation movement in the first quarter of this century made the City inevitably the centre of operations from which to establish I.C.F.C.'s activities. (Even that government agency set up

[10] *The Economics of Location*, Ch. 10.
[11] Cmd. 6153 of 1940, para. 413.
[12] Ibid. para. 428.
[13] *The English Provinces* by Donald Read, p. 286; and *London 2000* by Peter Hall, p. 37.

specifically to persuade businessmen not to set up offices in central London—the Location of Offices Bureau—finds itself with incongruous efficiency, at W.C.2).

A gap-filling institution naturally concentrates its attention on places where there are most gaps, and most gaps are likely to show themselves where there is most business: there *appears* to be little use in pressing finance for growth on firms which have no wish to grow, and in face of a sluggish economic environment. One needn't express surprise—or blame—if a man, on becoming richer, feeds his family less bread and potatoes, and spends more on record players, labour-saving domestic equipment, or installs central heating (which even when it is not oil, is likely to be much more efficient in the use of the indigenous fuels). The flow of I.C.F.C. finance, consequently, like the migration of labour, is the natural response of factors to differential income elasticities of demand, which in turn cause the differences in profitability and growth as between different industries and regions. The regional pattern of the Corporation's business is thus a reflection of the geographical distribution of the industrial and commercial activities over the different areas of Britain, i.e. it is basically determined by the varying density of economic life, as modified by the differing industrial structure of the regions, the differences in their growth rates, and in the regional availability of capital from sources of finance competitive with or complementary to those of the Corporation itself. These being the natural lines presenting themselves for investigation, we shall first examine the Corporation's financial flows into the Development Areas in the decade 1950 to 1960 (summarized in Table IV); secondly, we shall look at the wider regional picture in the seven years from 1960 (Table V). Having thus established the factual background we shall seek further to trace the causes of these differences in the broad regional pattern of industrial diversification (Table VI), relating this to a detailed industrial analysis of the Corporation's financial facilities (as given in Table VII).

Table IV gives the figures for the funds made available in the Development Areas, the hard core of the difficult regions, during the decade enclosing the 'Doldrums'. The Table also gives as a standard of reckoning, the figures for the London region. In 1950 London received—because it could make more profitable use of it on the whole—70 per cent more finance than did the Development Areas: in 1960 it received 268 per cent more. This degree of divergence was not exceptional, but typical of the average of the period from 1956 to 1960 inclusive. The main reasons for the poor showing of the Development Areas spring from their heavy concentrations of declining industries, and the related fact that the general amenities of these districts were such as to make them somewhat unpromising material for any substantial growth in small and medium firms.

TABLE IV

I.C.F.C. FINANCE FOR DEVELOPMENT AREAS COMPARED WITH LONDON 1950–60

Development area	*1950* *Amount*	%	*1955* *Amount*	%	*1960* *Amount*	%
	£'000		£'000		£'000	
Northern	990.6	4.8	836.2	3.0	482.7	1.3
Wales	592.6	2.9	641.0	2.2	772.2	2.0
West Cumberland	522.0	2.5	639.9	2.2	70.0	0.2
South Lancashire	300.0	1.4	345.3	1.2	324.2	0.8
Merseyside	385.0	1.9	482.7	1.7	621.0	1.6
Scotland	567.2	2.8	851.2	3.0	1,556.4	4.1
Total	3,357.4	16.3	3,796.3	13.3	3,826.5	10.0
London	5,752.2	27.9	10,649.6	37.2	14,128.6	36.8

Growth of Funds Invested in Development Areas in Decade 14%
Growth of Funds Invested in London Region in Decade 146%

The provision of subsidized finance by the Board of Trade and local authorities was often a reason for firms which might otherwise have received finance from I.C.F.C. not presenting and pressing their applications sufficiently forcefully. The combined result of these factors (reinforced by the lack of industrial diversification described below) contributed to the dismal record of the Development Areas as recipients of Corporation funds in the 1950's. The regions which had pressed hardest for the setting up of some such institution as I.C.F.C. were unable to find the means to benefit from its finances so much as other regions. Despite the 'bankers' clamp'—to use Lord Piercy's vivid description of the bankers' refusal to allow I.C.F.C. to attract funds from the public before 1959—and despite the generally restrictive government financial policy during most of the period, London-based business grew with remarkable vigour by 146 per cent during the decade, a rate ten times as great as the paltry 14 per cent increase in the Development Areas. It was this kind of contrast which gave rise to complaints typified by that of the council of the Scottish Chambers of Commerce in 1959 that: 'The Corporation seems to some extent to have lost sight of its original purpose and to have become too concerned with producing results from its own activities—in opposition to the risk function which it originally assumed.'[14] Strong echoes of the criticism are also found in Professor

[14] Cmnd. 827 of 1959: Radcliffe Memoranda Vol. II p. 100.

Bates' insistence of an 'economic gap', unfilled by I.C.F.C., which denied its existence.[15]

The coming of the Local Employment Act in 1960, with its emphasis on small districts flexibly selected on an administrative basis, rather than on statutorily fixed, wide areas, as previously, made it virtually impossible for I.C.F.C., or anyone else for that matter, to publish figures for such quickly changing districts on a consistent annual basis. There were a hundred changes in the places scheduled under the Local Employment Acts of 1960 and 1963 between the 'listed', 'removed', and 'stop-list' categories, before the Industrial Investment Act of 1966 significantly widened the localities into 'areas' (which are essentially 'Regions' with a few excised appendices), and removed much of the previous uncertainties. Consequently in the figures for the period since 1960, as given in Table V, we are concerned not only with the development districts as merged indistinguishably with the wider regions of which they form a significant part, but also with the other, richer regions. The Table shows the regional amounts of the Corporation's loans and investments during the seven years 1960 to 1966 inclusive. Though the general distribution is much as one would expect, with London and the Midland regions being by far the most successful in attracting funds, and with the regions north and west of the Tees-Exe line making a very poor show in comparison, it is the *extent* of these differences, and the relative movements up and down the percentage scale over these years which is the particular merit of the figures. The dominance of London, with well over a third of the total flow of finance, is perhaps more apparent still when contrasted with the picture it gives of the Northern, Western and Welsh regions. The average total finance for these three latter regions came to only 6 per cent of the country's total, so that London, with an average of 36 per cent had a lending rate six times as high as these three regions together: on a working population basis about three times as high at the very least. Nevertheless, in happy contrast to the Doldrums, the absolute figure for these regions is growing steadily, while the Western Region has picked up remarkably since 1960. Scotland in particular has in recent years made very considerable progress, its share of total finance rose from 6.6 per cent in 1962 to 9.7 per cent in 1965, almost equivalent to its share of the total population of the country. By 1966 its share had risen to 10.5 per cent slightly exceeding its population parity, indicating a remarkable revival since 1962. The figures for Wales, falling in 1963–64, rising sharply in 1966, show a hesitant progress, and yet are equivalent to

[15] J. Bates, *The Banker*, July 1961, and Lord Piercy, *The Banker*, October 1961.

TABLE V

DISTRIBUTION OF FINANCIAL FACILITIES BY REGIONS 1960 TO 1966

Region	Outstanding at March 31st, 1960		Outstanding at March 31st, 1961		Outstanding at March 31st, 1962		Outstanding at March 31st, 1963		Outstanding at March 31st, 1964		Outstanding at March 31st, 1965		Outstanding at March 31st, 1966	
	Amount £'000	*% of the whole*	*Amount £'000*	*% of the whole*	*Amount £'000*	*% of the whole*	*Amount £'000*	*% of the whole*	*Amount £'000*	*% of the whole*	*Amount £'000*	*% of the whole*	*Amount £'000*	*% of the whole*
Northern	707.3	1.8	820.1	2.0	843.3	1.8	860.0	1.7	1,084.1	1.9	1,214	1.8	1,507	1.9
East & West Ridings	3,028.2	7.9	3,442.6	8.2	3,771.6	8.0	4,314.9	8.5	5,227.5	9.1	6,577	9.9	6,973	8.9
North-Midland	2,634.2	6.9	3,334.2	7.9	3,701.2	7.9	4,515.7	8.8	5,320.9	9.3	6,137	9.2	7,672	9.8
Eastern	1,072.9	2.8	862.7	2.0	1,194.0	2.5	1,447.9	2.8	1,666.2	2.9	1,901	2.9	2,569	3.2
London	14,128.6	36.8	15,077.8	35.8	16,844.9	35.9	17,911.1	35.1	20,077.6	34.9	23,250	35.0	26,910	34.3
Southern	1,554.1	4.1	1,753.3	4.2	1,974.3	4.2	2,142.0	4.2	2,020.0	3.5	2,031	3.1	2,568	3.3
Western	317.0	0.8	546.1	1.3	1,038.0	2.2	1,356.6	2.7	1,944.3	3.4	2,159	3.3	2,886	3.7
Wales	778.2	2.0	843.6	2.0	1,020.1	2.2	951.2	1.9	872.5	1.5	1,012	1.5	1,570	2.0
Midland	6,178.2	16.1	6,797.2	16.1	7,343.7	15.6	7,110.5	13.9	7,183.3	12.5	7,972	12.0	9,385	11.9
North-Western	4,192.3	10.9	4,414.5	10.5	4,573.0	9.7	4,512.7	8.9	4,910.9	8.5	5,734	8.6	6,242	7.9
Scotland	2,734.1	7.2	2,908.6	6.9	3,080.5	6.6	4,015.7	7.9	5,505.4	9.6	6,469	9.7	8,200	10.5
South-Eastern	1,040.7	2.7	1,291.4	3.1	1,589.0	3.4	1,839.6	3.6	1,696.2	2.9	1,970	3.0	2,019	2.6
Total	38,365.8	100.0	42,092.1	100.0	46,973.6	100.0	50,977.9	100.0	57,508.9	100.0	66,426	100.0	78,501	100.0

only about a third of its population parity. They indicate the special problems I.C.F.C. faces in this Region despite the 'Welsh economic miracle' of the post-war period. The figures for the Northern Region tell a similarly depressing tale: the further special factors which help to account for these low figures will be looked at below.

TABLE VI

REGIONAL COMPARISONS IN THE DEGREE OF INDUSTRIAL DIVERSIFICATION

Region	*No. of industries with under 1000 employees*	*Rank*	*Group*
London & South-East	11	1st	A Highly Diversified
North-Western	13	2nd	
Midlands	15	3rd	
Scotland }	19	4th	B Moderately Diversified
Eastern & Southern }			
Yorks & Humberside	24	6th	
Northern	38	7th	C Poorly Diversified
South-Western	45	8th	
Wales	53	9th	

Source: Adapted from the Ministry of Labour Gazette, March 1966

The diversity of the industrial framework goes a long way towards explaining the regional differences in the flow of I.C.F.C. finance, for just as diversification is a kind of macro-economic insurance policy for a region, so is it on the micro level for a lender who does not like to have too many eggs in too few baskets. Table VI gives a regional ranking of such diversification as determined by the number of the 152 minimum list headings of the Standard Industrial Classification *not* represented, or poorly represented, in the region, i.e. those industries with fewer than 1000 employees in total. Here London clearly heads the list followed closely by the North-West (perhaps surprisingly to those who still think of this region purely in terms of cotton and coal), and, less surprisingly, by the Midlands. Together this Group A forms a contiguous Greater Region, a 'Golden Triangle' enjoying a very highly diversified economy and giving plenty of opportunities for the wide variety of small and medium firms which in the main make up the aggregate effective demand schedule for I.C.F.C. finance. Scotland, with its long-term average rate of unemployment double that of the country as a whole, has long been among the most vociferous in demanding assistance in becoming more highly diversified: and (while greater diversification would doubtless contribute to a strengthening of its economy), this has led to the mistaken belief that its industrial structure is relatively undiversified, instead of which it is in fact fairly highly diversified, ranking at the top of Group B with the Eastern and Southern region, and followed by Yorkshire and Humberside. This underlying favourable aspect of Scotland's industrial structure helps to explain the very marked upsurge in the Corporation's activities there, once certain special difficulties which had previously been holding back progress had been overcome.[16] There is a wide gap between Group B and the problem areas of Group C—Northern, South-Western and Wales—the difficulties of which are to be sought to a considerable extent in the fact that, despite the influx of new industries in the post-war period, they remain very poorly diversified when compared with the other regions: and this makes it heavier going for the Corporation's managers in these regions.

Table VII gives a detailed matrix of regional/industrial distribution by amounts of finance outstanding at March 31st, 1965. The industrial classifications are vertically arranged in descending order of importance, so far as I.C.F.C.'s finances are concerned. The regional groupings, between the double vertical lines, read from left to right also in descending order of quantitative importance for England, starting with the London regions and its subdivisions, with Scotland and Wales following. (Head Office and Leasing give the minor figures which cannot be regionally allocated.) Starting at the top left hand corner of the Table, the engineering and electrical goods industries form the first group of the ranking, with some 23 per cent of the total, almost twice as important as any other group: they produce a wide range of goods with a high income elasticity of demand. London, by far the most successful region, has a substantial representation in all the leading industries, except textiles, but has no stake at all in the unimportant industries at the bottom of the list. It is important to notice that the Corporation's successes in the London Region are greater than might be expected from an examination of the region's location quotients. For example, London's census of production location quotient for wireless apparatus and precision instruments is just over 2.0: yet I.C.F.C.'s London figures account for nearly 70 per cent of the similar category. Again London's location quotient for printing and publishing is also 2.0, but the Corporation's London figure accounts for 51 per cent of its national lending in this category. Employment in the

[16] For a more detailed treatment of the Scottish case, see G. Davies, *The Bankers' Magazine*, September 1966. Among these special difficulties were the very slow rate of economic growth in the fifties, and the Scottish Bankers' tradition of longer-term lending than was the case in England, which appeared to leave a smaller gap for I.F.C.C. to fill in Scotland.

CLASSIFICATION OF FINANCIAL FACILITIES BY REGIONS AND BY INDUSTRIES
(by amounts outstanding at March 31st, 1965)

–£'000 £'000–

Industry	*Rank*	*Percentage of total*	*Total*	*London*	*S.E. area East*	*S.E. area West*	*Cambridge*	*Birmingham*	*Leicester*	*Manchester*	*Leeds*	*Bristol*	*Newcastle*	*Edinburgh*	*Glasgow*	*Cardiff*	*Head office*	*Leasing*
Engineering and electrical goods	1	22.6	15,028	4,040	1,013	2,026	623	1,208	988	429	897	215	18	670	166		2,712	23
Distribution	2	12.0	7,955	1,408	249	213	681	691	194	1,045	944	423	438	631	243	387	326	82
Miscellaneous	3	11.7	7,776	2,130	108	97	32	403	138	48	284	399	125	312	244	16	3,047	393
Construction	4	8.0	5,287	1,637	398	421	73	751	358	200	426	14		265	309	92	319	24
Textiles	5	6.8	4,513	193			82	22	1,614	952	218		18	488	108		818	
Metal manufacture	6	6.1	4,035	1,307			75	1,717		155	125	140		159	140		209*	8
Paper, printing and publishing	7	5.4	3,560	1,342	86	449	587	52	137	82	109	163		354	16		161	22
Other metal goods	8	4.3	2,853	865	31	260	12	374	145	158	189	142	72	9	83	7	447	59
Food, drink and tobacco	9	4.1	2,732	375		126	573	340	33	39	319	9	142	466	124		176	10
Clothing, footwear and leather	10	3.2	2,110	701	23	9	189	43	183	427	32	60		129	18		276	20
Bricks, pottery, glass cement	11	3.2	2,092	427		110	61	518	346	158	192	38		84	32	10	116	
Transport and communication	12	2.9	1,950	456		29	48	545	29	4	100			17	223	101	354	44
Chemicals and allied industries	13	2.5	1,657	453	178	8	70	185	139	225	34	48	9				178	130
Timber, furniture, etc.	14	2.1	1,455	854	143	24	18	52	136	16	13	124		40	33			2
Vehicles and shipbuilding	15	2.1	1,415	571		83	121	228	73	180	56	5	42	41		9		6
Other manufacturing industries	16	2.0	1,313	161	124	87	46	95	264	331	54	6	12		100		25	8
Agriculture and forestry	17	·5	358		173		51		34			100						
Mining and quarrying	18	·5	337						19	8		154	46		72			38
Totals		100.0	66,426	16,920	2,526	3,942	3,342	7,224	4,830	4,457	3,992	2,040	922	3,665	1,911	622	9,164	869

* Includes miscellaneous metals not allocated elsewhere.

wider London Region has been growing in the post-war period at a rate of half a million a decade, and there are expected to be at least 3½ million more people living in South-East England by 1981. Much of the past growth has been because of the bright employment prospects and current wages in the engineering and electrical goods industries. Three-quarters of the total growth of employment has been in manufacturing industries, and of this a considerable amount is in the small and medium class.

A further feature of London's success is seen in the fact that, not only is its industrial structure favourable, but that the growth industries themselves have been growing at a greater pace in the London Region than have those same growth industries elsewhere. (The converse is true; and bringing growth industries to the North and West will not constitute in itself a guarantee that these regions will catch up with South-Eastern England—but it should still reduce the rate of divergence). The current emphasis on decentralization is likely to increase the dominance of the London *Region* in the Corporation's figures. Decentralization often involves the more-or-less forcible transfer (through area redevelopment, etc.) of workshops and small factories to the outskirts of the Metropolitan area, and this almost inevitably involves the small firms concerned in the need for more capital: they take the opportunity afforded by the move to a more spacious environment to re-equip and re-plan their lay-out on a more effective basis. By far the greater part of such moves keeps the firms within the London region, in sufficiently close contact with their previous suppliers, customers, government services and the skilled labour supplies which seem to be a particularly crucial factor for those small firms who cannot afford the interruption and costs involved in retraining local labour on the greater scale which a move to some other region would usually entail. 'The rate of movement to the Metropolitan zone (from locations nearer central London) is still rising, having been doing so more or less steadily ever since 1945.'[17] Despite the lip-service paid to the Barlow philosophy since 1940, and to Regional policy since 1959, when London businessmen are faced with the choice of Decentralization, Dispersal or Extra-Regional Transfer,[18] the first is by far the most frequently exercised; and much of the recent discussion on this topic by writers such as Hall, Holmans, Keeble and the official South-East

[17] D. E. Keeble 'Industrial Migration from North-West London', *Urban Studies*, May 1965.

[18] By Decentralization is meant movement to the outer edge of the continuously built-up area: by Dispersal is meant movement beyond the built-up area, though not necessarily far beyond: and by Extra-Regional Transfer is meant movement beyond the South-East Region.

Study reflect the realities of industrial location in the London Region, and form at the same time a sort of academic counter-attack against the more established and persistent regional out-pourings from the North and West.[19] Thus the limited geographical extent of decentralization reinforces the factors of favourable industrial size and structure, and of favourable growth rates, to make it a well-supported assumption that the present dominance of London in the total I.C.F.C. picture is unlikely to be diminished. Very similar arguments are applicable to the rest of the Golden Triangle—the Midlands (Birmingham and Leicester in the Table) and to southern Lancashire and southern Yorkshire (Manchester and Leeds).

At the bottom end of the ranking table come Agriculture and Forestry, 17th; and Mining and Quarrying, 18th. Together they take up barely 1 per cent of total I.C.F.C. finance; and their products have a low income elasticity of demand. Diversification of industrial structure is, as we have seen, a kind of regional insurance policy: but in the Corporation's case diversification is not enough. What also matters is *whether there is diversification among small and medium industries*. This important and sometimes neglected feature is demonstrated by the Welsh example, and helps to reinforce our above arguments in explaining her disappointing I.C.F.C. figures. Thus, by 1961 manufacturing accounted for 23 per cent of employment in Wales as compared with only 11 per cent before the war. In fact, 'in the ten years 1948–58 this sector expanded twice as fast as it did in Great Britain'.[20] Furthermore, when measured on a percentage basis, there was a very marked growth in just those categories that rank high on our list: miscellaneous goods, 3rd in our rank, expanded by 91 per cent; engineering, first in our list, grew by over 50 per cent; paper and printing, 7th, by 46 per cent and textiles (nylon), 5th, by 33 per cent. Since, however, these industries represented only a small proportion of Welsh industry at the base date, large percentage increases are compatible with relatively small absolute increases, still leaving 53 industrial categories negligibly represented, as shown in Table VI, and so still contrastingly strongly with the amounts of such industries in those regions with a more favourable overall industrial structure, and containing a much larger absolute amount of such growth industries. Of the 18 industrial categories only in 7 does I.C.F.C. finance play a part in Wales; and the mystery of why the Welsh miracle has passed the Corporation by, is to some considerable extent a consequence of its industrial structure. Similarly

[19] P. Hall, *London 2000*: A. E. Holmans, 'Industrial Development Certificates', *Urban Studies*, November 1964; D. E. Keeble, op. cit.

[20] Professor B. Thomas, *The Welsh Economy*, p. 190.

with that part of Northern England financed from Newcastle, only 10 of the industrial categories appear in its list.

Thus industries which have high location quotients in Wales, Scotland, and Northern England, like agriculture and coal mining, tend to have relatively little attraction for I.C.F.C. Conversely industries which have high location quotients in the 'golden triangle' are the favoured avenues of investment for I.C.F.C., so that the Corporation's contribution to their development tends to be even greater than their high location quotients would indicate. Differences in the typical size of plant and differences in ownership, as, e.g. in the heavy industries like iron and steel, and in the fuel industries—which are either large, or nationalized or both—and in agriculture, where specialist financial institutions exist strongly competitive with I.C.F.C., and the more favourable industrial incentives offered by the Board of Trade in Development Areas, help to account for the relatively low levels of activity by the Corporation wherever such industries predominate, as in the regions served by the Cardiff and Newcastle branches. In contrast, the smaller-sized plants, with less complex forms of ownership—family-owned, partnerships and private companies—and the more diversified mix of industries, combine to make areas like London, the Midlands, and the southern parts of Lancashire and Yorkshire, presenting less competition from the Board of Trade, ideally suited to throw up in abundance the very kinds of projects for which the Corporation was —principally—founded.

IV. CONCLUSION: A MATTER OF CONSCIENCE

In twenty-two eventful years I.C.F.C. has developed to fill a unique place as a mature City institution contributing significantly to the growth of a key sector of the economy—the miscellany of small and medium firms displaying an urge to expansion and inventiveness that, but for the existence of the Corporation would have been largely thwarted. Many of these assisted customers have already achieved a considerable importance both for the home and overseas markets and have become widely known; even more important as a basis for assessing I.C.F.C.'s achievement is the improved standing of the many hundreds of anonymous firms up and down the country. The economic life of the nation would have been very much poorer had their growth been stunted or had they been forced to the wall.

Furthermore, the Corporation has been able, without sacrificing its main role of financing growth in those areas of greatest potential, and within the framework of a private enterprise organization using unsubsidized funds from the banks and public in roughly equal quantities, to raise the level of activity in other regions as well, not only because of the profitability of so doing but also, in so far as the overall profit criterion allowed, because of a sense of public duty—although most observers, including the Corporation itself in its more introspective moments, would have liked to have seen more progress made in this direction. Though born with a well-developed social conscience, it has also, in the face of the strongly competitive and risky field of long-term capital provision, had to make sure that its institutional conscience exerted a pervasive pressure towards all-round efficiency. As a commercial venture, the Corporation cannot take on the guise of a Robin Hood of the Regions. The surprising thing in the circumstances, perhaps, is that it has done so well: and the beneficial influence of the Corporation in regions of special difficulty is strongly indicated by Professor Wilson's advice to the Northern Ireland Government to request I.C.F.C.-type assistance in her problems.[21]

For the future, official plans still project a promising scene for the Corporation's business. The National Plan (postponed rather than abandoned by the 1966–67 crisis) in putting the Corporation's primary-ranking industrial group of Engineering and Electrical Goods first in its Industrial Sector, indicated a required percentage increase in the rate of growth per annum from 4.7 in 1960 to 1964, to 5.8 in the period to 1970.[22] The economic Development Committees are busily revealing the need for a much higher rate of capital equipment among the smaller and medium firms in particular: 'The wool textiles industry foresees difficulties for some of the smaller firms in raising finance for the re-equipment they recognize to be necessary. The glassware industry foresees a similar problem.'[23] Hence, the greater opportunity for I.C.F.C. The South-East Study indicates, as we have seen, the opportunities which are bound to accompany its projected increase in population. The Selective Employment Tax offers a bounty to the Midlands and, if effective, is likely to release most labour supplies in the Corporation's leading region—London and the South-East—which has as much as one-third of the country's total employment in the services sector.[24] Thus the outlook for the Corporation's progress in the remainder of the sixties appears bright, particularly in those regions which now

[21] *Economic Development in N. Ireland*, Cmnd. 479, pp. 105–6.
[22] *The National Plan*, 1965 p. 101.
[23] Ibid. p. 59.
[24] See G. Davies, 'Regional Unemployment, Labour Availability and Redeployment', *Oxford Economic Papers*, March 1967.

account for the major part of its activities. This in itself, quite apart from the stepping up of public expenditures in the North-East and Scotland, should enable it to extend its finance toward the more marginal categories and more difficult regions. Not that business in the North and West is unprofitable! It is simply that, given the present regional imbalances, there is probably a larger proportion of marginal business of the kind that the I.C.F.C. would feel disposed to undertake in the North and West than it would feel free to take on in the South and East and in the Midlands, where it is more likely to come up against the restrictive 'directives' of the Bank of England and the Treasury.

If I.C.F.C. is to be encouraged in doing more lending in difficult regions, then applying brakes on its more profitable (in total) business in the Midlands and the South-East, merely in the hope that this would channel more funds to the North and West, would be a perverse, dog-in-the-manger and self-defeating policy, for the greater the amount of profit that the Corporation may reasonably make, the more it will be enabled (at the very least) to listen to its own—and other peoples'—social conscience. In the same way that the Corporation has adopted a variety of flexible methods for carrying out its main function of 'gap-filling', so it may begin to experiment more fully in the future with a variety of methods for carrying out its main ancillary function. Following its precedent with 'EDITH', 'Ship Mortgage', 'TDC' and 'Industrial Mergers' it might be possible for it to hive off a subsidiary specially to deal with particularly intractable sectors such as rural areas and the still relatively depressed areas, working in close conjunction with the branches most nearly concerned. One of the drawbacks of establishing a separate ancillary organization is that it might lose those very contacts with the main stream of activities from which fresh ideas and energy might flow. On balance, however, I.C.F.C.'s experience tends to push it towards setting up specialized undertakings to carry out such projects. It might even be worth considering the advantages and disadvantages of subsidizing such a subsidiary particularly in view of the fact that one of the main and avowed purposes of such an organization would be a social one. The valuable experience which I.C.F.C. has built up over the years could thus be harnessed to a strictly limited and clearly defined degree, for such urgent public purposes as, e.g. reversing the depopulation of rural areas and the small townships in parts of Northern England, Central Wales, Southern Scotland, and the Highlands; regions where the Corporation, in common with so many other institutions, has had little success in the past.

The provision of a subsidy is not a necessary condition for the establishment of an effective 'Special Loan Fund' or 'Development Agency' or whatever such a socially biased subsidiary might be called: it would, however, have two advantages, firstly in extending the range of possibilities available to it, and secondly in necessitating closer contact with other regional bodies. Possibly the preferred solution would be for any such subsidiary to work in close conjunction with the Branches of the Bank of England, thus enabling the I.C.F.C. to gain some of the powerful advantages available to its Canadian counter-part, the Industrial Development Bank. After reviewing its 20 years' experience the Porter report concluded in 'favour of the present arrangement under which I.D.B. is a subsidiary of the Bank of Canada' with the partial subsidization thereby involved, as, e.g. in being excused taxation, and in receiving all its equity and debenture capital from the central bank.[25] The I.D.B appears to have taken little notice of the Report's advice regarding its over-vigorous competition with private lending agencies; it has increased its branch coverage to some 28 offices and has recently reformed its organization in order 'to provide further administrative decentralization' so as to 'maintain closer contact with regional developments.'[26]

Little wonder that Canadian experience continues to be the most frequently used scale of reference for comparing the progress of I.C.F.C. and also for supporting the case for granting it privileged financial provisions so as to make it very substantially more than a capital lender of last resort, and in particular to strengthen its efforts in the more difficult areas. However, the disadvantages of subsidization are considerable, and would arise chiefly from three sides. The first would be its tendency to grow in answer to clamorous demands for the support of untenable projects. Secondly, there would be the related tendency for its administration to become involved in political and personal issues, particularly in small rural communities, in contrast with the greater impersonality and professionalism of business in larger towns.[27] Thirdly, the spectre, if not the reality, of 'unfair competition' would be raised, and this both from the side of rival suppliers of long term credit and rival borrowers.

With or without a subsidy, however, the co-operation of any such subsidiary with the new regional associations, official and voluntary, that are now springing up, would be to great mutual advantage. This would, in any case, be merely the extension of the kind of close co-operation with government departments that has

[25] Report of the (Canadian) Royal Commission on Banking and Finance (1964), p. 230.
[26] Industrial Development Bank, 22nd Annual Report, 1966, p. 8.
[27] This view has been, unfortunately, amply confirmed by the public controversy in the spring of 1967 over the activities of the Highland Development Board.

already been successfully carried out, for instance, in the administration by the Corporation of the Fuel Efficiency Loans Scheme on behalf of the Ministry of Fuel and Power.[28] If the Corporation were to be thus armed with a specialized subsidiary—and additionally, were this considered desirable, supported by a strictly limited subsidy—it would demonstrate, in a voice loud enough to silence at least some of its critics, its close concern with some of the most difficult problems connected with regional development.[29] In this way there would be little danger of alienating the essential co-operation of the banks; nor need anyone fear that I.C.F.C. might be tempted into becoming a slot-machine for feeding the smaller species of economic dinosaurs. Should the Corporation decide to carry on as it is at present without any formal division between its marginal and its supra-marginal activities, the more social side of its activities will still need to receive increasing attention in the course of the next five or six years, if it is just to hold its place in the expansion of I.C.F.C. as a whole. Failing such new departures, the Corporation is likely to follow the main lines of policy so successfully laid down in its early years. With its growing strength, its greater independence and maturity, ably demonstrated by its recent immunity from slumps, it should be able to avoid any return to the Doldrums. Nevertheless, its current pronounced success, a tribute to its spirit of enterprise and to its institutional conscience, would be enhanced by offering further scope for that social conscience which, after all, it inherited from the Regions.

UNIVERSITY OF STRATHCLYDE

[28] I.C.F.C. Eleventh Annual Report, p. 12.

[29] The setting up of the Industrial Reorganization Corporation has strengthened this argument regarding the need for greater co-operation between I.C.F.C., the banks and government agencies, to close the 'gap in the institutional framework' mentioned in para. 5 of Cmnd. 2889, January 1966.

THE DETERMINANTS OF STEEL PRICES IN THE U.S.: 1947–65

By Richard Mancke[1]

I

In this note we analyse steel prices during 1947–65 in order to establish the timing and cause of the change from near-constant increase to stability. Price is viewed as the resultant of (1) demand, (2) supply and (3) market structure, or the degree of monopoly. We assume the steel industry to set prices by imperfect collusion, and to get as close to maximizing industry profits as incomplete knowledge and limited collaboration will permit. But we do not light-heartedly assume monopoly, and go on from there. On the contrary: monopoly plus certain cost and demand conditions which we study in detail lead to some definite conclusions which are tested by a multivariate regression analysis and are not refuted.

In testing our hypothesis, we start with the simplest possible one, and add variables to see how much more can be explained. This makes for some repetition, but a cautious procedure is needed because of the limitations of the data.

II

The steel industry produces a tremendous variety of products (more than 50,000). However, they are standardized not differentiated products, mainly because purchased steel is an intermediate rather than a final good. Since it must meet a relatively detailed set of specifications, if any product differentiation exists it must be concentrated on the various selling services rather than on the physical product. Even more important is the relatively high elasticity of supply substitution among the different products. This implies that most of the industry's many products are merely permutations of its basic product: iron and steel.

The first problem is how to determine the industry's aggregate marginal cost curve (MC). All economists know the difficulty of trying to determine the MC curve directly but the industry's aggregate average variable cost curve (AVC) can be approximated and if AVC is horizontal it coincides with MC. The question thus becomes the empirical one of ascertaining the range of output over which AVC is nearly constant. For most years when output is

[1] The author wishes to thank Professor M. A. Adelman, and the referees of the original manuscript, for their helpful suggestions.

Table I

DEFINITIONS OF THE VARIABLES

SMP = steel mill prices
C = constant
AVC = average variable cost
AIMP = total imports of steel divided by total domestic output of steel
CU = capacity utilization
DUMB: Version 1 = 0 from 1947–58, 1 from 1959–65
Version 2 = 0 from 1947–61, 1 from 1962–65.
Z = DUMB·CU
AI = DUMB·AIMP
PLAP = Pittsburgh price of steel plate
PPLA = total imports of plate divided by total domestic output of plate
DPLA = DUMB·PPLA
SHEP = Pittsburgh price of sheet steel
PSHE = total imports of sheet divided by total domestic output of sheet
DSHP = DUMB·PSHE
BARP = Pittsburgh price of bars
PBAR = total imports of bars divided by total domestic output of bars
DPBR = DUMB·PBAR

Note. All prices were obtained from *Metal Statistics*, 1965. All other basic data was obtained from either the American Iron and Steel Institute's *Annual Statistical Reports*, 1947–65 editions, or from the *Wall Street Journal*.

Note: In the following four tables the results from estimating the regressions are presented according to the following schema. On line 1 is given the estimated coefficients, on line 2 is the estimated standard error of the coefficient, and on line 3 is given an indication of the degree of statistical significance of the estimated coefficients according to a two-tailed Student's *t* test. A single asterisk, *, mean the coefficient is significantly different from 0 at at least the 1 per cent level, ** means it is significant at at least the 5 per cent level, and *** means it is significant at at least the 10 per cent level. If there is no asterisk the coefficient is not significantly different from 0 at the 10 per cent level or lower.

Since we did not have *a priori* ideas as to what should be the appropriate sign for all of the coefficients (e.g. AIMP) a two-tailed test was utilized.

Note: In a discussion with a top marketing official of the Bethlehem Steel Company it was indicated that the steel industry considers the various government price indexes to be the best available estimates of the price of steel.

Steel

SMP =	C	+ AVC	+ AIMP	+ CU	+ DUMB	+ AI	+ Z	
1	−25.70	1.10						R^2 = .889
	(9.54)	(.095)						
	*	*						
2	−13.16	.93	205.01					R^2 = .918
	(9.92)	(.11)	(85.28)					
		*	**					
3	−4.61	.89	201.29	−.061				R^2 = .921
	(25.84)	(.15)	(88.30)	(.17)				
		*	**					
4	−15.02	.95	15.81	.018	1.93	125.47		R^2 = .922
	(32.3)	(.21)	(416.4)	(.22)	(11.3)	(447.7)		
		*						
5	−22.61	1.07	−195.71	0.05	−89.04		1.50	R^2 = .950
	(23.87)	(.14)	(171.7)	(.17)	(34.6)		(.55)	
		*			**		**	
Test for the effect of the guideposts								
5@	−15.52	1.07	−123.76	−.072	−69.11		1.17	R^2 = .945
	(23.84)	(.15)	(154.3)	(.15)	(39.7)		(.59)	
		*					***	

TABLE I *continued*

Plates

PLAP =	C	+ AVC	+ PPLA	+ CU	+ DUMB	+ DPLA +	Z	
1–P	—.58	.051						R^2 = .854
	(.52)	(.005)						
		*						
2–P	−.48	.049	5.58					R^2 = .870
	(.51)	(.005)	(3.98)					
		*						
3–P	1.13	.041	6.65	−.011				R^2 = .880
	(1.15)	(.008)	(4.07)	(.009)				
		*						
4–P	−.44	.043	−6.15	.006	.32	12.51		R^2 = .920
	(1.49)	(.007)	(6.26)	(.011)	(.33)	(8.21)		
		*						
5–P	−.53	.046	−5.58	.004	−4.63		.078	R^2 = .960
	(1.05)	(.005)	(3.76)	(.008)	(1.26)		(.019)	
		*	***		*		*	
			Test for the effect of the guideposts					
5@–P	−.11	.047	−4.57	−.002	4.02		.067	R^2 = .953
	(1.09)	(.006)	(3.73)	(.007)	(1.61)		(.023)	
		*			**		**	

Sheet

SHEP =	C +	AVC +	PSHE +	CU +	DUMB +	DSHP +	Z	
1–S	−.91	.006						R^2 = .848
	(.68)	(.007)						
		*						
2–S	−.54	(.061)	11.93					R^2 = .887
	(.63)	(.006)	(5.04)					
		*	**					
3–S	1.39	.052	12.09	−.013				R^2 = .896
	(1.79)	(.010)	(4.99)	(.012)				
		*	**					
4–S	−.16	.055	−33.94	.002	.40	41.21		R^2 = .916
	(1.98)	(.010)	(41.25)	(.014)	(.35)	(41.02)		
		*						
5–S	.30	.056	−8.44	−.004	−6.84		.112	R^2 = .945
	(1.46)	(.008)	(7.19)	(.010)	(2.55)		(.039)	
		*			**		**	
			Test for the effect of the guideposts					
5@ S	.42	.058	−8.50	−.008	−5.85		.097	R^2 = .943
	(1.48)	(.008)	(7.58)	(.010)	(2.81)		(.042)	
		*			***		**	

TABLE I *continued*

Bars

BARP =	C	AVC	PBAR	CU	DUMB	DPBR	Z	
1–B	−1.47 (.62) **	.062 (.006) *						$R^2 = .854$
2–B	.21 (.78)	.039 (.009) *	11.06 (3.81) **					$R^2 = .904$
3–B	.15 (1.6)	.040 (.010) *	11.52 (4.39) **	.003 (.012)				$R^2 = .904$
4–B	−.77 (1.47)	.039 (.011) *	16.64 (9.55)	.011 (.011)	2.09 (.88) **	23.50 (11.88) ***		$R^2 = .933$
5–B	−.24 (1.25)	.052 (.009) *	−2.47 (6.28)	−.006 (.009)	−4.49 (1.61) **		.076 (.024) *	$R^2 = .952$
Test for the effect of the guideposts								
5@ B	−.07 (1.31)	.051 (.009) *	1.21 (4.81)	.006 (.010)	−3.64 (2.07)		.061 (.030) ***	$R^2 = .946$

between 60 and 90 per cent of rated capacity the assumption of constant AVC is probably not violated to a substantial extent and hence AVC may be viewed as a good approximation for MC.

The second problem is with demand. Buyers of steel embrace the gamut of American industry. This means that even if we could ascertain every firm's demand for steel (a premise which is itself very dubious) any aggregate demand curve would be subject to the vagaries of a compositional effect for as the buyers of steel changed their relative positions in the general economy the aggregate demand for steel would fluctuate. For example, if GNP were to remain constant but there were a rise in auto production offset by a fall in clothing and housing production then the aggregate demand schedule for steel would shift upwards. This aggregation problem is theoretically insoluble; however, its practical significance is probably small. Nevertheless we will not neglect the opportunity to test for discrepancies between the demand for steel in the aggregate and in the small.

The demand for intermediate products is more inelastic than the demand for the final products which they help to build. Typically any intermediate good accounts for only a small fraction of the final product's total cost. Thus a dramatic rise in the cost of any such factor need not cause a dramatic rise in the cost of the final good and therefore the amount of the final good which is sold is not greatly affected. The result is that a sharp rise in the price of an intermediate need not be accompanied by a sharp fall in the amount demanded.

But although the short-run demand faced by all who sell steel in the market in which the U.S. industry competes is indeed inelastic, the *total supply* of steel and *the amount produced by the U.S. industry* are not identical. Even if there were perfect collusion among the members of the U.S. industry (and all available evidence indicates effective collusion to be very strong) so long as foreign competition is not stifled the short-run demand faced by the domestic industry may still be relatively elastic. One of the goals of this paper will be to see whether or not foreign competition has indeed played such a key role in limiting the short-run inelasticity of demand faced by the postwar domestic steel industry.

Finally, one more qualification is in order because even in the immediate run factor coefficients are not fixed; hence, as a factor's price is raised the demand for it becomes increasingly more elastic since substitutes become economically more attractive.[2] The implication of this is that at some point even a monopolist finds it unprofitable to continue to raise his prices at a rate faster than the general price level is rising. Could this be the case with steel in the 1960s?

III

Having separately considered the three determinants of steel prices we now present an ordinary least squares multivariate regression analysis of the determinants of aggregate steel prices and of the prices of three subsectors—plates, sheets and bars.[3] For each of these four product groups five (six for bars) regressions were estimated. We shall discuss in considerable detail the five regressions for the aggregate steel industry. Then, since the three subsectors have similar variables, we shall only consider any anomalous results which are revealed by their estimation. Finally we shall conclude with a discussion of the probable influence of the guideposts on steel prices.

Regression 1 represents the simplest theory for explaining steel prices. Observing that both AVC and steel prices rose constantly from 1947–58 and then displayed no apparent trend from 1959–65, it seemed obvious to regress steel prices on AVC.[4] The result as one

[2] M. A. Adelman, 'Steel, Administered Prices and Inflation', *Quarterly Journal of Economics*, February 1961, p. 26.

[3] The reasons for examining the three subsectors plates, sheets and bars were respectively: plate output is highly correlated with the output of the nation's heavy capital goods industry; sheet output is highly correlated with the nation's output of durable consumer goods, and bars have long been thought to be subject to more severe import competition than most other steel products.

[4] AVC = (total employment costs + total cost of intermediates)/(total ingot production).

would guess was highly significant and explained a considerable portion of steel price movements as is indicated by the correlation coefficient, $R^2 = .89$.[5]

There are, however, at least three deficiencies with this model. First, the Durbin-Watson Statistic for this regression has the value 1.13 (for the three subsectors its value is less than 1.00), indicating a high probability of positive serial correlation and hence inefficient estimation of the regression coefficients and an underestimate of their variances.[6] Serial correlation is often the result of the omission of one or more significant variables, since the theory of the firm implies that price is the resultant of three forces—demand, supply, and market structure—while regression 1 considers only one force, we have support for a second reason for feeling dubious about this naïve model. Finally, the estimated R^2 is an overestimate of the real explanatory power of changes in AVC resulting in changes in steel prices. Labor costs are the largest component of AVC and the fact that wages rose during the late 1950s when there was a labor surplus implies that the steel union was exerting monopoly power and collecting a share of the added income which resulted from any steel price rise. Thus we see that though one line of causation has higher AVC leading to higher prices, another has higher prices leading to higher AVC. We do not know to what extent AVC is price determined; however, we can be sure that the causal relation is not unidirectional from changes in AVC leading to changes in steel prices.[7]

If the domestic industry is collusive the main force preventing the industry from charging the monopoly price is the threat of imports.[8] Therefore the variable AIMP—total imports divided by total output—was introduced in regression 2. What sign should AIMP have? If the industry were competitive AIMP should be positive because when domestic prices are high this will encourage imports.[9] But we have assumed, particularly for the short-run,

[5] The constant, C, may be ignored throughout as its sole use is to improve the estimation. If we did not include the constant the estimated regression would be arbitrarily forced through the origin.

[6] J. Durbin and G. Watson, 'Testing for Serial Correlation in Least Squares Regression', parts I and II, *Biometrika*, 1950 and 1951.

[7] Professor Adelman brought this point to the attention of the author. In order to take account of the simultaneous equation bias which this implies the author has done some estimation of a model in which price is determined in a simultaneous framework. Appendix 2 gives some indication of the preliminary results—they tend to reinforce all of the conclusions of this paper.

[8] An opposing view allegedly advanced by some American steel men appeared in the *Wall Street Journal*, August 28th, 1963. Here it was stated that over capacity in Europe would lead to a fall in imports since the European firms would no longer be able to subsidize the 'low priced exports in the U.S. out of their now dwindling profits in the home market'. History has substantiated the naivety of this view.

[9] A flaw of this is that relative prices rather than absolute prices should determine the flow of imports.

that potential and actual foreign competition is the main force working to keep the essentially collusive domestic steel industry from charging the profit maximizing monopoly price. Therefore, relatively high imports would be expected to be a force tending to restrain price rises and hence we would expect, *ceteris paribus*, the import coefficient to be negative. Regression 2 tends to support the competitive hypothesis. It should also be noted incidentally that for regressions 2–5 the Durbin-Watson Statistic always has a value between 1.5 and 1.7 indicating that the likelihood of significant serial correlation is considerably lessened.

In regression 2 we introduced imports primarily as a proxy for market structure. In regression 3 we introduce CU—capacity utilization—in order to get an indirect indicator of both the level of demand relative to supply and of MC.[10] Since when demand rises, *ceteris paribus*, prices usually rise we would expect its coefficient to be positive. *Contra* to our expectations the coefficient is negative but not significantly so.

A look at our results up to this moment shows virtually no improvement as compared with the naïve cost-plus model of regression 1. Also the signs of AIMP and CU are the opposite of what our theory would predict. But so far we have assumed a constant universe over the whole period, and we now question that assumption. We may recall that 1959 was the year of the great steel strike (when any dialogue between labor and management disappeared) and also that for the first time since the war the strike settlement did not almost immediately lead to higher prices. These are indications of a structural shift. The hypothesis they suggest is that by 1959 steel prices had risen to such a level that further rises would be unprofitable. To test it, we now introduce a dummy variable, DUMB, which is 0 from 1947–58 and 1 from 1959–65. The use of this variable is seen to improve the specification of the model and to change significantly the nature of our results.

In regression 4 we now introduce two new variables, DUMB and AI—which is AIMP·DUMB. The estimated value of DUMB indicates if there was a shift in the level of the regression (constant) after 1959. For the purposes of this paper DUMB's coefficient may be ignored. The second variable AI should indicate if there was a structural shift in imports about 1959.[11] The fact that its coefficient is insignificant indicates no such structural shift and therefore imports were not, along with the changing pattern of AVC, the

[10] See Appendix 1 for a more detailed discussion of the variable CU.

[11] For an explanation of this use of dummy variables see Jack Johnston, *Econometric Methods* (New York: McGraw-Hill, 1960), pp. 221–8.

cause of the relative price stability after 1959. If imports were affecting prices at all it was in the same way that they had affected them in the decade before 1959.

Finally we come to regression 5. This is the key regression for explaining steel prices—both the aggregate price and the subsector prices. In regression 5 we drop AI and replace it with Z—defined as DUMB·CU. If Z has a significant coefficient it indicates that about 1959 there occurred a change in the relation of steel supply to demand. For the whole period CU was insignificant. Hence if Z's coefficient is significantly positive it indicates that starting in 1959 and not earlier the steel companies could now raise prices only when demand was relatively high and pressing capacity.

In fact the Z coefficient is significantly positive at at least the 5 per cent level for all four sets of regressions. This supports the hypothesis of a structural shift of the supply–demand relation occurring about 1959. Since we at last appear to have a well-defined model we shall next take a closer look at the coefficients of each of the variables in regression 5.

AVC has a positive coefficient and still is, as we would expect, by far the most significant variable. Also calculating the elasticity of steel prices with respect to AVC at the latter's mean yields the result $E = 1.003$. This shows that near the mean a given percentage change in AVC was associated with almost the same percentage change in prices. Again, however, the dual directional nature of causation between steel prices and AVC should be stressed. This means that the regression results yield an overestimate of the explanatory power of AVC. The coefficient of AIMP is now negative indicating support for the dominance of the second rationale; i.e. that over the entire period 1947–65 as imports rose prices fell due to increased foreign competition. This coefficient is significant only at the 20 per cent level; however, when we consider that at the same time the first reason—high prices leading to high imports—is also in operation we must appreciate that a significant force caused the dramatic switch in sign from being significantly positive as it was in what we now see was the poorly defined model of regression 2 to negative as it is in the well-defined regression 5. We therefore see that throughout most of the period (almost certainly from 1950–65) imports have not simply responded to higher prices but rather have played a key role in limiting the extent of the postwar rise in steel prices.

The coefficient for CU is still very insignificant showing that for the whole period this was not a good explanatory variable. Considering that Z is always positive and significant we must conclude that from 1947–58 steel prices tended to rise independently of demand relative to supply but not from 1959–65. Instead its price behavior began to parrot that of a more competitive industry since prices could now be raised only when demand pressed upon capacity. We conclude that the above empirical results give support to both the demand-shift and the mark-up price explanations of the behavior of steel prices since the war. This result should please the classical economist for all three elements—demand, supply and market structure—have been shown to have played an important role in determining steel prices.

IV

As indicated earlier, steel is not a homogeneous product; hence, we conducted a similar analysis of three subsectors: plates, sheets and bars. For plates and sheets all of the relevant coefficient signs are exactly the same as those for the aggregate industry. Also the coefficients all have approximately the same degree of significance. Finally the elasticities of plate and sheet prices with respect to AVC at its mean were .98 and 1.02 respectively. We therefore must conclude that the analysis of the aggregate steel industry carries over in its entirety to these two subsectors.

When we examine the bars subsector we observe minor deviations from the familiar pattern. First, in regression 4–B we note that DPBR (which equals DUMB·PBAR, where PBAR = total bar imports divided by U.S. bar output) the variable which represents a shift in the structure of imports in 1959 is barely significant.[12] For all of the other products a similar variable was insignificant. Further, the elasticity of bar prices with respect to AVC at its mean is 1.21—considerably higher than for the other products. This latter fact seems to give some explanation of the former since it implies that unlike the other products the price of bars rose considerably faster than AVC in the 1950s; hence, one would expect imports to have played an especially significant role in the bar market. Finally, since imports of bars did display a structural shift sometime around 1959, we estimated a sixth regression (not shown) which included both DPBR and Z. Since when DPBR was estimated alone it was only barely significant we did not expect any major differences between the basic regression 5–B and this regression 6–B. This expectation was not disappointed.[13]

[12] When we ran the same regression redefining DUMB so that it equaled 0 from 1947–61 and 1 thereafter PDBR was once again insignificant. This tends to verify that the shift occurred at or shortly before 1959.

[13] One referee has pointed out that the use of the variable CU in the three subsector models does not allow for the effect of compositional shifts in demand upon steel prices.

V

The foregoing model (given by the four versions of regression 5) seems to give a good explanation of postwar steel prices. Therefore we shall conclude this paper by attempting to see what light can be shed on the efficacy of moral suasion as exercised indirectly through the guideposts and directly by Presidential expressions of concern. Specifically we redefined DUMB to be 0 from 1947–61 and 1 from 1962–65. Then we recomputed regression 5. The reasons for choosing 1962 as the year when moral suasion first became a major policy tool were (1) in December 1961 the White House began to leak word that it would use its power to prevent price rises,[14] (2) in January 1962 the Annual Report of the Council of Economic Advisers for the first time explicitly stated the doctrine of the guideposts.[15] This is generally accepted as the beginning of guidepost action, (3) in April 1962 President Kennedy initiated his war against 'Big Steel'.[16]

The result of our calculation was that the signs of all of the variables of interest were the same regardless of which definition of DUMB was used.[17] However, using the 1959 definition we discover both (1) R^2 to three places is always slightly higher, and (2) the coefficients of interest to us are always considerably more significant. The reader should be cautioned against looking at the slight difference in R^2 and then jumping to the conclusion that these consistent differences are not significant—they are. The reasons are (1) the great (overstated) power which AVC exercises over the entire model; for example, for the aggregate steel industry regression 1 has $R^2 = .89$. Since adding additional variables cannot reduce and usually increases R^2—even if there were no relation it would reduce the degrees of freedom—the R^2 for any multivariate price model containing AVC must be of roughly the same order of magnitude,[18] (2) the standard error of the regression is always less using that definition of DUMB which defines the break as occurring

[14] 'The White House Role in Bargaining', *Business Week*, December 23rd, 1961, pp. 81–3.

[15] *Economic Report of the President together with the Annual Report of the Council of Economic Advisers* (Washington: U.S. Govt. Printing Office, 1962), pp. 185–90.

[16] During the Eisenhower administration there were intermittent rumbles about the need for price restraint in steel; however, these rumbles were from a source considered friendly to the industry and do not appear to have been seriously considered.

[17] An exception to this is that bars for DPBR changes sign—this is due to the shift in the role of imports which effected bars around 1959.

[18] See Appendix 2.

For example, CU may be relatively low but nevertheless the bars subsector may be pressing bar capacity. The author recognizes the validity of this criticism; however, since figures for capacity utilization of particular subsectors are unavailable he is forced to use CU as a proxy for the desired figures.

in 1959. Thus we must conclude that for the aggregate steel industry, as well as for the subsectors plate, sheet and bars, there is no evidence to support the conclusion that either President Kennedy's direct use of force or his indirect use of force through the guideposts exerted any significant effect on steel price behavior. Instead the evidence supports the conclusion that it has been market pressures which have led to the relative price stability of steel in the 1960s. Further, since using the second definition of DUMB did yield the result that all relevant coefficients were of the same sign but less significant we have further verification that the change which occurred about 1959 did not reverse itself in the 1960s.

The main policy conclusion to be derived from the foregoing is that if the government wishes to encourage lower steel prices there are two ways which are likely to be more efficacious than moral suasion: If the balance of payments is a problem the government should encourage lower prices by pursuing policies which will lead to lower AVC. Two such policies would be to encourage technical innovation or to grant subsidies. If the balance of payments is not a problem the government could lower tariffs thus encouraging foreign competition and hence lower prices.

MASSACHUSETTS INSTITUTE OF TECHNOLOGY

Appendix I

In the preceding analysis the data for capacity utilization (defined as CU = (total output of ingots)/(total capacity to produce ingots)) played a key role. As usual it is difficult to determine output precisely and even more difficult to determine capacity. For example, is the more relevant measure of output unfinished ingot or the output of the rolling mills and fabricating shops? What about quality changes over time? It should be obvious that what is desired is a vector of measures of output; however, since this is not practicable we chose only one measure—ingot production.

Having decided on our measure of output we still face problems in measuring capacity. Unlike output, the market process yields no numbers telling us the amount of capacity. We must instead appeal to the estimates of acknowledged experts in the industry and we do not ask much—only that they be consistent.[19] Beginning with 1961 the industry no longer released its estimates of ingot capacity; for this period we must rely on outside information.

[19] The industry capacity estimates used here closely parallel the Bureau of the Census Performance Potential estimates found in U.S. Dept. of Commerce, Bureau of the Census, *The Measurement of Performance Potential in Manufacturing Establishments*, Working Paper, No. 18 (Washington: U.S. Govt. Printing Office, 1965).

Since the measure of capacity is crucial the author was especially concerned about what results would occur using different estimates for post 1960 capacity. As a result each regression was estimated using four different estimates of capacity. They were

1. The Council of Economic Advisers' estimate that from 1961–65 capacity increased 2 per cent per year.
2. The *Wall Street Journal* estimates which are obtained from information gleaned from sources close to the industry. These are probably the best estimates; however, the *Journal* acknowledges that they could result in an overestimate because since 1963 the massive introduction of basic oxygen furnace (BOF) capacity has not been accompanied by the official junking of much obsolete open hearth capacity.

In order to try to take account of the possible overestimate by the *Wall Street Journal* the author constructed two other estimates:

3. A minimum estimate assumed that since most industry sources state that by the start of 1963 it had become profitable to replace relatively modern open hearths with BOFs implying that the average cost of BOFs was less than the AVC of open hearths; then, if this were in fact the case, the steel companies would spend all available capital on BOFs and every bit of new BOF capacity would simply replace open hearth capacity.[20] Therefore this measure assumes that from 1963–65 there was no rise in capacity.
4. An estimate derived by assuming that due to its relative efficiency the rate of capacity utilization of BOFs was 100 per cent and therefore output of BOFs equaled BOF capacity. Given this identity the yearly absolute increase of BOF capacity could be calculated. If we assume that all of the new BOF capacity is for replacement of obsolete open hearths, then the total yearly increment to real (as opposed to the *WSJ's* measure of nominal) capacity can be found by subtracting this amount from the *WSJ's* capacity estimates.

The four sets of estimates follow (in millions of tons):

	1961	1962	1963	1964	1965
1. CEA	151.6	154.6	157.7	160.8	164.0
2. *WSJ*	150.0	157.0	162.0	168.0	174.0
3. Minimum	150.0	157.0	157.0	157.0	157.0
4. Medium	150.0	157.0	160.1	160.5	160.4

The results of the four sets of regressions showed that there was not one significant change in the important coefficients regardless of which capacity measure was used. However, the CEA's estimates

[20] See for example the special section on BOFs in the Annual Report, 1966, Bethlehem Steel Corporation.

generally yielded coefficients with the highest significance. It was closely followed by the *Wall Street Journal's*. The one exception to this ranking was that the minimum and medium estimates of capacity yielded the coefficients for AIMP which were most significant.

Because the model yielded robust results regardless of which capacity estimate was used and because the *Wall Street Journal* figures seem to be derived from the best source, the estimates presented in this note were all based on these figures.

Appendix 2

The coefficients estimated by ordinary least squares are not unbiased due to the simultaneous nature of the relationship between the dependent variable, SMP, and three of the independent variables, AVC, AIMP and CU. To meet this problem and perhaps to shed more light on the extent to which higher prices lead to higher labor costs leading to higher AVC, the author had made some preliminary estimates of a model which treats all four variables as endogenous. Initial 2-stage least squares estimates of the six price regressions for the aggregate steel industry and for the three subsectors yielded coefficients for the key variables which were always of the same sign as the ordinary least squares estimates and usually even more significant in the desired direction. Further, the 2-stage estimates showed the guideposts to have played a much less significant role than was earlier indicated. We shall not present the simultaneous equation model at this time; however, we shall present two tentative regressions—5 and 5@—in order to indicate what qualitative changes the 2-stage estimation makes in the results.

SMP =	C +	AVC +	AIMP +	CU +	DUMB +	Z
5	−9.87	1.053	−237.29	−.122	−167.39	2.642
	(32.8)	(.206)	(294.0)	(.220)	(57.62)	(.922)
		*			*	*
	R^2 = .923		Durbin-Watson = 1.70			
5@	3.28	1.057	−273.67	−.267	−231.17	3.523
	(38.7)	(.248)	(275.6)	(.260)	(100.4)	(1.486)
		*			**	**
	R^2 = .866		Durbin Watson = 1.54			

A more complete account of the nature of the linkage of labor costs, AVC and steel prices awaits a subsequent paper.

REFERENCES

M. A. Adelman, 'Steel, Administered Prices and Inflation', *Quarterly Journal of Economics*, February 1961, pp. 16–40.

American Iron and Steel Institute, *Annual Statistical Reports*, 1947–65 editions.

American Metal Market, *Metal Statistics* 1966 (New York: 1966).

'The White House Role in Bargaining', *Business Week*, December 23rd, 1961, pp. 81–3.

Economic Report of the President together with the Annual Report of the Council of Economic Advisers (Washington: U.S. Govt. Printing Office, 1962).

Ezekiel Mordecai and Kathryn Wylie, 'Cost Curve for Steel Production', *Journal of Political Economy*, December 1940.

Hearings before the T.N.E.C., Part 26, Iron and Steel Industry, 'Steel Prices, Volumes, and Costs' (Washington: 1940).

Jack Johnston, *Econometric Methods* (New York: McGraw-Hill, 1960).

Report to the President on Steel Prices (Washington: Council of Economic Advisers, April 1965).

The Wall Street Journal, August 28th, 1963 and January 26th, 1967.

L. Weiss, 'Business Pricing Problems and Inflation Reconsidered', *Journal of Political Economy*, April 1967, pp. 177–87.

Wholesale Prices and Price Indexes (Washington: U.S. Dept. of Labor, Bureau of Labor Statistics, 1955–65).

PUBLICATIONS RECEIVED

Account for Your Profit, commissioned by the National Vehicle Committee of the Motor Agents' Association from Ronald L. Sewell, a Guide to the Understanding and Use of Management Accounts in the British Retail Motor Trade, published by the Economic Development Committee for Motor Vehicle Distribution and repair, N.E.D. Office, 1967.

Africa and the Common Market, by P. W. C. Origbo, Longmans, Green & Co. Ltd., 1967, 27s. 6d.

L'Agricoltura Negli Stati Parmensi dal 1750 al 1859, by Pier Luigi Spaggiari, Banca Commerciale Italiana, Milano, 1966.

Agricultural Development of African Nations, Volume II, by S. C. Jain, Vora & Co., 1967, $6.

Aims and Methods of Soviet Planning, by Mikhail Bor, Lawrence & Wishart, November 1967, 50s.

Alternative Commercial Policies – Their Effect on the American Economy, by Mordechai E. Kreinin, MSU International Business and Economic Studies, Institute for International Business and Economic Development Studies, Division of Research, Graduate School of Business Administration, Michigan State University, 1967.

An Approach to the Training and Development of Managers, a report by the Management Training and Development Committee, H.M.S.O., 1967, 1s. 6d.

Les Avantages Comparitifs Dans le Marché Commun European, by Felix Irappeniers, Editions Nauweloerts, Louvain, 1967.

Basic Research, Applied Research and Development in Industry, 1965, National Science Foundation NSF 67-12.

Capital Budgeting and the Use of DCF Criteria in the Corporation Tax Regime, by G. H. Lawson and D. W. Windle, Oliver & Boyd Ltd., November 1967, 57s. 6d.

Changing the United States Commitment to Gold, by Eugene A. Birnbaum, Essays in International Finance, No. 63, Princeton University, November 1967.

A Comparative Study of Consumption and Production of Selected Materials and Intermediate Goods in Missouri 1964, by Floyd K. Harmston and Raleigh A. Garcia, No. 11 of a series of studies defining the problems and prospects for Missouri's economy, Research Center School of Business and Public Administration, University of Missouri, 1967.

Consumer Expenditures and Incomes in Greece, by Jean Crockett, 17th in the Center of Planning and Economic Research Monograph Series (joint publication with the National Statistical Service of Greece, Constantinidis & Mihalas, 1967, $4.

Credit Facilities or Reserve Allotments?, by Fritz Machlup, Reprints in International Finance, No. 7, 1967, I.F. Section, Department of Economics, Princeton University.

Data Processing Managers, by R. J. Harper, Lyon Grant & Green Ltd., 1967, 21s.

Decisive Forces in World Economics, by J. L. Sanpedro, Weidenfeld & Nicolson, World University Library, November 1967, Paperback 14s., Hardback 25s.

Demand for Energy in North-West India, by P. N. Dhar and D. V. Sastry, Asia Publishing House, Rs. 18.

Development Planning, by Jan Tinbergen, Wiedenfeld & Nicolson, World University Library, 1967, Paperback 14s., Hardback 25s.

An Economic Profile of Tucker County, West Virginia, by James H. Lord, M.B.A., (Economic Development Series, No. 10), Bureau of Business Research, College of Commerce, 1967.

Economics and Industrial Efficiency, an introduction to Managerial Economics by H. Speight (Second Edition), Macmillan & Co. Ltd, 1967, 36s.

The Economics of Subsistence Agriculture, by Colin Clark and M. R. Haswell, Macmillan & Co. Ltd., 1968, 36s.

The Economics of Transporting Oil, by Michael Hubbard, McClaren & Sons Ltd., 1967, 50s.

The Economy of Nepal, by B. P. Shreshtha, a study in Problems of Industrialization, Vora & Co., 1967, $6.

The Economy of Pakistan, A Select Bibliography, by Akhtar H. Siddiqui, Pakistan Institute of Development Economics, Karachi, Pakistan.

The Efficiency of Control Strategies, Communication and Decision-Making in Organizations, by Dick Ramström, Almqvist & Wiksell 1967, Sw. Kr. 90.

The Enterprise in Transition, An Analysis of European and American Practice by H. van der Haas, Tavistock Publications Ltd., November 1967, 63s.

Essays on Finance, by S. L. N. Simha, Vora & Co., September 1967, $6.

The Exporters: A Study of Organization, Staffing and Training, by Douglas Tookey, Eleanor Lea and Camilla McDougall, Ashridge Management College, November 1967, 21s.

The Framework of Price Theory, by Clark Lee Allen, Wadsworth Publishing Co. Inc., 1967, text $7.95, trade $10.50.

The Free Trade Area Option: Opportunity for Britain, by Maxwell Stamp Associates, (The Atlantic Trade Study), 10s.

From Dormant Liabilities to Dormant Assets, by Fritz Machlup, Reprints in International Finance, No. 8, October 1967, Princeton University.

Geographical and Occupational Mobility of Workers in the Aircraft and Electronics Industries, Regional Trade Union Seminar, Paris, September 1966, final report, International Seminars, 1966-3, O.E.C.D., Paris, 1967, $2., 12s. 6d., F. 8, Sw. Fr. 8, DM 6.60; and Supplement to Report.

Gold: Barbarous Relic or Useful Instrument?, by Miroslav A. Kriz, Essays in International Finance, No. 60, June 1967, International Finance Section, Department of Economics, Princeton University Press.

Imports of Pakistan: Growth and Structure, a Statistical Study by Nurul Islam, Pakistan Institute of Development Economics, September 1967, U.S. $4.

Incomes Policy and the Individual, by Behrend/Lynch/Thomas/Davies, Oliver & Boyd Ltd., October 1967, 17s. 6d.

The Indian Rupee, by R. S. Kapuria, Vora & Co., 1967, $5.

Industrial Marketing Management and Controls, by L. A. Williams, (Management Studies Series), Longmans, Green & Co., 63s.

The Industrial Society, by Raymond Aron, Three Essays on Ideology and Development, Wiedenfeld & Nicolson, 1967, 36s.

Integrated Managerial Controls, by R. O. Boyce (Management Studies Series), Longmans, Green & Co., November 1967, 75s.

Integrated Marketing, by B. G. S. James, Modern Management Series, B. T. Batsford Ltd., 1967, 84s.

International Seminars 1966–2: Manpower Problems in the Service Sector, Background report for a Trade Union Seminar, O.E.C.D., Paris 1967, 14s.; and Supplement to report.

An Introduction to a Mathematical Treatment of Economics, by G. C. Archibald and Richard G. Lipsey, Weidenfeld & Nicolson, 1967, 50s.

Introduction to Managerial Economics, by Christopher I. Savage and John R. Small, Hutchison University Library, Hutchinson & Co. Ltd., 1967, 30s.

The Keynesian Revolution (Second Edition), by Lawrence R. Klein, Macmillan & Co. Ltd., October 1967, 42s. (published simultaneously in Papermac 21s.)

The Labour Market and Inflation, edited by Anthony D. Smith, Macmillan & Co. Ltd., Febuary 1968, 70s.

The Machinery of Finance and the Management of Sterling, by A. T. K. Grant, Macmillan & Co. Ltd., November 1967, 30s.

Management in the Printing Industry, by C. Spector, Management Studies Series, Longmans, Green & Co. Ltd., 1967, 75s.

Mathematics Observed, by Hans Freudenthal, Weidenfeld & Nicholson, World University Library, 1967, Paperback 12s. 6d.

Modernizing State Government, a Statement on National Policy, by the Research and Policy Committee of the Committee for Economic Development, C.E.D., 1967, $1.

The New Ordeal by Planning, by John Jewkes, Macmillan & Co. Ltd., 1968, 42s.

Optimum Adjustment Processes and Currency Areas, by Delbark A. Snider, Essays in International Finance, No. 62, October 1967.

Organizacion Comercial: Situacion asteral de la industria barcelonesa, Escuela de Administraction De Empresas, Barcelona.

The Pattern of Investment and Economic Development, by Hannan Ezekiel, University of Bombay, 1967, Rs. 9.50.

The Politics of International Money and World Language, by Charles Kindleberger, Essays in International Finance, No. 61, August 1967, Princeton University.

Problems and Prospects of Management Education and Research in Germany, Developments in Organizational Theory and Organizational Practice, Summary report of the 12th annual conference of I.U.C. held in Nuremburg, June 17th–21st 1965.

Regional Economic Development in Italy, by Lloyd Saville, Duke University Press, September 1967.

Regional Employment Premium, Notes for Employees with Manufacturing Establishments in Development Areas, Ministry of Labour, H.M.S.O., 1967.

Relative Rates of Growth Agriculture and Industry, by Ashok Rudra, (Series in Economics, No. 14) University of Bombay, 1967, Rs. 8.

A Report on the Seminar on the Population Problems in the Economic Development of Pakistan, Pakistan Institute of Development Economics, Karachi, September 1967.

Research Papers 7: Employers' Associations: The Results of Two Studies, Royal Commission on Trade Unions and Employers' Associations, H.M.S.O, 1968, 10s. 6d.

The Science of Wealth, by C. F. Carter (Second Edition), Edward Arnold (Publishers) Ltd., October 1967, 25s.

Selected Papers from Symposium on Housing Finance, National Buildings Organization and U.N. Regional Housing Centre (ECAFE), New Dehli.

Some Data about Sweden 1967–68, Stockholms Enskilda Bank, April 1967.

9A *Studien und Berichte*, Bibliographische Materialien zur Hochschulforschung by Klaus Hüfner: Institut für Bildungsforschung in der Max-Planck-Gesellschaft, Berlin, 1967.

Studies in Innovation in the Steel and Chemical Industries, by J. A. Allen, December 1967, Manchester University Press, 45s.

The Structure of the Defense Market 1955–64, by William L. Baldwin, Duke University Press, 1967, $8.

Teaching Economics, edited by Norman Lee, Economics Association, 1967, 15s.

Techniques of Sectoral Economic Planning: The Chemical Industries, Industrial Planning and Programming, Series 1, United Nations Industrial Development Organization, United Nations New York, 1966, $1.

Voluntary Foreign Investment Curbs: a Plan that really Works, by Benjamin J. Cohen, Reprints in International Finance, No. 6, April 1967, International Finance Section, Princeton University, Princeton, New Jersey.

Wage Drift Origins Measurement and Behaviour by Judith Marquand, Woolwich Economic Papers, No. 14, 3s.6d.

Why Growth Rates Differ, Postwar Experience in Nine Western Countries by Edward F. Denison assisted by Jean-Pierre Poullier, The Brookings Institution, 1967, Paper $4.95, Cloth $12.50.

Working Group Reports No. 1. Patents (September 1967), European Industrial Research Management Association.

LIMIT PRICE AND THE MARKET SHARE OF THE LEADING FIRM

by B. PETER PASHIGIAN[1]

IN 1949, Bain[2] suggested that price is set below the monopoly price in a number of highly concentrated industries to block the entry of potential competitors. This would help to explain why the market share of the leading firm(s) did not decline. Bain noted that it may be more profitable in some cases to set prices above the limit price and accept entry. Subsequent contributions by Bain and Modigliani[3] have largely ignored this latter point and have stressed the size of the discrepancy between the limit price and the competitive price. What has not been explained is: When should and when should not the monopoly price be reduced to the limit price to block entry? Why do any firms enter an industry? Or, if entry does occur, why and when does it stop? In its current state, the limit price theory does not provide answers to these questions because it deals primarily with the mechanics of setting a limit price and does not specify when this type of pricing will be adopted.

In the first section of the paper the assumptions of the static limit pricing model are reviewed. In the second section a simple dynamic extension of the limit price theory is presented. This extension specifies the conditions which make it optimal to charge the monopoly price and allow entry *or* charge the limit price and block entry. The main empirical implications of the theory are then presented. In the last section the theory is evaluated on its ability to explain certain other empirical regularities that have emerged from postwar studies of concentration and profitability.

ASSUMPTIONS OF THE STATIC LIMIT PRICE MODEL

It will be convenient to assume an initial monopolist, whose price policy will either favor (by monopoly pricing) or block (by limit pricing) the entry of new firms. Once a short review of the elements of the limit price theory has been presented, the assumptions of the limit price theory will be discussed in more detail.

[1] The author is Professor in the Graduate School of Business at the University of Chicago. He would like to thank members of the Industrial Organization Workshop for helpful comments and criticisms. Funds were supplied by the Research Committee of the Graduate School from a Ford Foundation grant.

[2] J. Bain, 'A Note on Pricing in Monopoly and Oligopoly', *Amercian Economic Review*, XXXIX (1949), 448–64.

[3] J. Bain, *Barriers to New Competition* (Cambridge, Mass.: Harvard University Press, 1956); Franco Modigliani, 'New Developments on the Oligopoly Front', *Journal of Political Economy* (June 1958), 215–32.

Limit pricing has been discussed in the context of situations where the minimum efficient scale represents a non-negligible share of the market. Under these conditions the market price will decline if entry does occur and if the output of the monpolist remains constant. The decision to enter is based on the expected profits at the post-entry price. A limit price will by definition not yield a competitive return to the entrant and a higher than competitive return to the monopolist. These are the bare mechanics of limit pricing.

One assumption of the limit price theory is that the monopolist is not able to charge the monopoly price and yet block entry by threatening to lower the price if entry is attempted. Such a policy would be more profitable and hence superior to a limit price policy. To enforce it, the monopolist would incur additional 'short'-run costs. He must be prepared to produce the larger output required to meet demand at the limit price with a plant primarily designed for efficient production of the smaller monopoly output. To achieve this output flexibility, the monopolist will either sacrifice some plant efficiency for greater plant flexibility than is otherwise required, or incur higher short-run cost in trying to produce the larger output with a specialized plant designed for the monopoly output, or carry higher inventories, again at additional cost. In contrast the entrant is able to design a plant for the optimum rate or range of outputs, with a cost advantage over the monopolist. If costs depend on the rate of change of output as well as the rate of output, the monopolist will incur even higher costs while he attempts to block entry by changing his rate of output.

These are formidable difficulties, which will not often be overcome. It is, therefore, proper to assume that the monopolist is unable to have the best of both worlds and exclude entry while charging the monopoly price. Such cases will occur, and it is desirable to analyze them, but it seems more profitable to deal first with the others, where the monopolist must choose a limit price or a monopoly price.

A second assumption of the limit price analysis is that the limit price does in fact forestall entry. But one may ask: Why cannot the entrant ignore the limit price and enter, expecting the monopolist to curtail his output and accommodate the entrant? It is true that the monopolist has constructed enough capacity to supply demand at the limit price. But this is not an immovable barrier. A determined entrant could lower or eliminate the monopolist's profits by entering and even could cause the monopolist to suffer larger losses, if he maintained output, than the entrant. The limit price theory does not satisfactorily explain why this does not occur.

One way of salvaging the theory is suggested here but would need a complete investigation. Suppose there is a cost of expanding too rapidly. The entrant incurs a cost of growth if the increase in its rate of output from one period to another exceeds some specified value. Economies of scale and the high cost of increasing the rate of production too rapidly will allow the monopolist to raise the price above his long-run cost and yet thwart entry. If the initial output of the entrant is much less than optimum and if costs incurred by growing rapidly are high, the monopolist may find a price above his long-run marginal cost (and average cost) which yet reduces the present value of the entrant's income stream to zero.

The chief criticism of this suggestion is that the monopolist will still have more to lose than the entrant if entry nevertheless does occur. The entrant can present a very credible threat. While both the monopolist and the entrant suffer, the monopolist has more to lose. To deal with this criticism, it seems preferable to define a limit price as that price which causes the entrant to suffer a larger present value of losses than the monopolist suffers if entry did occur. If the monopolist chose such a price and if entry did occur, the entrant would suffer a larger loss than would the monopolist. Under these conditions the entrant does not present a very credible threat and there would be less reason for the monopolist to reduce his market share and share his profits with the entrant. Under this interpretation the limit price would be determined by the cost structure and would be higher, the larger is the extent of economies of scale and the larger is the cost of increasing the rate of output. This approach is not pursued here, but it appears to be a more satisfactory explanation of why entry does not occur when the limit price is charged.

AN OPTIMAL PRICE POLICY

It is convenient to list the assumptions of the standard model of limit pricing and to present some notation before discussing the properties of an optimal price policy.

For purposes of dicussion, the industry demand curve is assumed constant throughout the analysis.[4] Long-run average cost of each firm declines until output reaches $\bar{q}$ and thereafter remains constant for output larger than $\bar{q}$. $\bar{q}$ will be referred to as minimum efficient scale. Once the demand and cost conditions have been specified, monopoly profits of the industry Π_m, and limit profits of the industry,

[4] The discussion will be limited to long-run problems and the optimal price policy is derived under the assumption that costs of adjusting the rate of output can be ignored. However, the discussion in the first part of the paper does stress the importance of these costs in evaluating the feasibility of a monopoly price which could block entry. To this extent there is an asymmetrical treatment of costs.

Π_L, can be determined. $S(t)$ will denote the market share of the monopolist at time t with $S(0) = 1$ and r denotes the discount rate.

Suppose the monopolist begins by charging the monopoly price. This price is above the limit price so entrants are attracted to this industry and the market share of the monopolist declines. While there are many theories about the behavior of rivals, we begin by assuming that entrants collude with the monopolist and do not engage in price chiseling. As the monopolist's market share declines, so does his share of monopoly profits. As entry continues, the decline in his market share may accelerate so that at some time it pays for the (former) monopolist to lower the price to the limit price to block the entry of additional firms. At the limit price, the monopolist obtains his current share of the limit profits of the industry. Because demand and cost conditions are stationary, the market share of the leading firm remains constant thereafter.

To determine the characteristics of the optimal price policy, we must specify the determinants of the market share of the monopolist. As a first approximation, we assume that the rate of entry is a function of the elapsed time during which price has been above the limit price.[5] The form of $S(t)$ will depend on those factors which impede entry into the industry. When the current market share is independent of current and past prices, an optimal price policy must necessarily be a two parameter price policy. At any point in time the monopolist will either choose the monopolist price or the limit price. If he chose a price between the monopoly price and above the limit price, total industry profits would be less than monopoly profits and the decline in the market share would be the same as it would have been if the monopoly price was chosen. Consequently, the monopolist will find it profitable to charge the monopoly price as long as entry is accepted, *or* the limit price if entry is to be blocked.

Since an optimal price policy is a two parameter price policy, it remains to determine when the monopoly price should be lowered to the limit price. In Fig. 1, the undiscounted income stream of the (temporary) monopolist is shown under the assumption that the monopoly price is lowered to the limit price at $t = T$.

[5] This assumption simplifies the solution considerably but at the cost of some loss in realism. The simple model can be generalized by making the rate of change of the market share a function of the difference between the market price and the limit price, i.e.

$$\frac{dS}{dt} = f(P(t) - P_L) \text{ where } \frac{dS}{dt} = 0$$

when $P(t) = P_L$. In both models the decision to lower the price to the limit price is governed by the same considerations. Hence, the simple model contains several interesting aspects of the pricing problem; see footnote 16.

This income stream is ABCP. Now consider an alternative policy identical with the previous price policy in every respect except that the monopoly price is lowered to the limit price at $V = T + \mathrm{d}T$. The income stream is ABEGH. Because the monopoly price is maintained

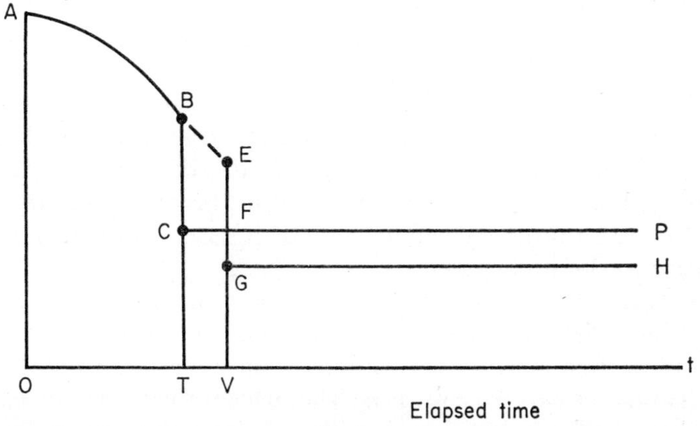

Fig. 1

for an interval $\mathrm{d}T$, the market share of the monopolist continues to decline. Hence, his share of limit profits will be lower once the price is lowered to the limit price at $T + \mathrm{d}T$. It can be shown that the optimal time at which to lower the price to the limit price is when the following condition is satisfied.[6]

$$\Pi_m S(T) = \Pi_L S(T) - \Pi_L \frac{\mathrm{d}S}{\mathrm{d}T}\frac{1}{r} \tag{1}$$

where $\mathrm{d}S/\mathrm{d}T$ is the rate of change in the market share.[7] Figure 1 may

[6] The present value of the firm is

$$P.V.(T) = \int_0^T \Pi_m S(t) e^{-rt} \mathrm{d}t + \int_T^\infty \Pi_L S(T) e^{-rt} \mathrm{d}t. \tag{1a}$$

When $0 \leqslant t \leqslant T$, the monopoly price is charged and the market share of the monopolist declines. The first integral represents the discounted value of the monopolist's share of monopoly profits. For $t > T$, the limit price is charged and the market share remains constant at $S(T)$. The second integral represents the discounted value of the monopolist's share of limit profits. (1a) is a function of (T). The first order condition for a maximum is given by (1). The second order condition is

$$\frac{\mathrm{d}^2 (P.V.)}{\mathrm{d}T^2} = \left\{ \left(\Pi_m - \Pi_L \right) \frac{\mathrm{d}S(T)}{\mathrm{d}T} + \Pi_L \frac{\mathrm{d}^2 S}{\mathrm{d}T^2} \frac{1}{r} \right\} e^{-rT} < 0. \tag{1b}$$

[7] If Π_m and Π_L are functions of time because demand and cost conditions are changing, (1) becomes (1c)

$$\Pi_m(T) S(T) = \Pi_L(T) S(T) - \Pi_L(T) \frac{\mathrm{d}S}{\mathrm{d}T}\frac{1}{r} \tag{1c}$$

be used to interpret equation (1). At $t = T$ the firm has a choice of charging the monopoly price for an interval dT and then lowering the price to the limit price or lowering the price at T. If the firm charges the monopoly price, it receives its share of monopoly profits, $\Pi_m S(T)$ (the area BEVT). What does the firm sacrifice by maintaining the monopoly price over an interval dT? It loses (a) its interim share of limit profits, $\Pi_L S(T)$ (the area CFVT) which it would have received if it had charged the limit price; *and* (b) the present value of the income stream lost because its market share continued to decline during dT, $\Pi_L/r \; dS/dT$ (the area FPHG). When the left-hand term of (1) is equal to (greater than) the sum of the two terms on the right-hand side of (1), the firm will (not) lower the price to the limit price.

The optimal value for T may be $T = 0$, in which case the limit price is established immediately: entry does not occur and the firm remains a monopolist. This solution may be expected to occur infrequently for two reasons. First, the market share may be expected to decline slowly at first since it will take time for rivals to determine the profitability of the industry. Second, it will take time for substitutes to be developed for this product and consequently demand may be sufficiently inelastic that profits at the monopoly price will be severalfold higher than profits at the limit price. In most cases the limit price will be charged after some entry has occurred. The reason why there are so few industries with the leading firm supplying the complete market is that is is seldom profitable to remain a monopolist by always charging the limit price.

The theory suggests that the limit price will be reached at one time or another in every industry where the assumed type of cost conditions exist. This conclusion may be modified if we relax the assumption of successful collusion at the limit price. If T is large, many firms will have entered the industry in the past and successful collusion at the limit price may not be realized. If collusion is reasonably effective when the monopolist is reducing his market share but becomes less effective once the limit price has been set and market shares have stabilized, the monopolist will find it profitable to delay before reducing the price to the limit price. Once the price has been lowered, the price will not remain at the limit price but decline to the competitive price because of price cutting by members of the cartel. It also seems reasonable to expect the time required for the price to decline from the limit price to the competitive price will be smaller the larger the number of firms in the industry at the time when the price is lowered to the limit price. Whether the price will settle more frequently at the limit price or at the competitive price cannot be settled by *a priori* argument but both possibilities may occur under the theory.

SOME COMPARATIVE STATISTICS

Associated with this optimal price policy is the terminal market share of the temporary monopolist. It is appropriate to determine how changes in the extent of economies of scale, the discount rate and the parameters of the market share function change the terminal market share of the leading firm.

A. *Economies of scale:* The terminal market share of the monopolist depends on the ratio of Π_m/Π_L, the ratio of monopoly profits to industry profits at the limit price. A smaller ratio will be associated with a larger value of $S(T)$. The ratio of Π_m/Π_L will be smaller, the larger is the minimum efficient scale. Thus, the theory predicts that for a given market demand the terminal market share of the leading firm will be higher the larger the minimum efficient scale.[8] The monopoly price will be lowered to the limit price sooner in industries where minimum efficient scale accounts for a larger proportion of the market. One prediction of the theory is that the terminal market share of the leading firm will be larger in such industries given the other parameters of the model.

There is some evidence in support of this hypothesis. In their cross-sectional studies Evely and Little found a positive correlation of .60 between average plant size and concentration once the absolute size of market was held constant.[9] This result suggests that concentration is lower in industries where minimum efficient scale accounts for a smaller proportion of the total market.

Another test of this hypothesis can be made by comparing concentration in different countries. Since markets are frequently relatively larger in the United States than in Canada or England, the market share of the leading firm would be expected to be lower in the United States. This prediction assumes that the other factors in the model are held constant. Along with differences in other variables, differences in discount rates between countries can be expected to cause differences in the market share of the leading firm between countries. Also, cross-country comparisons implicitly assume that the market share of the leading firm declines in roughly the same way in the two countries.

[8] The ratio of Π_m/Π_L will also decline if unit costs rise for outputs below $\bar{q}$.

[9] R. Evely and I. Little, *Concentration in British Industry* (Cambridge University Press, 1960), p. 15. Average plant size may be a good proxy for minimum efficient scale of plant and measure the extent of technical economies. For additional evidence see P. Pashigian, 'The Effect of Market Size on Concentration', *International Economic Review* (forthcoming).

The evidence is sparse but tends to confirm the predictions of the theory. Rosenbluth did find that concentration was lower in the United States than in Canada and attributed this largely to differences in the size of market and not to differences in size of firm.[10] Pashigian finds concentration in British industries tends to exceed concentration in comparable U.S. industries and attributes these differences to differences in market size.[11]

B. *Discount rate:* Total monopoly profits, Π_m, and total limit profits, Π_L, are functions of factor prices.[12] If T is defined as the optimal time at which to lower the price to the limit price, a change in r causes T to change in the following way.[13]

$$\frac{dT}{dr} = \frac{-\left\{\frac{d\Pi_m}{dr}S(T) - \frac{d\Pi_L}{dr}S(T) + \frac{dS}{dT}\frac{d\Pi_L}{dr}\frac{1}{r} - \frac{dS}{dT}\frac{\Pi_L}{r^2}\right\}}{\left\{(\Pi_m - \Pi_L)\frac{dS}{dT} + \frac{\Pi_L}{r}\frac{d^2S}{dT^2}\right\}} \qquad (2)$$

The second order condition for a maximum requires the denominator to be negative. However, the numerator cannot be signed from *a priori* considerations alone.

The reason for this indeterminacy is that an increase in the interest rate lowers total monopoly profits and total limit profits but not necessarily in the same proportion. The first two terms in the numerator measure this effect. In addition an increase in r lowers the present value of the sacrificed income stream because of (a) the fall in total limit profits and (b) the higher discount rate. This last effect would ordinarily cause T to increase. Though unlikely, the higher discount rate could lower total monopoly profits by a sufficiently larger amount than it lowers total limit profits and T could decrease.[14]

C. *The market share function:* The ultimate market share of the monopolist will depend on the particular way the market share declines, other than that differences exist.[15] Among the variables

[10] G. Rosenbluth, *Concentration in Canadian Manufacturing Industries* (Princeton University Press, 1957), pp. 75–85.

[11] B. P. Pashigian, 'Market Concentration in the United States and Great Britain', *Journal of Law and Economics* (forthcoming).

[12] I am indebted to Harold Demsetz for emphasizing this point and for correcting an error in an early draft of this paper.

[13] Differentiation of equation (1) with respect to T and r leads to (2).

[14] A similar interpretation of (2) is required if a change in some other factor price is permitted except that the last term in the numerator of (2) will not appear. To this extent, an increase in T is more likely to occur in response to an increase in the interest rate than to an increase in (say) the wage rate. To the extent that a change in the discount rate causes Π_L and Π_m to change in approximately the same degree, an increase in the discount rate will lead the firm to trade future profits for present profits.

[15] M. Vidale and H. Wolfe, 'An Operations Research Study of Sales Response to Advertising', *Operations Research*, vol. 5 (1957), pp. 370–81.

under the firm's control, price, and advertising policy are undoubtedly the more important variables affecting the decay rate.[16] While these variables may be important, the characteristics of the product and the expense required to control the flow of technical information to competitors may be of greater importance. In some industries, the product and associated services can be duplicated and customer loyalties established relatively inexpensively. In these industries the function of the monopolist decays. In practice, the rate of decay of the market share will depend on a number of variables, only a few of which are under the firm's control. To a considerable extent, this is an area of ignorance. Very little is known about the causes of differences between industries in the rate at which the market share of the monopolist will decline rapidly if the monopoly price is charged. For other products, the establishment of trade connections, product reputations and customer loyalties requires considerable time even when market research and promotional activities are undertaken. In these instances the market share of the monopolist will decline less rapidly if the monopoly price is charged.

Even though little is known about the differences between industries in the rate of decline in the market share, the derivation of implications of particular forms of the market share function may be suggestive.

The market share may be thought of as a function of elapsed time and a parameter α.

(3) $$S = S(t, \alpha)$$ (3a) $$\frac{\partial S}{\partial \alpha} < 0.$$

(3a) states that the larger the value of α, the smaller the market share for any given value of t. To determine whether the optimal value of T

[16] The model presented may be regarded as a first approximation, useful to analyze price behavior in industries where price is not an important determinant of the decay rate of the market share. In some cases this would not be a good approximation and a more general model should be considered. A more general model would relate rate of decrease in the market share to the difference between the market price and the limit price, i.e.

$$\frac{dS}{dT} = f[P(t) - P_L]$$

The decision to lower price in the more general model will be based on the same considerations as in the simple model. The price would be lowered to the limit price when

$$\{\Pi_m\{P(T)\} - \Pi_L\} S(T) = -\frac{\Pi_L}{r} f[P(T) - P_L]$$

where Π_m denotes industry profits at $t = T$ when the optimal price is $P(T)$ and where $f[P(T) - P_L]$ denotes the rate of decrease in the market share when the market price is $P(T)$. The interpretation of this equation is similar to the interpretation given to (1).

increases or decreases with change in α, differentiate (1) with regard to α and T

$$\frac{dT}{d\alpha} = \frac{-\left\{(\Pi_m - \Pi_L)\dfrac{\partial S}{\partial \alpha} + \dfrac{\Pi_L}{r}\dfrac{\partial^2 S}{\partial T \partial \alpha}\right\}}{(\Pi_m - \Pi_L)\dfrac{\partial S}{\partial T} + \dfrac{\Pi_L}{r}\dfrac{\partial^2 S}{\partial T^2}}. \tag{4}$$

The denominator of (4) is negative. However, the sign of the numerator is indeterminate and depends on the sign of $\partial^2 S/\partial T \partial \alpha$. If $\partial^2 S/\partial T \partial \alpha < 0$, then $dT/d\alpha < 0$. Otherwise, the sign of $dT/d\alpha$ is indeterminate. Consequently, the sign of

$$\frac{dS}{d\alpha} = \frac{\partial S}{\partial T}\frac{dT}{d\alpha} + \frac{\partial S}{\partial \alpha} \tag{5}$$

is ambiguous, and it is not possible to say whether the terminal market share of a monopolist will be lower in industries where the market share declines more rapidly. These results may be explained by noting that in an industry with a larger α the leading firm will have a smaller market share for a given value of t. This implies that the difference between the monopolist's share of monopoly profits and his share of limit profits will be smaller. By itself, this effect would lead to a smaller value for T. However, (1) shows that the present value of the sacrificed income stream increases (decreases) if $\partial^2 S/\partial T \partial \alpha$ decreases (increases). By itself, this effect would lead to a smaller (larger) value for T. It is possible for these two effects to oppose each other, and because of this it is not possible to say whether the price will be lowered to P_L sooner in industries where the market shares function declines more rapidly.

There is some reason to expect that the terminal market share will be higher the larger is α. It can be shown that the terminal market share is higher the larger α if the market share is linear in t or if $S(t)$ is a weighted exponential.[17] Under these conditions the market share of a temporary monopolist will be larger in industries where entry appears to be easy. In this connection consider the effects of sales promotional activity on entry. Suppose advertising lowers the value of α by decreasing the rate at which consumers shift allegiance

[17] The form of the linear market share function is

$$S(t) = 1 - \alpha t \qquad 0 < t < \frac{1}{\alpha}$$

The weighted exponential is

$$S(t) = 2e^{\alpha t}[e^{-2\alpha t} + 1]^{-1} 0 \leqslant t \leqslant \infty.$$

to the products of entrants. A smaller value of α leads to a lower terminal market share for the temporary monopolist. This may sound paradoxical because it suggests that the market share of the leading firm will be larger in precisely those industries where the market share is expected to decline more rapidly. This result can be understood if one recognizes that the decrease in profits suffered by the monopolist as a result of entry is smaller the smaller α. Because of this, the monopolist is willing to tolerate entry. While brand loyalty is an entry deterrent, it is also the reason for entry to occur.[18]

SOME IMPLICATIONS OF THE THEORY

Given the market share function, the terminal market share of the leading company will be lower the larger Π_m/Π_L. The size of Π_m/Π_L will depend on the price elasticity of demand and the shape of the cost curve at sub-optimal outputs as well as the minimum efficient scale. For a given cost curve, Π_m/Π_L will be larger in industries with larger arc elasticities between the monopoly price and the limit price.[19]

The theory predicts that a large terminal market share will result if the market share declines rapidly when the price is above the limit price even though the minimum efficient scale may be relatively small. Industries of this type may appear to an outside observer as low-barrier industries. Yet, the market share of the leading firm in industries of this type will be larger and could not be justified on the basis of efficiency requirements alone. Under these conditions the market share of the leading company should decline rapidly when an exogenous increase in demand or a change in the cost curve increased Π_m/Π_L.

Another implication of the modified limit price theory is that the measured price elasticity will be lower when the market share is declining than when it is stable.[20] Under the theory we would expect the price elasticity to be lower in the early stages of the life cycle of a product when demand is growing rapidly and when the market share of the leading firm declines than in the latter stages of the cycle when demand has stabilized and when the terminal market

[18] Usually, advertising will increase the size of the market and cause the market share of the provisional monopolist to fall. The implications of this model conflict with the more common view that advertising blocks entry through its effect on demand conditions.

[19] The price elasticity will be defined as a negative number. The theory implies that the terminal market share of the leading firm will be smaller in industries with less elastic demand schedules, given the other factors of the model.

[20] In this simple model the price elasticities would be evaluated at the monopoly price and the limit price. In a more general model where the rate of decrease in the market share is larger the greater the gap between the market price and the limit price, the rate of decrease in the market share would be positively related to the estimated price elasticity.

share has been reached. The theory also implies that price elasticities in the more rapidly growing industries will tend to be smaller than the price elasticities in industries with stable demands.[21]

In its present form the modified limit price theory predicts that the rate of return should exceed the competitive return when the market share of the leading firm is large. However, there is nothing in the theory which suggests a monotonically increasing relationship between market share and rate of return. The market share of the leading firm will be large while the rate of return is relatively low if economies of scale are small relative to the size of market and the market share declines quickly when the price is raised above the limit price. The predictions of the modified limit price theory are very similar to the predictions of the traditional price theory except that the limit price theory tries to explain the market share of the leading firm while the traditional theory takes this as given.

Because little is known about the effect of number of sellers on the costs of collusion, it may be preferable in empirical tests to compare the mean return of industries with very high concentration with the mean return of industries with very low concentration. If no significant differences exist, the evidence would contradict the predictions of the theory.[22]

The existence of a significant difference would be consistent with the predictions of the limit price model and of the traditional price theory. The profit test can be used to reject the limit price model but cannot confirm the theory. The available empirical evidence is contradictory and hardly one-sided. Perhaps, the weight of evidence leans somewhat in favor of a small but significant difference between the means of the measured rates of return of the two groups of industries.[23]

The limit price theory predicts an inverse relationship between the level of concentration and relative market size. This type of relationship is often observed in cross-sectional studies of concentration.

Short-term studies of changes in concentration over time show an inverse relationship between changes in concentration and changes in relative size of market.[24] This inverse relationship is consistent

[21] To conduct these tests, adjustments would have to be made for changes in minimum efficient scale.

[22] Profit tests must be considered with care because of imperfections in the profit data, and the capitalization of earnings will reduce all returns to the competitive return.

[23] The most recent and comprehensive summary of profitability studies can be found in N. Collins and L. Preston, *Concentrations and Price-Cost Margins in Manufacturing Industries* (unpublished manuscript).

[24] The postwar studies which show an inverse relationship between changes in concentration and changes in a measure of relative size of market are: P. Pashigian, 'The Effect of Market Size on Concentration', Report 6710, Center for Mathematical Studies in Business and Economics, Department of Economics and Graduate School of Business,

with the prediction of the theory. The apparent stability of concentration in a number of industries over longer periods of time does not fit nicely with the implications of the modified limit price theory. The stability of the concentration ratios of these industries in the face of persistently increasing demand cannot be explained by the modified limit price theory (or by other maximizing theories) without also assuming that the minimum efficient scale has been increasing at approximately the same rate so that the relative size of market has not changed appreciably over time.

CONCLUSION

To be useful, the limit price concept must become a systematic analysis of the terminal market share of the leading firm(s). Thus modified, it explains why and when entry occurs, given profit maximizing. The original purpose or rather suggestion of the limit price concept—to explain why entry does not occur—can not be sustained.

UNIVERSITY OF CHICAGO

University of Chicago; and L. Weiss, 'Factors in Changing Concentration', *Review of Economics and Statistics*, XLVI (February 1963), 70–7. Evely and Little did not observe a relationship between changes in market concentration and changes in absolute market size once changes in plant size were taken into account; Evely and Little, op. cit., 18–22.

THE RELATION OF PROFIT RATES TO OPERATING RATES

by Reed Moyer

Two important indices of performance in industry studies are the degree of utilization of productive capacity and some measure of rate of return. Analysis usually focuses on various structural conditions that influence these and other measures of performance as well as on the effect of market conduct on performance. It is easier to describe structure and conduct than to show the relation of the two to performance criteria; nonetheless, empirical research reveals evidence of linkages among structure, conduct, and performance that support industrial organization theory.

Analysis of the impact of structure and conduct on the degree of utilization of productive capacity (hereinafter referred to as the operating rate) may take several forms. The analyst may study the effect of the ease of entry into and exit from the industry on the rate of utilization of capacity. Also he may show the impact of pricing policies on capacity utilization. For example, a policy of maintaining a price 'umbrella' over inefficient producers may lead to the maintenance of excess capacity.

Similarly, certain relationships between structure and market conduct on the one hand and profit rates as an indicator of performance on the other are postulated, and the theoretical relationships are tested with empirical studies.[1] Attempts are made to measure the degree and extent of association among the relevant conduct and performance criteria.

Instead of tracing the effect of structure and conduct on capacity utilization and earnings rates, this study shows the interaction between these two performance criteria themselves. It tests the impact of operating rates on profits.

Knowing the relation between operating rates and profit rates may serve two useful purposes. First, the operating rate may be a reliable predictor of profits. If the correlation between an industry's operating rate and its profit rate is high, knowledge of one will permit a good prediction of the other. It may be easier to predict profits in this way—by estimating a single independent variable (operating rate)—than to estimate costs, prices, and other factors necessary for predicting profits directly.

[1] See for example Joe S. Bain, 'Relation of Profit to Industrial Concentration: American Manufacturing, 1936–40', *Quarterly Journal of Economics*, August 1951, pp. 297–304, and Leonard W. Weiss, 'Average Concentration Ratios and Industrial Performance,' *Journal of Industrial Economics*, July 1963, pp. 237–54.

Second, it is useful to study the operating rate–profit relationship for public policy purposes. Reduced operating rates usually set in motion several forces that result in reduced earnings. Other things being equal, where competition is viable and prices flexible, a lower operating rate should cause proportionately lower profits than would occur in a less competitive industry with sticky prices. There are exceptions to this rule, and to understand them requires analyzing changes in marginal revenue, marginal cost and the elasticity of demand. I make this analysis a little later in the paper.

Intuitively, a relationship between operating rates and profits makes sense. A composite of demand and cost factors determines profits. Those factors also enter into the determination of the operating rate or flow impliedly from it. A change in demand reflects itself in a change in the level of production which in turn alters the operating rate. This development affects costs which feeds back to a change in the rate of return. Likewise the change in the operating rate influences the price level which also affects profit rates.

The operating rate is defined as O/C where O represents total output for a given period of time and C signifies capacity for the same period. Ideally, both O and C are expressed in physical units although each quantity can be translated into financial units. An operating rate of 100 obviously indicates an operation conducted at full capacity although, depending on how one defines capacity, it is feasible for operating rates to exceed 100.

A change in the operating rate can stem from several factors and can have different results depending on the conditions prevailing in each instance. A change in the operating rate may result from a change in the output rate, in the level of capacity or from a combination of the two. Thus a reduced operating rate does not necessarily reflect itself in lower production. And even if it does result in lower production, lower profits do not *necessarily* follow. We need to look at the changes in marginal revenue and marginal cost conditions.

We should ask first *why* the operating rate fell. An increase in demand, *ceteris paribus*, will increase profits. But to know whether output rises with an increase in demand, requires knowledge of the relative elasticity of the new demand curve. The firm's reaction to an increase in demand if the demand curve is relatively inelastic may be to curtail output to maximize profits. Should the decline in output stem from a reduction in demand, however, profits must fall necessarily unless there is a corresponding reduction in marginal costs (from a downward shift in the marginal and average cost curves), sufficient to overcome the lower marginal revenue. If the firm is a profit-maximizer, it will take whatever action is consistent with equating

MR and *MC* whether that action results in an increase or decrease in output.

A number of forces can operate to reduce the elasticity of demand and thus temper the adverse effects on profits of a reduction in demand. Though output and profits may fall in the short run from reduced demand, the lower earnings may discourage entry with its probable attendant effect of decreasing the elasticity of demand. There may be dynamic effects on costs as well, the lower prices for one firm's products spelling reduced marginal costs for its customers.

The fulfillment of the profit-maximizing principle of the equality of *MR* and *MC* may find firms producing either short of or beyond the minimum points on their average cost curves. Usually operations are conducted short of the minimum. In these situations, if a reduction in the operating rate results from lower output, a firm operates in the short run with higher average costs, the amount of the increase depending on the slope of the firm's marginal cost curve and the ratio of its fixed–variable costs.

Thus one must study both the structure of costs as well as the industry's reponse to a change in demand (reflected in its prices) and the nature of the demand change to know the extent to which the industry's profits will reflect changes in the operating rate. If, as in the usual case, the operating rate declines from a reduction in demand, the result is lower output for each firm and declining profits. But the reductions will be proportionately greater in industries with relatively high fixed–variable cost ratios. Industry A with relatively inflexible prices will witness less of a decline in profits than industry B with flexible prices unless A's fixed–variable cost ratio is sufficiently more favorable than B's to counterbalance the unfavorable effect of A's proportionately greater reduction in prices.

The outcome depends upon conditions surrounding each case. If capacity increases from the entry of new producers, the pressure on prices (overall demand remaining unchanged) will likely lead to lower profits. However, the added capacity may come from existing firms replacing old equipment with new. The effect here may be not only to increase capacity but to lower average costs as well. (The firm would install the cost-saving equipment only if the average costs with the new equipment were below average variable costs with the old.) If we can assume that *MR* remains unchanged with the new equipment, then profits will rise despite the fall in the operating rate, unless pressure on prices from the new capacity overcomes the reduced costs.

If one were to regress profit rates on operating rates the slope of the regression line should reflect the impact on profits of the fixed-variable cost ratio and the degree of price flexibility. If prices are relatively inflexible and fixed costs relatively low, the slope should be slight. One would associate a steep slope with a high degree of price flexibility and high fixed costs. A moderate degree of slope could result from a combination of moderate price flexibility and fixed costs or from low fixed costs and high price flexibility or the reverse. Figures 1-*A*, *B* and *C* graphically portray the three possibilities.[2]

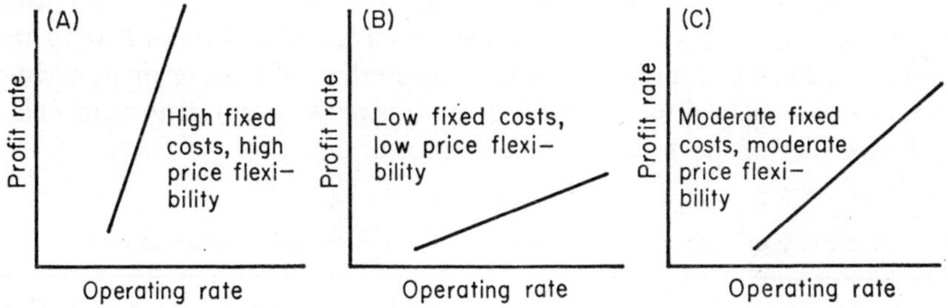

FIG. 1. Relation of operating rate to profit rate: three possibilities.

The degree of monopoly power, reflected in the extent of price flexibility, will affect the regression in another way. In addition to reducing its slope it should also affect the *height* of the regression line. *Ceteris paribus*, the greater the monopoly power in an industry, the more likely are prices—hence profits—in that industry to be abnormally high at any given operating rate. The fixed–variable cost ratio, however, should affect only the slope, not the height of the regression line.

RESULTS OF ANALYSIS

Table I summarizes simple least squares regression results for ten industry groups for the period 1954–65. For operating rates I used the Wharton index of capacity utilization; the source for the earnings data is F.T.C. & S.E.C., 'Quarterly Financial Report, U.S. Manufacturing Firms'.[3] The industries (all but autos being two-digit) are those for which both operating rate and earnings rate data were available. The regressions take the form: $y = a + bx$ where y is after-tax profits as a percentage of net worth and x is the operating rate. All but one of the r values are significant at the .01 level; each is significant at the .05 level. In most cases, however, the degree of fit is not especially high. The intercept values are all negative as we would

[2] Obviously there are gradations among these three possibilities.

[3] For the Wharton data see Laurence R. Klein and Robert Summers, *The Wharton Index of Capacity Utilization*, Economics Research Unit, Wharton School of Finance and Commerce, 1966. Quarterly profit rates are the ratios P/E where P is after-tax profits for each quarter and E is equity at the end of the quarter. Included in equity is capital stock and surplus, earned surplus and surplus reserves.

expect them to be. Using the regression coefficient, the assumed break-even points appear to be 'reasonable' except for rubber, autos and parts and electrical machinery which appear to be unrealistically low.[4]

A linear function appears to fit adequately the observed data, most of which involve moderately high operating and profit rates. But one can not necessarily extrapolate downward a linear regression particularly in the area where operating rates are relatively low and profits low or negative. In this area a curvilinear function may be more appropriate. This would have the effect of raising or lowering the break-even points depending on competitive conditions in each industry during periods of weak demand.

TABLE I

REGRESSION OF PROFIT RATES ON OPERATING RATES, 1954–65, QUARTERLY DATA

Industry group	*Estimating equation*	*Standard error of estimate*	r	*t values*
Textiles	$-31.06+.415x(.048)^2$	1.538	.786	8.59**
Pulp and paper	$-20.49+.349x(.035)^1$	0.872	.830	10.05**
Chemicals	$-19.52+.348x(.040)^1$	0.991	.785	8.59*
Petroleum	$-12.64+.250x(.124)^2$	1.795	.286	2.06**
Rubber	$-5.27+.184x(.033)^1$	1.472	.638	5.64**
Stone, clay and glass	$-27.14+.460x(.089)^1$	3.290	.605	5.23**
Fabricated metal products	$-25.96+.383x(.069)^2$	2.091	.633	5.48**
Non-electrical machinery	$-11.18+.254x(.026)^1$	1.468	.820	9.75**
Electrical machinery	$-2.27+.168x(.042)^2$	1.664	.507	4.02**
Automobiles and parts	$-7.93+.294x(.054)^1$	4.601	.627	5.47**

*Significant at .05 level.
** Significant at .01 level.
N.B. Standard error of regression coefficient in parentheses.
[1] Reject hypothesis of serial correlation at .01 level using Durbin–Watson test.
[2] Accept hypothesis of serial correlation at .01 level using Durbin–Watson test.

To test this possibility I fitted a curvilinear regression to the data by adding a squared operating rate term as another independent variable. The *r* values for these regressions are not appreciably different from those in Table I using linear regression. In no case do the correlation coefficients differ by more than 3 points; in 7 of 10 cases the *r* values are within a single point. The results might have been different had there been more low and negative values for profit rates and correspondingly low operating rate values.

A study of this type encounters problems of selecting profit rate data. One involves the choice of using pre-tax or after-tax earnings and the question of how to handle different depreciation practices. The

[4] These three were 28.6, 26.9 and 13.5 per cent of capacity respectively. The other seven ran from 44.0 per cent for non-electrical machinery to 74.8 per cent for textiles, the average break-even point for the seven being 58.7 per cent.

regressions in Table I use after-tax figures. Regressions using profits before taxes and including depreciation allowances were also computed, but in most instances the *r* values are not appreciably different from those cited in Table I.[5] The slope coefficients obviously are higher, being, as might be expected, almost twice as high as the values obtained in the previously discussed regressions.

TABLE II

PROFIT RATE AT AVERAGE OPERATING RATE

Industry	*Average operating rate*	*Regression profit rate at average operating rate (per cent)*
Textile	89.2	5.95
Pulp and paper	85.4	9.48
Chemicals	94.3	13.29
Petroleum	96.8	11.56
Rubber	89.2	11.14
Stone, clay and glass	83.5	11.27
Metal working	90.4	8.66
Non-electrical machinery	83.9	10.13
Electrical machinery	82.1	11.52
Automobiles and parts	79.3	15.38

Table II adds another dimension to the analysis. It shows both the average operating rate for the ten industry groups in Table I and the profit rate at the average operating rate using the regressions in that table. There is no correlation between the degree of capacity utilization and profit rates *among* industries, though, as the regressions show, there is *within* each industry group. There obviously are other factors at work within each industry influencing the reaction of that industry's profit rates to its operating rates. I suggested two such forces in the discussion of the two slope hypotheses.

TESTS OF SLOPE HYPOTHESES

Previously I discussed the potential impact on profits of different degrees of competition and different cost structures. A crude taxonomy of operating rate–profit rate slope coefficients was suggested. This section describes the results of tests of the validity of the taxonomy.

The responsiveness of an industry group's prices and profits to changes in operating rates should depend, in part, on the degree of

[5] The only industry group potentially affected by using one form of profit rate over another is petroleum, presumably because of the influence of percentage depletion allowances on earnings. Regressions of pre-tax and after-tax earnings reveal correlation coefficients between .916 and .990 for nine of the industry groups, but only .701 for petroleum.

competition in the industry. A measurement of a structural characteristic which should influence the degree of competition is the concentration ratio. Thus I regressed adjusted concentration ratios on the *b* values in Table I.[6] This is a test of the hypothesis that the slope of the operating rate–profit rate regression line is related to the concentration ratio, higher *b* values presumably being associated with lower concentration ratios and vice versa. The correlation ($r = -.394$) is not strong (not significant at the .05 level), but it is negative which, *a priori*, we would expect.

Testing the hypothesis that the *b* values and industry cost structures are related produces slightly different results. It was postulated in the taxonomic discussion above that the slopes of the operating rate–profit rate regressions should depend, *ceteris paribus*, on the relation of the industry groups' fixed to variable costs. Those with relatively high fixed costs should see their earnings fluctuate rather sharply as operating rates change. As a test I regressed the ratio of total capital to value added (K/V) on the *b* values in Table I for the nine industry groups in that table for which adequate K/V data were available.[7] The *r* value again is low and negative; however, the results are distorted by the petroleum industry whose *b* value is substantially higher than those of all the other industries but whose K/V ratio is proportionately even higher (4–8 times higher than the other eight industries). The correlation coefficient excluding petroleum is .72, significant at the .05 level.

For purposes of macro-economic forecasting it would be useful to determine the relationship between operating rates and profit rates for the combined manufacturing industries. Fitting a linear regression to the quarterly data, for the period 1954–64, the estimating equation is $-16.7+.316x$ where x is the aggregated operating rate.[8] The *r*

[6] I used adjusted concentration ratios in Leonard W. Weiss, op. cit., p. 242. Weiss adjusted the ratios to account for local and regional markets (ratios based on the assumption of the existence only of national markets often understate concentration) and to correct for overstating and understating ratios resulting from aggregation of data. My regression included the nine industry groups for which Weiss's definitions and mine agreed. Included were the following industries: non-electrical machinery; electrical machinery; stone, clay and glass; chemicals; rubber; metalworking; petroleum; paper and textiles.

[7] The K/V data came from C. E. Ferguson, 'The Elasticity of Substitution and Regional Estimates of Capital and Capital Ratios in American Manufacturing Industry, 1954–58', in *Essays on Southern Economic Development*, Melvin L. Greenhut and W. Tate Whitman (eds.), (Chapel Hill: The University of North Carolina Press, 1964), p. 429–33. The industries mentioned in footnote 6 were used in this regression.

[8] Sources: for profits: F.T.C.–S.E.C., 'Quarterly Financial Report for Manufacturing Corporations'; for operating rates: 'Measures of Productive Capacity', Hearings before Subcommittee on Economic Statistics, Joint Economic Committee, 87th Congress, 2nd Session, p. 129, and 'Productivity, Prices and Incomes', materials prepared by Committee Staff for Joint Economic Committee, 1967.

Profit rates exclude the newspaper publishing industry.

value is .824, significant at the .01 level.[9] A change in slightly over 3 percentage points in the aggregate operating rate is associated with a movement of 1 point in the profit rate. The implied break-even point for manufacturing industry is 52.8 of capacity.

CONCLUSION

The problem of measuring the relationship between operating rates and profits is not easily solved. There are serious data limitations, not the least of which is the selection of a technique for determining operating rates. This study chose one from among several because it appeared to be fairly reliable and fitted in with the selection of earnings data.[10]

As a practical predictive and analytic tool, the regression relationships would be more valuable if calculated on a less aggregated basis. Needed are studies of the operating rate–profit rate relationships in, at least, four-digit or, if possible, five-digit industries. A few studies have been done for specific industries (e.g., paper) and more are possible for others where operating rate data are readily available. But analyses of the relationships for many industries must await the collection of better operating rate data.

This study, therefore, is but a beginning step. It postulates relationships between the variables, and derives crude statistical estimates of those relationships. This study concludes with the same melancholy observation that applies to many other economic studies: more work in this area remains to be done.

MICHIGAN STATE UNIVERSITY
EAST LANSING

[9] This reasonably good fit does not contradict the conclusion concerning the data in Table II that 'there is no correlation between the degree of capacity utilization and profit rates *among* industries . . .' (see p. 183). The regressions for each industry show that as operating rates rise, profit rates also rise. The *level* of profits for each industry at a given operating rate, however, is higher than it is at a lower rate. The regression of operating rates and profit rates for all manufacturing combined simply averages out the different figures for each industry.

[10] For a summary of sources of operating rate data and their shortcomings, see 'Measures of Productive Capacity', op. cit.

PRIVATE CAPITAL INVESTMENT: A CASE-STUDY APPROACH TOWARDS TESTING ALTERNATIVE THEORIES

by C. M. Cannon

This paper considers the information collected and used by four businesses, and their formation of expectations, during their generation and appraisal of proposals for four factory investments. The businesses were very large, each with an international reputation, and were members of The Centre for Business Research of Manchester University. They selected fourteen investments for investigation by The Centre for Business Research; I selected the four large-capacity expansion investments from among these fourteen, for further study.[1] All the case-studies were ex-post so that they could refer to matters no longer secret or controversial. Case-study evidence is complex, lengthy and detailed, drawing on reports, letters and statements. Consequently this paper can only substantiate inferences with particular illustrations from synthesized and camouflaged material; I provide instances of specific actions from one case-study.

Case W[2] was a diversification investment, executed by acquisition of an existing producer at a cost of over £300,000. The parent business made a deliberate search for new markets because its income growth and profitability were low; liquidity was very high from 1953 to 1961. The time-span from first identifiable idea to visible documentation was seven years, and from then until sanction nineteen months. Formulation of proposals began while the economies of Western Europe and the U.S.A. were expanding rapidly. But uncertainty strongly influenced final specification when U.K. economic growth slowed in 1961–62. There were several well-established producers in the product market.

Case X was a pioneer factory investment in an economically underdeveloped country. The business had long experience of such projects, and made a deliberate search for such opportunities. Total initial capital expenditure was over £1.5 million. Five years separated first identifiable idea from visible documentation, and fifteen

[1] This paper uses material collected by The Centre for Business Research, to which the author was seconded while a Research Associate in Economics at Manchester University. I thank Professor B. R. Williams who supervised the writing of the thesis upon part of which this paper is based, and I thank Mr. R. W. Shaw for his comments upon an earlier draft of this paper.

[2] Evidence from fourteen C.B.R. case-studies, including these four, is outlined in *Investment Proposals and Decisions*, 1965, by B. R. Williams and W. P. Scott. My notation W, X, Y and Z corresponds with their Cases G, B, A and C. Outcomes are compared with predictions in Ch. 5, pp. 30–53.

months elapsed from then until sanction. Establishment was accomplished in the face of intense competition from powerful rivals for the privileges expected from the local government. The income growth and profitability of the whole business group were about the average for U.K. manufacturing industry over the period 1953–61; the business was illiquid.

Case Y was a factory investment incorporating a novel process of production, producing a product previously available as a by-product of traditional processes. This investment was forced on the business because some sources of supply had been eliminated by the decision of the parent business group to use a changed, cheaper process to produce its main product. Total initial capital investment was over £600,000. Time-span from first identifiable idea to visible documentation was three months; from then until sanction nine months. Excess demand threatened market position, for coeval with loss of supplies, demand was growing rapidly. The parent business had very high income growth and profitability during the period 1953–61, and was liquid.

Case Z was a factory investment to expand production, made after a deliberate enquiry into market opportunities. Total initial capital expenditure was £800,000. Two years elapsed from first identifiable idea to visible documentation, and eighteen months from then until sanction. Several other producers were firmly established. The 1961–62 business recession influenced the progress of the project. High income growth and profitability distinguished the parent business during the period 1953–61; liquidity was high.

THE FOUR INVESTMENTS. I—THE ENQUIRY AND RECOGNITION STAGE

The extent of possible outcomes was thought to be important while the opportunities for three of the projects were still to be recognized and determined, and while fundamental information was sought. In Case W a U.S. producer suggested a joint entry into the U.K. market for the product; the choice faced was whether to investigate this potential partner, or to reject the suggestion outright. In Case Y there was awareness of cost estimates for various novel processes of production; the immediate question to be considered was whether or not to endorse these estimates as an account of techniques available to replace traditional processes. In Case Z a proposed reorganization of management responsibility was closely connected with the question of expansion of facilities to produce the product; the choice to be made about the immediate progress of the project became whether or not to approve of the management reorganization.

Two outcomes of these positive acts, to investigate, to endorse and to reorganize, were selected. These two outcomes were possible success and possible disaster. This displayed a dichotomy of attitude. Nevertheless, valuation of each act was not effectuated by comparing these two prospects. Instead, the poorer of the two was eventually ignored, and the act assessed on the basis of the better which was then compared with a standard of acceptability; although always this exercise was performed with the stipulation that future re-examinations of the issues should take place. This behaviour resulted from an awareness of extreme uncertainty, from a lack of useful information, and from an appreciation of calamitous possibilities. So some opposition to the projects was aroused when each venture was sufficiently tentative for this to be influential. But these conflicts in expectations were nullified rapidly, and long before formulation and submission of expenditure proposals.

Next, I describe in more detail the choice made in Case W. The Board was informed of the approach by the U.S. producer, but only after five months of delay did the Board agree even to a formal investigation of the worth of joint entry. Despite suspicion of the motives of the potential associate business, the usefulness of its expertise led to the visualization of two extreme possible outcomes. One was a 'success', employing help necessary for successful market entry. The other was a 'disaster', with acceptance as an unnecessary joint operator a powerful unscrupulous rival in other product markets, which would be enabled to infiltrate, then obtain and exploit information useful to it. The 'success' was sufficiently attractive to permit intensive investigation eventually, but it was not then thought to be more likely.

THE FOUR INVESTMENTS. II—THE FORMULATION STAGE

Once the existence of opportunities for investment had become a subject for investigation, attention turned to the formulation of the precise characteristics of the opportunities: market area, product types, product mix, production capacity, production process and production and marketing organization. In considering these matters the business outlook on all four projects encompassed only a narrow and composite set of prospects, with an assured and confident attitude. Businessmen neither selected a few from foreseen outcomes, nor summarized the range of foreseen outcomes by weighting possibilities within it. This account of business expectations by the investigator is of overwhelming importance. The best way to substantiate it with evidence is to outline the character and manner of collection and use of the information which formed the bases for the formation of expectations at this stage.

Future total market size was always forecasted. Estimates for up to three years ahead were made by extrapolating recent and current sales of the product, sales of associated products, and movements of output in the whole national economy and other economies. Records were used of company and industry sales for as much as ten years previously and, too, surveys were taken of trade and customer opinion. As the passage of time provided results which were inconsistent with predictions, so the forecasts on this short range ahead were adapted freely. For longer-range forecasts on prospects more than three years ahead, there were also assertions about influences upon the motion of demand—influences which, it was believed, would not be anticipated by competitors capable through expansion of 'eliminating' excess demand, and so the investment opportunity.[3] These assertions were not questioned by the businessmen and did not give rise to the perception of alternative future events. They were qualitative, general, concerned the very long run and were vital in the generation of all the ventures. Quantitative forecasts of total market size were usually for up to five years ahead, the furthest was for ten years. Only one quantitative range was admitted in any forecast of total market size. This was made about W over a year before submission of expenditure proposals, but was supplanted with a changed and single figure estimate long before capacity was determined.

Market share was always forecasted. But X, Y and Z assumed throughout that competitors' future behaviour and attitudes would not differ from those judged to be current: that there would be continued stability in competitive relations and little reaction to an increase of demand. Only Z did not expect its market share to increase. X experienced three widely differing quantitative forecasts of market share in about one year, the last more than double the first for some products. But each was single-valued and used confidently while considered valid. Later, the diversifying W made an allowance for product price to fall 10 per cent below current price, this was in the only calculation of any expected profitability of these projects at other than current product price.[4] Throughout the

[3] This is consistent with Williams' hypothesis that businessmen short-circuit complex calculations by concentrating on 'key factors'. B. R. Williams, *Melbourne Lectures*, unpublished, 1962, p. 13. C. F. Carter and Williams, *Industry and Technical Progress*, 1957, p. 83. A. Keynes uses examples to illustrate the complexities of technical, 'political' and social factors which underlie 'facts' about projects, and contain the really crucial issues. 'The Importance of Assumptions', *Journal of Management Studies*, 1966.

[4] Other reasons than the short-sightedness of competitors have been suggested for the use of current prices in calculations about the future. J. M. Keynes has maintained that

projects at this stage, these expansions supposed that growth of *excess* demand would provide investment opportunities without damaging dislocation of either price 'stability' or the profit margins of producers: that competitors themselves would not fully anticipate these future long-term shifts of demand by their own capacity expansions.

Next, I describe in more detail the compilation of a forecast of demand at this stage in Case W. A large U.S. producer approached the business to suggest an associated entry into the U.K. market. They agreed that first a detailed study of the market be made and discussions take place afterwards. Current and future demand and the likely capacity of existing producers were the objects of a survey of hundreds of potential customers. The recent rapid growth of sales of this product in the U.S. was known; suppositions were that U.K. per capita absolute demand would soon grow rapidly itself, towards the present U.S. level, a distinct rise in market size. W saw quantitative forecasts of physical market size and of the productive capacity of existing producers for five years ahead; there were qualitative impressions of still further ahead. On one product type the market demand forecast admitted an error range, but only ±15 per cent of the mean estimate, with a single-valued forecast of the capacity of existing producers. While about the other product type, which was to be rejected, all forecasts were qualitative. Well in advance of a plant capacity decision all these estimates were replaced with new and single-valued forecasts.

At this formulation stage the physical dimensions of all these expansions of capacity were strongly influenced by expected physical sales, by the difference between expected absolute demand and the expected capacity of the industry to produce.

THE FOUR INVESTMENTS III—THE PROPOSAL AND APPROVAL OF EXPENDITURE STAGE

In this stage, choices were whether to invest in a plant or acquire an existing producer, whether to rent or purchase plant, and where

---

necessity for decision in business conditions compels one to use techniques. First, one is compelled to act as though the present is a much more serviceable guide to the future than a candid examination of past experience would show it to have been hitherto. Second, one is compelled to rely upon an assumption that present prices and output in the market are based on a correct summing-up of future prospects. And third, one is compelled to fall back on conventional judgement. 'The General Theory of Employment', *Quarterly Journal of Economics*, 1937.

R. Mack has found that 'points of major reliance' in planning by the individual and by the market are current sales, deliveries and prices. Taking current values involved less responsibility than predicting definite changes. 'Business Expectations and the Buying of Materials', M. J. Bowman (ed.), *Expectations, Uncertainty and Business Behaviour*, 1958, p. 115.

to site any factory. Then required capital expenditure and its profitability was calculated, and the worth of the proposed capital expenditure was appraised. It is essential to appreciate that the specification of none of these substantial expansions in the formulation stage had admitted quantitative ranges for variables such as product price, factor costs and sales. Some ranges of possibilities were incorporated in calculations of the profitability of planned capital expenditures, that is *only after* assessment of demand and *after* choice of the capacity of plant and product mix. So profitability estimates relied upon information bases and project dimensions already established. Then about profitability, either percentages of full capacity working and percentages of current product price reflected various assumptions, or allowance was made for the effects of the regular oscillations of the shorter business cycle. Yet still the figures within the resulting ranges displayed no importunate disagreement; for their bases of information were common, and they were not markedly dissimilar assessments. Differences were small for such substantial expansions with significant innovation, and summed up to most of the effects of the recurrent business cycle.[5]

In submission of first expenditure proposals on W, profitability[6] was estimated at from 13 to 32 per cent; the difference between the limits and the midpoint as a percentage of the midpoint was 41 per cent. One limit assumed full output with current product price and current factor costs in the specified plant, and the other 80 per cent of full output with 90 per cent of current product price and current factor costs. But within six months market conditions had deteriorated, planned capacity was reduced, and estimated returns had fallen to 10–22 per cent, an error range of 37.5 per cent. X did not see even these quantitative allowances, it expected a profitability of 16 per cent. Y admitted current product price and current factor costs, and from full to 75 per cent of full working capacity, with profitability extending from 22 to 40 per cent, an error range of 29

[5] Therefore, evidence from all these cases is consistent with T. A. B. Corley's evidence on short-run output and stock investment decisions. These expansions of capacity were determined not with reference to anticipated revenue and costs, but to expected physical sales. 'How Do Businessmen Plan Production?, A Case-Study of the Radio and T.V. Industry', *Journal of Industrial Economics*, 1962.

One can see a similar predisposition in Robinson's three-stage approach to business forecasting: The Economic Forecast, The Market Demand Forecast, The Market Share Forecast. But Robinson, of course, advocates a far more extensive reference to details than is shown by my case-studies. C. Robinson, a Senior Planning Economist in Esso Petroleum, 'Some Principles of Forecasting in Business', *Journal of Industrial Economics*, 1965.

[6] The rates of profit return calculated were after depreciation provision and before tax; they were estimated for the first normal year of working, that is after running-in, in one venture, and for each year up to the quantitative time horizon in the other three. Annual profits were calculated on total fixed and annual working capital invested in three instances, on fixed capital only in Y.

per cent. Z expected yield to oscillate between 10 and 15 per cent with trade conditions, assuming current prices and costs, an error range of 20 per cent. These error ranges were all small,[7] and the expected profitabilities of projects W, X and Z were barely marginal.[8]

Expectations during these proposal and approval choices in Cases X and Y never disclosed any importunate conflict. But after approval of W and Z these two projects were postponed and revised, for risk and uncertainty was believed to create formidable difficulties. Then businessmen expressed doubt and displayed caution, and the projects were evaluated solely on the basis of their poorer or poorest foreseen worth. The investigator cannot be confident that these businessmen did reckon with only the worst prospect because there is some evidence that even in these instances they still felt themsleves to be taking some chances of even poorer results. Also, observation of mental processes is a hazardous undertaking. This behaviour occurred as the business cycle moved into a down-phase in 1961–62. As well as low business confidence, another cause may have been the reaction in such circumstances to a 'feedback' of continuing inadequacy in predictions, and fear of earning the opprobrium of controlling committeees by over-optimism.

Next, I describe in detail a choice made during the final stage of Case W. In W in the same month as a reduction in planned plant size had been approved, the proposers suggested instead that, 'it would be less of a gamble to acquire an established producer'. Actual sales were disappointing by diverging downwards from predictions as business moved into a down-phase of its cycle in 1961–62, so less credence was given to the activating forecasts of excess demand. Estimates were made of the difference between the required capital outlays for plant and for acquisition 'at least', and of the difference between profits from plant and from acquisition 'at most'. That is, the performances of plant and acquisition were compared in the poorest set of circumstances envisaged, when plant investment would be restricted nearest to the cost of the acquisition and when profit from an untried plant in a novel market would diverge downwards furthest from that in a flexible 'going concern'. Critical calculations were of 'start-up' losses, of the flexibility in

[7] Carter and Williams found from a sample of investments in 250 British companies that the difference between actual and expected return was 50 per cent or more of expected return in 75 per cent of the individual cases, and more than 100 per cent in 25 per cent of the cases. Carter and Williams, *Investment in Innovation*, 1958, pp. 89–90.

[8] There is likely to be a close relation between these businesses' alleged 15 per cent minimum 'cut-off' rates and recent costs of capital. C. M. Cannon, 'Profitability Calculations and Business Practice: An Inquiry Into Academic and Business Stereotypes', *Journal of Industrial Economics*, 1967.

operation and speed of implementation of the two proposals, and of the effects of the elimination of an established competitor and acquisition of its staff, plant and reputation. So, it was the results in the poorer and poorest possible circumstances which aroused fear and arrested attention, although there was awareness of better prospects.

CONCLUSIONS

Formation of expectations in the enquiry and recognition stage of these projects was consistent with some hypotheses of Shackle's and of Carter-Egerton's models.[9] Two outcomes of each act were selected, possible 'success' and possible 'disaster', displaying a dichotomy of attitude. Nevertheless, inconsistent with one of Shackle's hypotheses, valuation of these acts was not effectuated by comparing these two prospects. Instead, the poorer of the two was eventually ignored and the act assessed on the better of the two. Such conflicts in expectations were nullified in the formulation stage when project dimensions were established, then businessmen believed in their ability to foresee the future accurately. It was on the basis of these dimensions that the expected profitabilities of the proposals were calculated. So businessmen neglected revenue and costs in their reckonings, they relied heavily upon unchallenged assertions about the long-term movement of physical demand. Nevertheless, short-term expectations were continually proved mistaken; they were liable to sudden and violent adjustment, albeit from faith in one cohesive 'non-conflicting' set of possibilities to faith in another, quite different set. This business conviction continued throughout the progress of Cases X and Y, and until reappraisal of approved expenditure proposals in Cases W and Z. In these reappraisals businessmen were abruptly led to admit in their reckonings the extent and significance of risk and uncertainty; they recoiled quite shocked and dismayed. Such apocalyptic events occurred when deterioration in the condition of trade had lowered their confidence[10] in prospects, and aroused their fear of controlling committees. In such circumstances businessmen displayed consternation and apprehension. They relied upon the poorer and poorest possibilities so that their formation of expectations was consistent with the hypothesis of a maximin theory: they became unwilling to take any chance.[11] No

[9] G. L. S. Shackle, *Expectation in Economics*, 1949. C. F. Carter, 'The Present State of the Theory of Decisions Under Uncertainty', *Uncertainty and Business Decisions*, Carter *et al.*, 1957, pp. 142–52.

[10] Mack superimposes a 'coefficient of sureness' on to distributions of belief in possible events. Bowman, op. cit., p. 115.

[11] W. Baumol, *Economic Theory and Operations Analysis*, 1965, p. 552.

evidence from these case-studies is consistent with the frequent belief of economists that typically businessmen in large modern organizations are calculating gamblers.

A convincing reason still needs to be found for this neglect of expected revenue and costs and for this frequent apparent unawareness of the problems likely to be caused by risk and uncertainty in such large and marginally attractive capacity expansions. For in Cases W, X and Y competitive conflict was intense, only in Z was market share not expected to increase but even about Z there were several well-established competitors. Oligopolistic collusion was not apparent. In Cases W and Y there were severe technological uncertainties. In Case X there was severe political uncertainty, and uncertainty about the geographical extent and growth of the economy. Only Case Y was not begun as an initiative of the business itself. Nor did these investments appear to possess sufficient modification potential to permit a neutral attitude towards all uncertainty or the risk component of it. Nor was there evidence of the employment of a heavy time discount rate to lessen or to remove the significance of future risk and uncertainty.[12]

One cause of this 'unawareness', and this reliance upon assumptions about changes in market size, was that some interested businessmen became involved with the spirit of these ventures even before formal investigation, and somctimes depended upon career opportunities in the enterprises to be set up. So pressure was exerted upon investigators to make worth appear obvious. Another cause was the adoption of assertions about the future inaction of competitors, even in situations of intense conflict when market shares were expected to change considerably and when excess capacity could have arisen. In forecasting market share X, Y and Z assumed that competitors would not adopt a similar or related policy of expansion; W, which did not make such a rigid assumption, made the only calculation allowing for a price change. Another possible explanation of this business behaviour may have been the existence of imperfectly competitive markets for funds within these businesses.[13] Perhaps target budgeting set a total to be spent by each business sub-unit.[14] After all, only the business which generated X was illiquid. The high liquidity of the other parent businesses could have led them to ignore the opportunity cost of capital spent even on projects whose valuation was a feasible exercise, such as these capacity expansions.

[12] See footnote 8, above.

[13] The perfectly competitive internal market for funds is a major implicit assumption of the theory of the firm. R. H. Coase, 'The Nature of the Firm', *Economics*, 1937.

[14] This would be consistent with one explanation of simple calculations in businesses by Cyert and March. *A Behavioral Theory of the Firm*. 1965, p. 80.

Many other empirical studies have revealed the complexity of the private capital investment decision. They have been unable to substantiate solely one within the two major groups of theories of determination of changes in the level of private capital investment: accelerator and marginalist theories. My case-study evidence too is consistent with an absolute sales-capital stock form of accelerator relation, if the subjective character of expectations of market size is admitted.[15] At the same time my evidence is consistent with marginalist theories if allowance is made for the following elaborations. The first elaboration is a frequent apparent ignorance of problems created by risk and uncertainty, but an inability to gamble when the existence of risk and uncertainty is recognized. The second elaboration is the strong influence of unchallenged assertions, first an assertion on the future level of demand, second an assertion on lack of reaction of competitors to a demand increase, and third an assertion on lack of reaction of competitors to a large-scale expansion by other producers in the industry, or lack of reaction to large new entrants. The third elaboration is that businessmen can be attracted by the career opportunities created by expansion, and can be capable of action to discriminate in favour of expansion at the expense of the business. The fourth elaboration is the existence of a highly imperfect market for funds within a business.

If a marginalist approach admits such rigidities in expectations and such imperfections in planning and financial control, it will provide a similar prediction to that of one accelerator relation: changes in the ratio of expected absolute sales to capital stock will determine changes in the level of private capital investment. On the other hand my evidence suggests that this accelerator relation was abruptly recognized as an inadequate rule of thumb by businessmen who were experiencing a down-turn in the business cycle. It was then, when confidence had 'broken', that attention turned to a financial summary of the worth of expenditure proposals, but to a summary only of the poorer and poorest possibilities.

UNIVERSITY OF LEEDS

[15] This is consistent with Meyer and Glauber's conclusions on U.S. evidence. Their best measure was a capacity utilization or absolute sales-capital stock form of accelerator. But accelerator effects required substantial supplementation with measures of business expectations such as changes in stock price values. J. Meyer and R. R. Glauber, *Investment Decisions, Economic Forecasting and Public Policy*, 1964, pp. 248–9.

ENTROPY, MARKOV PROCESSES AND COMPETITION IN THE BREWING INDUSTRY

by Ann and Ira Horowitz

INTRODUCTION

In an earlier paper we discussed trends in demand and concentration in the brewing industry.[1] Our empirical analysis encouraged the following suggestions: (1) The pronounced decline in the number of firms in the industry has in the main resulted from the inability of the less efficient smaller brewers to withstand the competitive pressures exerted by the larger firms in the face of fairly fixed industry demand; and (2) the increase in industrial concentration in the industry reflects the exodus of both the smaller and medium-sized firms from the industry and this trend will likely continue; but (3) competition in the industry has been maintained through the emergence of many economically healthy firms who of necessity will actively compete for their share of industry demand.

The present paper presents additional fuel in support of our previous arguments. In particular, the analogy is drawn between the entropy concept of communication theory and industrial concentration. Concentration in the brewing industry between 1944 and 1964 is then analyzed with respect to this measure. A rather unique picture of the trends and degree of concentration and competition in the industry evolves from this analysis. Further, we derive a transition probability matrix involving most of the leading brewers. This matrix reflects shifts in market shares within the industry. An analysis of the transition probabilites clearly reveals the likely prospect of the continuing disappearance of the vast majority of the smaller brewers as well as the continuing strengthening in the position of the growing regional brewers.

ENTROPY AND COMPETITION

In communication theory and the physical sciences, *entropy* is a measure of the degree of disorder, uncertainty, or randomness in a system.[2] Suppose there are $i = 1, \ldots, n$ possible events that can

[1] 'Firms in a Declining Market: the Brewing Case', *The Journal of Industrial Economics* vol. XIII, no. 2 (March 1965), pp. 129–53.

[2] For a discussion, see Claude E. Shannon and Warren Weaver, *The Mathematical Theory of Communication* (The University of Illinois Press: Urbana 1964), particularly pp. 8–22, 36–50. Michael O. Finkelstein and Richard M. Friedberg, 'The Application of an Entropy Theory of Concentration to the Clayton Act', *The Yale Law Journal*, vol. 76, no. 4 (March 1967), pp. 677–717, have independently suggested the use of entropy as

occur. Let the probability of occurrence of the ith event be denoted by p_i. The entropy in the system, or the disorder or freedom of choice, is defined to be the negative of the weighted average of the logarithms to the base 2 of the p_i, where the p_i are the weights. In symbols, the entropy H is given by

$$H = -\sum_i p_i \log_2 p_i$$

If the jth event is the only possibility, then $p_j = 1$, all other $p_i = 0$, and $H = 0$. That is, there is only a single event and therefore neither any freedom of choice nor any disorder or entropy in the system.

If there are two equally likely possibilities, then $p_i = \frac{1}{2}$ and

$$H = -\tfrac{1}{2}\log_2(\tfrac{1}{2}) - \tfrac{1}{2}\log_2(\tfrac{1}{2}) = 1$$

There is a unit of entropy in this situation. Doubling the number of equally likely possibilities will double the entropy, doubling the number again will increase the entropy by an additional unit. In general, each time the number of equally likely possibilities doubles from any base level, H increases by one unit. Furthermore, for a given number of n possibilities, the disorder in the system is greatest and H assumes a maximum value of $\log_2 n$ when the n possibilities are equally likely to occur. That is,

$$H = -n(1/n)\log_2(1/n) = -\log_2 1 + \log_2 n = \log_2 n.$$

Relative entropy is defined as the ratio of the actual to the maximum entropy in a system.

There would seem to be a ready, useful, and intuitively appealing analogy between the entropy of a communication source and the 'competitiveness' of an industry. The greater is the degree of competition, the greater the uncertainty as to which of a given number of firms will secure the business of a buyer chosen at random. In particular, if entropy is used as a measure of the degree of competition and the p_i are likened to actual market shares, then H would equal the weighted average of the logarithms of the market share of

---

a measure of industrial concentration. Their measure, denoted by C, is given by

$$\log_{10} C = -\Sigma p_i \log_{10} p_i$$

Thus, C corresponds to the equivalent number of equal size firms discussed in this paper. Finkelstein and Friedberg give three derivations of C: (1) a competitive activities derivation based on a weighted average (the weights are the p_i's) of the competitive activities of the firms using the assumption that a firm's competitive activities are described by the function $\log 1/p_i$; (2) a permutations derivation based on the number of permutations of customers that could occur given that all firms retain the same share of the market; and (3) a 'probabilities' derivation based on the probability that each firm will retain the same number of customers.

each firm in the industry. In a monopolistic situation with only one p_i, H would equal $-1 \log_2 1 = 0$. There is no entropy for the buyer has no freedom of choice. In the situation where there are n firms, H is larger the more equally sales are distributed among the n firms. Thus, H assumes a maximum value, given the number of firms, when competition is at what presumably would be its greatest level, i.e., when each firm holds an equal share of the market.[3] With n equal-size firms in the industry, we would then have $p_i = 1/n$ and $H = \log_2 n$. Of course, H may assume higher values for industries with a greater number of firms but for a given number of firms $\log_2 n$ is an upper bound of H.

As a measure of industry *concentration*, then, entropy has the very nice property of being truly analogous to industry *competition*. That is, H varies directly with the degree of competition and uncertainty as to which firm a buyer chosen at random would purchase from. Although independent of the size of the industry, H *is* dependent upon the number of firms in the industry to the extent that the number of firms determines the upper bound of H. With respect to competition, the implication is that the *potential* degree or intensity of competition is greater, the greater is the number of firms. The only lower bound, however, is zero in the monopoly case. This means that H could be smaller, indicating less competition, for industry A than for industry B even though industry A has significantly more firms. This result could occur, for example, if a few firms in A tended to dominate the industry in terms of market shares while the remaining firms were roughly the same size. Hence, the entropy measure reflects differences in the concentration of market power as well as differences in the number of firms in the industries.

Furthermore, a movement towards equal market shares will not necessarily result in either greater competition or a higher value of H if, concurrently, the number of firms has decreased. Indeed, since the upper bound of H is $\log_2 n$ we see that in such a situation there are two opposing forces operating on the entropy measure as well as on the competitiveness of the industry. On the one hand, the equalization of market shares will tend to raise the entropy and the degree of competition. On the other hand, the trend to fewer firms will tend to reduce the entropy and the competition. In general, the combined effect will reflect each of these conflicting tendencies, the essential point being that the effect of each on the entropy measure will correspond to its presumed effect on competition. Nevertheless, an equalization of market shares resulting from a merger of two or

[3] This is a property of H. Indeed, any change towards equalization of market shares, of the p_i, raises H (Shannon and Weaver, op. cit., pp. 51–2).

more relatively small firms with the shares of all other firms remaining unchanged will necessarily reduce H. Specifically, it can be shown that if two firms with market shares of p_1 and p_2 merge, H falls by $(p_1+p_2) \log (p_1+p_2)-p_1 \log p_1-p_2 \log p_2$.

Distinct from, and in addition to, the degree of competition, it is also meaningful to recognize the extent to which the competitiveness of an industry approaches the maximum level that is attainable *given* the number of firms actually in the industry. The relative entropy, $R = H/\log_2 n$, provides an appropriate measure of this. Relative entropy does not tell us anything about the degree of competition. Rather, it accepts the fact of the limitation imposed on the industry's competitiveness by the finite number of firms in the industry, and proposes to measure the extent to which the degree of competition is achieving its maximum potential. Thus, whereas H seeks to answer the question of how competitive an industry is, R seeks to answer the question of how competitive it is relative to how competitive it could be. Certainly each of these issues could be of relevance in policy decisions.[4]

In addition, once one has computed H for an industry one can determine the number of equal size firms which would result in the same amount of entropy. This is done by setting the computed value of H equal to $\log_2 n$ and solving for n. The equivalent number of equal size firms can be used to compare the degree of competition in one industry with that in another (or to compare the degree of competition at one period of time with that at another).

ENTROPY IN THE BREWING INDUSTRY

Trends in concentration and competition in the United States brewing industry are placed in a most interesting light when viewed through the entropy measures. Both H and R have been calculated for the industry for the years 1944 through 1964.[5] These figures are presented in Table I.

The second column in Table I presents the values for H. The figures reveal a slow but steady decline in the degree of concentration and disorder in the industry since 1946. The 1964 value of H is approximately two units less than the 1946 value. A reduction of

[4] We are, therefore, departing from the view that a measure of concentration should be unambiguous or one dimensional (Marshall Hall and Nicolaus Tideman, 'Measures of Concentration', *Journal of the American Statistical Association*, vol. 62, no. 317 (March 1967), p. 163). More than one issue is involved here. Each entropy measure does, however, satisfy the properties of being unambiguous, independent of industry size, raised by an equalization of market shares, and an increasing function of n (ibid., pp. 163–4).

[5] The data used in this analysis were taken from various issues of *Brewing Industry Survey* (Research Company of America: New York).

two units is equivalent to reducing the number of equally likely possibilities (or equal size firms) by three-fourths.

As indicated in column 5 the number of firms in the industry has declined from 374 in 1944 to 129 in 1964.[6] For comparative purposes column 6 shows the concentration ratio for the leading 25 firms. The ratio rose from 39.2 in 1944 to 85.4 in 1964, increasing steadily in every year since 1946. Thus, both the concentration ratio for the leading 25 firms and *H*, the degree of disorder among *all* firms in the industry, indicate a steady decline in competition during the

TABLE I
THE ENTROPY MEASURES

Year	*H*	*R*	*Equivalent number of equal size firms*	*Actual number of firms*	*Concentration ratios for the leading 25 firms*
1944	7.31	.86	159	374	39.2
1945	7.31	.86	159	374	40.1
1946	7.33	.86	161	374	38.1
1947	7.15	.84	142	373	43.3
1948	6.95	.82	123	367	46.8
1949	6.62	.81	92	260	49.6
1950	6.49	.80	90	271	51.4
1951	6.35	.79	82	260	54.6
1952	6.29	.79	78	252	55.7
1953	6.35	.79	81	259	57.9
1954	6.29	.80	78	239	59.1
1955	6.14	.79	71	223	61.0
1956	6.11	.78	69	221	62.0
1957	5.97	.78	62	200	64.7
1958	5.85	.78	58	184	66.7
1959	5.73	.77	53	179	73.8
1960	5.67	.76	51	174	75.2
1961	5.55	.76	46	162	77.5
1962	5.40	.75	42	148	79.7
1963	5.25	.74	38	137	84.3
1964	5.20	.74	37	129	85.4

postwar period. The values of *H* follow approximately the same pattern as the concentration ratios for the top 25 firms. *H* has the advantage, however, of taking all firms into consideration while the results for the concentration ratio depend on the number of firms for which the ratio is computed. The percentage of the market held by firms outside the top 25 in 1964 is one-fourth the percentage in 1946. It is interesting to note that this decrease corresponds to the reduction in equal size firms indicated by the values of *H* for 1946 and 1964.

[6] The list of firms includes only those firms that were listed as having any sales in a particular year. This would account for the minor discrepancy between the figures in Tables I and IV.

The third column of Table I presents the calculations for $R = H/\log_2 n$, the ratio of actual competition to the maximum level that would be attained if each firm held an equal share of the market. This ratio will range from a value of zero for a monopoly to a value of one when each firm in the industry has an equal market share. Again the slow but steady decline since 1946 appears in the data. Still, it would seem apparent that despite the decline in the number of firms in the industry, the extent to which in any one year the industry has failed to achieve its maximum possible degree of competitiveness, *given the number of firms* operating in that year, has remained fairly small and comparatively invarient. Indeed, even after over a decade of decline, the recent figures stand only slightly below those of the late 'forties. The figures appear to indicate that as an oligopolistic industry, brewing represents the many-firm case of monopolistic competition, with little national dominance on the part of individual brewers.[7] Further, the trends in R would reinforce our earlier conclusions to the effect that the *relative* dominance of individual firms has not been significantly expanded. Indeed, the comparatively slight diminution in R would seem to imply that, in the main, the decline in H is more a reflection of the disappearance from the industry of a host of smaller brewers who were the least effective competitors, rather than the emergence of a few dominant firms to overwhelm the rest.

Finally, the fourth column of Table I indicates the number of firms that would have had to share equally in sales to give the same degree of competition, as measured by H, as actually existed in the brewing industry in each year. These are simply the antilogs of the H's to the base 2. These figures will perhaps help to place those of column 2 in better perspective. For example, an industry composed of 37 firms with equal sales would yield a value of $H = 5.20$, the same degree of competition provided by the 129 firms in the brewing industry in 1964. The post-1946 trend towards concentration of sales in fewer hands is emphasized here. The results indicate that between 1945 and 1948 competition in the brewing industry was equivalent to that in an industry composed of 123 to 159 equal size firms. During the early 1950s, however, competition had decreased to the point where the brewing industry was equivalent to an industry with 78 to 90 equal size firms. This period corresponds to the time when many of the relatively small regional brewers such as Falstaff, Hamm and Carling were rapidly expanding their marketing areas.

[7] Here we consider only the national market. Since not all brewers sell in each and every submarket, individual brewers may well dominate in any one geographical sub-market.

During the late 1950s, the number of equal size firms yielding an equivalent amount of entropy fell from 71 to 53 firms. The decline has continued into the 1960s so that between 1962 and 1964 competition in the industry has been roughly equivalent to that of an industry with 37 to 42 equal size firms. Thus, in 1964, when 25 firms accounted for 85 per cent of industry sales, competition was equivalent to that of an industry composed of 37 equal size firms. Notwithstanding this decline, however, nor to underestimate its significance, it should be emphasized that this number of equal size firms is by no means 'negligible'. It is 'low' only by earlier industry standards.

MARKET SHARES AND THE MARKOV PROCESS[8]

In order to appreciate the *extent* to which the trend towards fewer brewers will continue as well as to obtain some insight as to *how* it will proceed, let us assume that consumer purchases among firms in the brewing industry follow a first order Markov process. This is equivalent to assuming that the probability that a consumer purchases from *firm* j in period $t+1$ depends upon whether or not he purchases from *firm* i in period t. This probability is denoted by p_{ij} and is assumed to be fixed over the 1944–64 period.

Specifically, we form six groups of breweries: I, Anheuser-Busch, Miller, Pabst, Schlitz; II, Drewrys, Carling, Falstaff, Hamms; III, Coors, Jackson, Olympia, Pearl; IV, Schaefer, Ballantine, Liebmann, Ruppert; V, Schmidt, Stroh, National, Duquesne; VI, all others. The first five groups represent the major national premium brewers, the growing regional giants who now market their popular price brands throughout the country, the emerging West Coast and South Western giants, the major Northeastern producers, and the major Mideastern brewers, respectively. Using a technique suggested by Theil and Rey,[9] we estimate the transition probability matrix $P = [p_{ij}]$ where, for example, p_{23} represents the probability that a consumer of a group II beer in year t will be a group III consumer in year $t+1$. These probabilities are based upon percentages of sales for the 1944–64 period. They reflect *both* shifts in demand between groups and shifts in purchases that result when firms merge. Thus, $p^6{}_4$, say, may be influenced by consumers shifting from group VI to group IV brands as well as the merger of group VI with group IV firms.

Now, if p_t is a column vector of market shares in year t, then

[8] See J. G. Kemeny and J. L. Snell, *Finite Markov Chains* (Van Nostrand: Princeton, N.J., 1959).

[9] H. Theil and Guido Rey, 'A Quadratic Programming Approach to the Estimation of Transition Probabilities', *Management Science*, vol. 12, no. 9 (May 1966), pp. 714–21.

$P'p_t = p_{t+1}$, where the 'prime' indicates transpose. The Theil-Rey procedure applied here was to minimize the quadratic form $\sum_t (p_{t+1} - P'p_t)' \, I(p_{t+1} - P'p_t)$, where I is the identity matrix subject to the constraints $\sum_j p_{ij} = 1$, $p_{ij} \geqslant 0$. The unconstrained matrix, $\tilde{P}$, as well as P, is displayed in Table II. The unconstrained estimate of p_{23} would be .1448; the constrained estimate is .0842. The approach used here uses least squares to minimize the variance in the error terms, while successively applying constraints to assure that all the probability estimates will be non-negative. It is, therefore, of particular interest to note that the p_{16} and p_{56} estimates which are positive in $\tilde{P}$ are forced to zero in P.

The analysis is confined to these rather arbitrary although meaningful six groups in order to hold the complex computational burdens within practical bounds.[10] The possibility of a nonbeer drinker in year t being a group j drinker in year $t+1$ is neglected as is the possibility that a brand j drinker in year t will be a non-consumer in year $t+1$. The results must therefore be considered at best to be strongly suggestive of general trends and should not be interpreted literally nor considered conclusive.

The transition probability matrix calculated from the sales data is immediately seen to be of the canonical form.

$$P = \begin{bmatrix} C & O \\ R & Q \end{bmatrix}$$

where C is a 5×5 closed matrix, O is a 5×1 zero vector and R is a 1×5 transient probability vector, and Q is a 1×1 transient probability matrix. A matrix of this form may be interpreted as follows. Once a customer enters states $i = 1, \ldots, 5$, he *never again* enters state 6 since all $p_{i6} = 0 (i = 1, \ldots, 5)$. Still further, it is a well-known property of this type of matrix that $N = (I - Q)^{-1} = 23.2$ is the expected number of years before the average customer will be absorbed in one of the closed sets of C. The variance, however, is given by $\sigma_N{}^2 = N(2N_D - I) - N_{SQ}$, where N_D is a diagonal matrix with the diagonal elements of N, and N_{SQ} is a matrix with the elements of N squared. Here, $\sigma_N{}^2 = 514.8$. Thus, the standard deviation is 22.7. This would indicate that any precise predictions would be on most shaky ground.

The year-to-year group brand loyalty, as indicated by the fairly sizable diagonal elements, is quite interesting. It is also interesting to note that when group III buyers switch purchases between two

[10] We are grateful to Messrs. James C. Hershauer and William A. Ruch for invaluable programming assistance.

years they will switch to a premium, group I, brewer. Moreover, the fact that $p_{43} = p_{53} = p_{24} = p_{25} = p_{34} = 0$, and $p_{35} = .0017$ is most reassuring, since in the past these beers have in the main not been in *direct* competition, although their marketing areas are widening. This is further illuminated by considering the matrices μ and σ_μ of Table II. These give the mean first passage times and

TABLE II

THE MARKOV MATRICES

$\tilde{P}$	I	II	III	IV	V	VI
I	.5898	−.1556	.0600	.2779	−.0825	.3104
II	.5257	.7051	.1448	−.0108	−.2323	−.1325
III	.1229	.3186	.6718	−.3065	.4406	−.2474
IV	.6615	.5186	−.0290	.3785	.3033	−.8328
V	−.9839	.1888	−.1017	.3203	.9368	.6398
VI	.0049	−.0453	−.0011	.0439	−.0233	1.0207

P	I	II	III	IV	V	VI
I	.8242	.0107	.0281	.1244	.0127	0
II	.0339	.8819	.0842	0	0	0
III	.2630	0	.7353	0	.0017	0
IV	.2033	.0439	0	.6600	.0928	0
V	0	.1931	0	.0368	.7701	0
VI	.0066	0	0	.0365	0	.9569

μ	I	II	III	IV	V
I	2.4814	24.7971	28.3269	11.0951	37.7130
II	11.2174	4.2373	16.6011	22.3101	48.7027
III	3.8755	28.4641	8.4890	14.9497	41.2501
IV	8.5258	19.8217	28.2514	6.3776	31.7802
V	15.1477	7.5225	22.8167	23.0888	11.5741

σ_μ	I	II	III	IV	V
I	4.9873	20.9382	23.7898	12.8487	37.7493
II	8.6736	11.4558	19.7477	15.4959	38.7064
III	3.5467	21.1855	17.4770	13.3174	37.8868
IV	9.4065	20.0490	23.0876	11.7389	37.0978
V	9.6343	11.5048	21.1115	16.8280	26.8948

their standard deviations, respectively, based upon C. That is, the element $\mu_{23} = 16.6$ indicates that, given a consumer who is a group II beer drinker, it will be an average of 16.6 years before he switches to a group III beer. Again, the high standard deviation of 19.7 indicates the uncertainty surrounding the estimate. Note, however, that the shortest switching times tend to involve switching to a group I beer. The comparatively low estimates of $\mu_{31} = 3.9$ and $\sigma_{\mu 31} = 3.6$ are particularly noteworthy. The diagonal elements tend to be low reflecting brand loyalty, although the relatively high values for μ_{33} and μ_{55} are somewhat surprising.

It is also a well-known property of an ergotic regular submatrix such as C (one in which it is possible to get from one state to any other) that $C^m \to W$ as $m \to \infty$. Here, W is a matrix all of whose rows are given by $w = (w_1, w_2, w_3, w_4, w_5)$ where $wC = w$. The elements of w represent equilibrium probabilities. In the present context these represent the share of the market that will eventually accrue to the ith group. For the transition probability matrix of Table II, w is readily found to be the vector $w = (.4030, .2360, .1178, .1568, .0864)$. This suggests that the 4 major national brewers will ultimately claim about 40.3 per cent and the 4 widely marketed regionals 23.6 per cent of the market; while the Western, Northeastern and Mideastern firms will claim 11.8, 15.7 and 8.6 per cent, respectively. Their current (1966) shares are 34.9, 20.1, 9.2, 11.7 and 7.5 per cent, respectively. Based upon P and 1964 market shares, the 1966 *estimates* would be 30.6, 17.6 8.6, 13.8 and 7.2 per cent, respectively.

These results are, as previously emphasized, merely suggestive. They are strongly influenced by the selected groupings. Alternative groupings would undoubtedly lead to slightly altered statistics. In fact, the discrepancies between the actual and the estimated 1966 market shares is at least partially attributable to such developments as Schlitz's wide-scale promotion of a popular price brand, Old Milwaukee, and the conversion of Pabst from the premium price to the popular price category. In addition, the market shares would have been affected by Drewrys' merger with another growing regional, Associated, and Falstaff's acquisition of Narragansett in 1965. Thus, it is not necessarily true that the twenty firms in the first five groups will survive and the remainder will ultimately disappear. It is, however, interesting to note that the transition probability matrix results do suggest that there will be a sharp and continued decline in the number of firms in the industry; and, though the survivors might be different, there is the extremely strong suggestion that the national and regional brewers will, by the turn of the century, completely supplant the smaller local brewers.

Now, the transition probability matrix is estimated from data which includes the effects of mergers. We cannot, however, determine what the transition probability matrix would look like if mergers had *not* taken place. It would seem undoubtedly true that the disappearance of the smaller firms and the inferred continuance of their disappearance would be slowed. The fact that many group VI firms are technologically efficient would seem to imply that mergers result in the demise of some firms which have the technological capacity to survive. Internal Revenue Service figures on net profits or losses before taxes by size of assets for breweries filing returns, however, tends to support our view that many small firms would be unable to survive even if mergers were completely disallowed. Average net profits per firm as a percentage of the midpoint of the asset classes is substantially lower for firms with assets below the five million dollar asset mark. Between 1955 and 1961 firms with assets between one and five million dollars had an average rate of return of 2.6 per cent while firms with assets between five and ten million dollars earned an average of 9.4 per cent of assets. The corresponding figures for the ten to fifty million and fifty to one hundred million classes are 8.3 and 9.3 per cent, respectively.

The suggestion that many small firms may disappear is by no means novel. Indeed, portents of this have caused the majority of brewers great concern for the past several years. A central issue involved here is whether the possibility of the disappearance of so many firms is incompatible with our previous comments with respect to the degree of competition in the industry, or whether in fact it is precisely because of the keen competitive climate in the industry that so many firms have fallen, and will continue to fall, by the wayside. In our earlier study we indicated that a combination of economies of firm scale and fairly fixed industry demand imposed economic pressures on the smaller brewers that they simply could not, in general, withstand; nor could it be expected that the larger brewers would fail to take advantage of the situation. The issue that we now turn to is whether the larger firms in the industry have resorted to policies, in particular a policy of expansion by merger and acquisition, which would seem to be out of the purview of 'fair competition'.

THE EFFECTS OF MERGERS

In line with the previous discussion this section is particularly concerned with the effects mergers have had in determining the relative sales positions of the firms in groups I, II, III, IV and V. There is considerable difference in the number of mergers involving firms in these five groups. Between 1947 and 1964 the four firms in group I acquired a total of six brewers operating in the continental United States; the four firms in group III acquired only one; the four in group IV acquired four; the four in group V acquired five; while the four in group II were involved in seventeen mergers. Thus, it is the group II firms which have been most active in the merger game.

Each of the four firms in group II has acquired several rather lively competitors. Between 1948 and 1957 Falstaff acquired six firms with brewing capacities ranging from 120,000 to 1,200,000 barrels and averaging 512,000 barrels.[11] Shipments for these firms in the last year prior to merger, however, averaged only 202,000 barrels with a range from 70,000 to 360,000 barrels. Between 1951 and 1962 Drewrys acquired five other firms with an average capacity of 715,000 barrels and a range from 225,000 to 2,000,000 barrels. Shipments for these five companies in the year prior to acquisition ranged from 137,000 to 1,360,000 barrels and averaged 449,000 barrels. Between 1953 and 1960 Theo. Hamm acquired three companies, two of which had capacity of 500,000 barrels, and the other, 1,000,000 barrels. Shipments for the three acquired firms in the last year prior to acquisition averaged 254,000 barrels with a range from 56,000 to 616,000 barrels. Between 1954 and 1964 Carling acquired three firms with brewing capacities ranging from 250,000 to 2,000,000 barrels and averaging 967,000 barrels as compared to shipments which averaged 677,000 barrels and ranged from 147,000 to 1,483,000 barrels. It is interesting to note that each of the four firms in group II has acquired another firm with capacity of at least 1,000,000 barrels. Twelve of the thirteen other group II acquisitions have involved firms with capacities of 500,000 barrels or less.

Both Carling and Drewrys, in addition to each acquiring a firm with capacity of 2,000,000 barrels, have tended to acquire firms operating closer to capacity than the firms acquired by Falstaff and Hamm. The three firms acquired by Carling were operating at an average of 65 per cent of capacity at the time of acquisition and the five acquired by Drewrys at an average of 60 per cent. This compares to an average of 45 per cent and 30 per cent of capacity, respectively, for Falstaff's six acquisitions and Hamm's three acquisitions.

Since 1964 there have been three mergers involving firms in the groups under consideration. In addition to the acquisitions of Associated and Narragansett by Drewrys and Falstaff, respectively, two firms in group IV, Liebmann and Ruppert, merged. At the time of the merger of Drewrys and Associated, Drewrys was the larger of the two companies with shipments of 2,610,000 barrels a year compared to Associated's shipments of 1,485,000 barrels. Drewrys, therefore, should be considered the acquiring company despite the fact that it assumed Associated's name. It is interesting to note that Associated itself evolved from a long series of mergers. It was formed initially as the result of the 1962 merger of Pfeiffer and E. & B. Brewing Company. Pfeiffer, the larger of the two, had previously acquired two other brewers. In 1964, Associated also acquired Sterling with capacity of 750,000 barrels and sales of 660,000 barrels.

[11] Any capacity figures are necessarily going to be somewhat suspect. Those used here are taken from the *Brewing Industry Survey*.

To help put the effects of these mergers in perspective, we consider an approach suggested by Weiss.[12] In this approach, the acquired company's shipments as a percentage of total industry shipments at the time of merger is taken as a measure of the merger's effect on concentration ratios. In this paper, the market shares of the acquired firms in the year of merger is used as a measure of the effect of mergers on the 1964 market share of the firms in the various sales groups. If it is assumed 'that the acquired plant would survive and grow at the same rate as the industry does if left independent and that acquiring firms would build new capacity no faster or slower if prevented from merging than they do when merger occurs',[13] then the acquired firm's market share at the time of merger does measure the effect of the merger on concentration. For each firm in the five sales groups, the market share of each acquired firm at the time of the merger is totaled in order to obtain a measure of the increase in the firm's market share which is attributable to merger. The results are presented in Table III.

TABLE III

INCREASE IN MARKET SHARE ATTRIBUTABLE TO MERGER 1947–64

Group I		*Group II*		*Group III*		*Group IV*		*Group V*	
Pabst	2.2	Falstaff	4.6	Pearl	.4	Schaefer	.6	Schmidt	.6
Schlitz	1.0	Drewrys	2.6	Olympia	0.0	Liebmann	.5	National	.4
Anh.-Busch	.3	Carling	2.2	Coors	0.0	Ruppert	.2	Duquesne	.3
Miller	.2	Hamm	.9	Jackson	0.0	Ballantine	0.0	Stroh	.2
Total	3.7		10.3		.4		1.4		1.5
1964 Market Share	29.6		17.0		8.5		13.4		7.2
1947 Market Share	13.9		4.7		2.0		11.6		3.8

It is apparent from the figures in Table III that although the increase in market shares attributable to merger for groups IV and V is a significant part of their total increment between 1947 and 1964, this increase is comparatively minor. Only the group II firms have increased their market share as a result of acquisitions to any *significant* extent. This is further emphasized when the total increase figures are compared with the 1964 market shares of the five groups. For group I, this is at least partially due to the threat of Justice Department interventions or as in the case of Anheuser-Busch (and more recently Schlitz) to court orders prohibiting acquisition of

[12] Leonard W. Weiss, 'An Evaluation of Mergers in Six Industries', *The Review of Economics and Statistics*, vol. XLVII (May 1965), p. 172.

[13] Ibid., p. 173.

competitors. The group I total includes Blatz's market share of 1.5 per cent in 1958 and Burgermeister's market share of .8 per cent in 1961 prior to acquisition by Pabst and Schlitz, respectively. Recently, these acquisitions have been dissolved by court orders. The .3 per cent for Anheuser-Busch represents its acquisition of Regal in 1958 which was dissolved in 1961. With the exclusion of these now-dissolved mergers, the increase in market share for group I firms attributable to mergers is only 1.1 per cent.

A second approach for gauging the effect of mergers has been suggested by Stigler.[14] In this approach, the Herfindahl index—the sum of the squares of market shares—is the concentration measure. When firms with shares of p_1 and p_2 merge, the index rises by $2p_1p_2$. Summing all such increments provides a measure of the merger activity. Again, not only is the Herfindahl index for the brewing industry quite low—.0138 in 1947 and .0427 in 1964—but the increment attributable to merger is only .0108. To give these numbers some perspective, the brewing industry's index in 1947 was lower than the 1954 index for each of 150 industries for which Grossack[15] has provided data; further, only 35 industries had lower indexes, in 1954, than the brewing industry had in 1964.

Moreover, for the industry as a whole acquired firms typically are moderate size firms whose sales have been declining and whose prospects appear very dismal indeed. Thus, for the sixty-eight firms which were acquired by other firms between 1948 and 1964, average annual sales in the year prior to merger were 270,000 barrels. This figure is about 10 per cent *less* than the average of their annual sales during the four years prior to the mergers. Also indicative of their deteriorating positions, we note that sales in the last year prior to acquisition divided by average sales in the previous four years, average 86 per cent. Furthermore, only eighteen of the sixty-eight firms had final year sales which were at least as large as the previous four-year average. On the average, sales in the year prior to merger were only 58 per cent of sales in the firm's best year since 1947 and only 45 per cent of capacity. This is not the result of a phase-out in anticipation of the merger. During the four years prior to the last year of operation, the firms were operating at an average of only 53 per cent of capacity. In fact, the largest percentage of capacity utilized in any one year between 1947 and the year prior to acquisition averages 75 per cent for these sixty-eight firms.

[14] G. Stigler, 'The Economic Effect of the Antitrust Laws', *The Journal of Law and Economics*, vol. IX (October 1966), pp. 225–8.

[15] I. M. Grossack, 'Towards an Integration of Static and Dynamic Measures of Industry Concentration', *The Review of Economics and Statistics*, vol. XLVII, no. 3 (August 1965), pp. 305–7.

The relatively small size of the acquired firms is also attested to by the fact that their average market share at the time of acquisition was .3 per cent. Neither did the acquiring firms tend to be exceptionally large—their market share in the year prior to merger averaged less than 2 per cent with only six acquiring firms having a market share in excess of 5 per cent, the largest share being 8.4 per cent. The market share of the acquiring and acquired firms combined averages 2.2 per cent, the largest being 8.7 per cent.

The post-1947 sales history of the companies operating in 1947 is displayed in Table IV. This table indicates the number of firms active in 1947 by sales size class, the number which have since been acquired by other firms, the number which have disappeared, and the growth in sales between 1947 and 1964 for those still operating in 1964. The table shows that: (1) the vast number of disappearances, 75 per cent, were firms with sales of less than 100,000 barrels; (2) 50 per cent of the acquisitions consisted of firms with sales between 101,000 and 500,000 barrels; (3) some firms in all size classes have enjoyed high growth rates but the majority of the surviving firms in the two smallest size classes have been experiencing declining sales. The findings are not surprising in view of the fact that our earlier analysis indicates that the marginal producer in the brewing industry would brew approximately 100,000 barrels a year which suggests that 100,000 barrels a year is the minimum efficient size of a firm in the brewing industry.[16] Clearly, the decline in the number of firms in the brewing industry has been so pronounced because of the inability of inefficient firms to survive. This decline has also been contributed to by the trend towards merger of moderate size firms with deteriorating market positions, firms operating well below

TABLE IV

SALES HISTORY OF 1947 COMPANIES

1947 Sales group	Acquired	Disappeared	*Ratio of 1964 to 1947 sales for surviving companies* 0–.50	.51–1.00	1.01–1.50	1.51–2.00	2.01–2.50	2.51–3.00	3.01–more
0–100	17	151	17	16	12	3	1	2	4
101–200	12	30	4	8	5	2	1	0	2
201–500	22	13	2	2	8	1	1	0	4
501–1500	17	6	1	4	3	2	2	1	5
1501 or more	0	0	0	1	2	2	1	1	0
Total	68	200	24	31	30	10	6	4	15

[16] Op. cit., p. 145.

capacity, who in combination with other firms can, in fact, find competitive strength. It should be noted that we are not using the data in Table IV to determine minimum efficient scale via the 'survivor technique', nor do we feel that such a use is justified.[17] Rather, we are using our earlier results as a 'given' serving as a point of departure. Once these previous estimates are accepted (and they are, in fact, in complete accord with other independent estimates from industry sources) the inferences that we have drawn from the data appear to be warranted.

CONCLUSIONS

The results of the analysis of competition in brewing through the concept of entropy, and the analysis of trends in the industry through the transition probability matrix, reinforce our earlier suggestion that despite the continuing decline in the number of firms in the industry, relative competition among the survivors has not suffered severely. It is industry performance rather than bare concentration ratios that is important.[18]

This competition has been maintained in the face of a sizable number of industry mergers. With the exception of a few firms and a few mergers, the mergers that have taken place have had insignificant effects. A few mergers may have been detrimental to competition; but several others undoubtedly contributed to a more lively competitive atmosphere.

The shake-out in the brewing industry will continue. The merger movement will continue. If the courts will consider each merger on its individual economic merits and overcome the tendency towards concentration ratio myopia, we can preserve the historically strong competitive atmosphere that has been traditional in brewing.

INDIANA UNIVERSITY

[17] For a discussion of the survivor technique see G. Stigler, 'The Economies of Scale', *The Journal of Law and Economics*, vol. 1 (October 1958). We are in substantial agreement with W. G. Shepherd's critique of this method of analysis in 'What Does the Survivor Technique Show About Economies of Scale', *Southern Economic Journal*, vol. XXXIV, no. 1 (July 1967). It is interesting to note, however, that in his application of the technique, Weiss (Leonard W. Weiss, 'The Survival Technique and the Extent of Suboptimal Capacity', *Journal of Political Economy*, vol. LXXII, no. 3 (June 1964)) found that in 1954, 43.2 per cent of brewing industry shipments came from suboptimal plants. In this year, group VI firms accounted for 46.4 per cent of industry sales.

[18] For an interesting discussion see Albert J. Simone, 'Scientific Public Policy, Market Performance, and Size of Firm', *The Antitrust Bulletin*, vol. XII (spring 1967), pp. 99–108.

VERTICAL INTEGRATION AND THE MARKET FOR REPAIR PARTS IN THE UNITED STATES AUTOMOBILE INDUSTRY[1]

by ROBERT CRANDALL

THE current Clayton Act litigation involving Ford's purchase of certain assets from the Electric Autolite Company,[2] serves to emphasize a curious phenomenon. The largest producers of motor vehicles in the United States have continued to expand their production capabilities in 'upstream' components markets despite the competitive structure of these markets. During the period 1947–65, components firms realized average after-tax profits of 13.8 per cent on net worth,[3] compared with 13.2 per cent for all manufacturing.[4] During this same period, motor-vehicle procedurs were earning 20.2 per cent on net worth, and the Big Three producers were realizing over 25 per cent.[5] Why have the largest assemblers of vehicles continued to integrate backward when it would seem that they could procure their components requirements at prices approximating their own incremental cost of production?

I. VERTICAL STRUCTURE OF THE AUTOMOBILE INDUSTRY

The domestic motor-vehicle industry is composed of three major firms, one smaller firm and a few producers of specialty vehicles. This is a remarkable distillation of the 1500 firms which have attempted motor-vehicle assembly during the past seventy years.[6] The surviving Big Three—General Motors, Ford and Chrysler—are highly integrated into components manufacture, and all are more highly integrated than the assemblers which have failed. American Motors, the least integrated firm among current manufacturers,

[1] This study is taken from chapters 2 and 3 of the author's doctoral dissertation, 'Vertical Integration in the U.S. Automobile Industry' (Northwestern University, 1968). The dissertation was written while the author held a Johnson Research Fellowship at the Brookings Institution, Washington, D.C. Helpful suggestions and criticisms were received from M. A. Adelman, Charles H. Berry, M. L. Burstein and R. B. Heflebower.

[2] *United States v. Ford Motor Company and the Electric Autolite Company*, U.S. District Court, Eastern Division of Michigan, Civil Action no. 21911.

[3] First National City Bank of New York, *Monthly Letter*, April 1948–66. Actually, this probably represents an overstatement of the rate of return for components production since the largest producers have been diversifying rapidly into more lucrative markets.

[4] A student's t statistic was computed: $t = 23.8$ for 38 degrees of freedom. Thus, the difference was not significant at the 1 per cent level of confidence.

[5] First National City Bank, op. cit., and *Moody's Industrials*, 1948–66.

[6] See the testimony of George Romney before the United States Senate Subcommittee on Antitrust and Monopoly, *Hearings, Administered Prices*, part 6, 85th Congress, Second Session, 1958, p. 2862.

teeters perilously close to extinction. These observations suggest that integration is a requirement for success in the production of motor vehicles. Often heard is the assertion that General Motors, the most integrated producer, could easily initiate price reductions which would leave it as the sole assembler of vehicles since it is the lowest-cost producer, but we shall argue that its greater integration might lead to similar results even if its costs were identical to those of its rivals. Before so doing, however, it is necessary to examine the vertical structure of the industry more closely.

The measurement of a firm's vertical integration is not easily accomplished. Since integration is a preemption of the price mechanism, it is intuitively appealing to attempt to utilize a measure of value added relative to the value of final output toward which the firm's activity is directed. If the automobile industry were merely a vertical arrangement of firms transforming original factors into final consumer products independently of other sectors, one could simply sum payments to factors by assemblers and express them as a ratio of the value of the final vehicles sold to consumers. Given the inter-relationship among sectors of the economy, this computation is impossible. Motor-vehicle companies produce outputs for other markets. Their suppliers also serve other sectors, and the division of their activities and factor payments cannot be accomplished. As a substitute, several economists have suggested a ratio of value added to sales (*VA/S*),[7] a measure which will be utilized below.

The *VA/S* measure is liable to considerable distortion since it is not invariant to the forwardmost stage of production occupied by the firm. In addition, it is affected by changes in relative prices due to variations in market power at various stages or to technological change. The former criticism need not be of great concern in estimating integration of vehicle assemblers since all have been integrated into distribution of repair parts, the wholesaling of vehicles and, to a minor extent, the retailing of vehicles. There have been no major changes in this pattern in the past twenty years.

The problem caused by technological change are more severe, however. The complexity of motor vehicles has increased, and the value added required, say, to build a transmission is far greater than that required in past decades. Thus, a measure of *VA/S* may show an increase where the assembler has undertaken no new components manufacture. On the other hand, if similar changes occur

[7] This measure is utilized by M. A. Adelman in 'Concept and Statistical Measurement of Vertical Integration', *Business Concentration and Price Policy*, National Bureau of Economic Research, Princeton: Princeton University Press, 1955, pp. 281–330. It is also used by Michael Gort in *Diversification and Integration in American Industry*, Princeton: Princeton University Press, 1962, pp. 79–91.

in raw materials markets, there may be no change in *VA/S*. The use of the *VA/S* statistic for intertemporal comparisons must be considered as tentative, and we shall support any inferences drawn from these data with additional observations culled from the trade literature.

In Table I, we present estimates of *VA/S* for the major automobile manufacturers since World War II. Value added is simply the difference between annual sales and annual purchases, and sales are measured in current dollars. Ford and Chrysler data exclude purchases of special tools and dies which results in a maximum overstatement of *VA/S* of .02 to .03 in various years. Since there are no data for Ford's or Chrysler's purchases of these special tools, it is impossible to make the necessary correction. Instead, we resort to a summation of factor payments (*VA′*) over total sales (*S*) for the Big Three. These estimates appear in Table II, *VA′/S* measuring payments to labor, net income before taxes, interest and depreciation divided by net sales. The only defects in the data arise from the exclusion of supplementary employee compensation for Ford from 1946 through 1954 and for G.M. from 1946 through 1948—an exclusion which results in an understatement of value added of .02 to .03 for each year. While it might be argued that value added should exclude depreciation, the omission of depreciation in the numerator does not alter cross-sectional or intertemporal comparisons.

The evidence contained in both tables demonstrates that General Motors is and has always been the most integrated assembler. Ford and Chrysler follow in that order, and the minor firms have been less integrated. The relatively high figure for Nash from 1947 through 1953 is probably a reflection of the fairly large contribution of the Kelvinator Division to total value added. Such a problem does not arise for the Big Three since over 90 per cent of their output is for the motor-vehicle and parts industry.[8]

Interpretation of the trends displayed requires greater caution. The data for 1946 and 1947 reflect artificially low output which resulted from reconversion problems and labor boycotts. Since firms had to meet high fixed costs, this would result in larger *VA/S* for those years. There is a continual increase in the ratios for the Big Three from 1948 through 1962, allowing a tentative conclusion that firms had been increasing their self-sufficiency in inputs to the assembly process. The slight decline in 1962–65 is undoubtedly a

[8] See the registration statements (Form S–1) filed by each of the Big Three with the Securities and Exchange Commission. For the years 1959–64, the share of total sales represented by shipments of motor-vehicle products was .89 for General Motors, .92 for Ford, and .93 for Chrysler.

reflection of record levels of output which have forced assemblers to increase their dependence upon suppliers in the short run. Whether there will be further investment upstream by assemblers in order to restore the self-sufficiency of the early 1960s cannot be foretold at this time.

Another inference which might be drawn from Tables I and II is that Ford and Chrysler have increased their degree of integration at a more rapid rate than General Motors, but despite these efforts they continue to rely upon suppliers to a greater extent than G.M.

TABLE I

RATIO OF VALUE ADDED TO SALES (VA/S)—DOMESTIC ASSEMBLERS

Year	*General Motors*	*Ford*	*Chrysler*	*American Motors*	*Studebaker*	*Packard*
1946	N.A.	N.A.	N.A.	N.A.	.310	N.A.
1947	N.A.	N.A.	.338	.468	.312	.227
1948	N.A.	N.A.	.347	.475	.328	.284
1949	.495	N.A.	.359	.393	.336	.254
1950	.530	N.A.	.367	.384	.340	.249
1951	.502	N.A.	.327	.364	N.A.	.298
1952	.511	N.A.	.387	.366	.265	N.A.
1953	.469	N.A.	.340	.347	.268	.271
1954	.485	N.A.	.372	N.A.	N.A.	
1955	.512	.440	.397	N.A.	N.A.	
1956	.499	.423	.369	N.A.	N.A.	
1957	.494	.402	.401	N.A.	N.A.	
1958	.483	.393	N.A.	N.A.	N.A.	
1959	.510	.464	.377	N.A.	N.A.	
1960	.504	.453	.387	N.A.	N.A.	
1961	.520	.444	.398	N.A.	N.A.	
1962	.542	.445	.422	.328	N.A.	
1963	.544	.438	.420	.326	N.A.	
1964	.547	.434	.425	.305		
1965	.541	.434	.421	N.A.		

N.A. = Not Available.
Source: Annual Reports of assemblers.

Supporting evidence for Ford's and Chrysler's backward integration is not difficult to find. Despite Henry Ford's preoccupation with integration at River Rouge, Ford found itself greatly dependent upon its suppliers in 1948, according to Nevins,[9] and immediately launched upon a program of acquisitions and construction. New plants were constructed to produce axles and forgings in Dearborn and Canton, and a new transmission facility was constructed in Cincinnati. In 1949, Ford acquired the Kelsey-Hayes wheel plant at Monroe, Michigan, and constructed a pressed-steel plant in Buffalo, New York. A new engine plant and a foundry were scheduled for construction in Cleveland in the same year. At the same

[9] Allan Nevins (in collaboration with Frank Hill), *Ford: Decline and Rebirth*, New York: Charles Scribner's Sons, 1963, p. 340 ff.

time, the glass, steel, and blast furnace facilities were refurbished and expanded.[10] Since this period, Ford has purchased Auto-Lite's battery plant, spark-plug facility, and trade mark and the Philco Corporation, which manufactures automobile radios and tape decks among other appliances.

TABLE II

VA'/S FOR THE BIG THREE ASSEMBLERS

Year	*G.M.*	VA'_d/S *Ford*	*Chrysler*
1946	.474*	.394*	N.A.
1947	.470*	.370*	.288
1948	.465*	.352*	.287
1949	.481	.358*	N.A.
1950	.515	.384*	.306
1951	.484	.379*	.254
1952	.500	.401*	.301
1953	.459	.373*	.249
1954	.474	.382*	.340
1955	.500	.413	.353
1956	.487	.388	.338
1957	.479	.367	.355
1958	.464	.348	.333
1959	.492	.437	.333
1960	.486	.471	.319
1961	.499	.410	.340
1962	.527	.416	.379
1963	.522	.409	.380
1964	.525	.399	.386
1965	.522	.404	.373

* Excludes supplementary employee compensation.
N.A. = all data not available.
Sources: Annual Reports of assemblers.
Forms 10K—Securities and Exchange Commission.

For Chrysler, the evidence is quite similar. In 1965, the Company stated that:

> The Corporation over the last *fifteen* years has been engaged in expanding, modernizing, replacing, and *integrating* its facilities and operations. This has involved, among other things, the acquisition and expansion of facilities for making automotive stampings, castings, gears and axles, the consolidation and expansion of engine and transmission building operations . . ., and the construction and installation of facilities to permit unitized body construction and the manufacture of substantially all of the Corporation's requirements of alternators, voltage regulators, distributors and starting motors, and for the fabrica-

[10] Allan Nevins, loc. cit.

tion of about three-fourths of its total requirements of windshields, side and back glass[11] [emphasis supplied].

The most important single step in this integration process was the purchase of Briggs in 1953, making the firm nearly self-sufficient in body stampings and assemblies.

This trend toward vertical integration can also be discerned in the published records of automotive suppliers who have remarked upon their loss of original-equipment components markets to the assemblers' own operations. During this period, none of the assemblers has attempted additional production of primary metals or glass. Ford's self-sufficiency in steel, for example, is no greater than 50 per cent of its requirements, while the Company has begun to produce such items as spark plugs, batteries, bumpers and trim sets which it purchased from outside suppliers before the elder Harry Ford's death.[12]

In summary, there is very strong evidence that present assemblers of motor vehicles are more integrated than they were two decades ago. Since none have ventured into retailing of motor vehicles or parts to any appreciable extent, this increase must be focused upstream.

II. VERTICAL INTEGRATION IN ECONOMIC THEORY

Only a brief survey of the literature on vertical integration can be presented in this paper.[13] Vertical integration may be defined as a preemption of the price mechanism caused by a firm performing two or more successive functions which could be performed by independent entities. The traditional 'theory' of integration is rooted in the literature of technological joint economies and of imperfect markets. Firms seek to obtain the benefits of rolling steel while it is still hot from the refining process, to treat metals with finishes before they are corroded by exposure to oxygen, or to utilize slack inputs in adjacent production processes.[14] On the other hand, integration may be a means to obviate the inefficiency of bilateral monopoly,[15]

[11] Chrysler Corporation, *Annual Report*, 1965.

[12] Securities and Exchange Commission, Form S–1, Ford Motor Company, Nov. 1963.

[13] The reader is referred to Fritz Machlup and Martha Taber, 'Bilateral Monopoly, Successive Monopoly, and Vertical Integration', *Economica*, May 1960, pp. 118–19 for an excellent bibliography.

[14] W. A. Paton and Robert Dixon testified before the United States Senate Committee on Antitrust and Monopoly, *Hearings*, *Economic Concentration*, 89th Congress, 1st Session, 1965, pp. 1668 ff., that motor-vehicle firms produce their own dies in order to fully utilize their die repairmen who often would stand idle awaiting malfunctions in stamping operations otherwise.

[15] See William Fellner, 'Prices and Wages under Bilateral Monopoly', *Quarterly Journal of Economics*, August 1947, pp. 503–9 for a rigorous analysis of this problem.

to prevent substitution against a firm's monopolized output in subsequent production,[16] or to extract consumers' surplus through price discrimination.[17] Finally, integration as an industry practice may serve to heighten entry barriers and consolidate monopoly power.

Of the above hypotheses to explain vertical market structure, we immediately reject the notion of obviating substitution in downstream production functions as irrelevant to the problem of backward integration by assemblers of motor vehicles. The bilateral-monopoly argument deserves closer consideration, however.

Given the indeterminancy of equilibrium in markets characterized by bilateral-monopoly power, integration may allow more efficient allocation of resources. In the absence of enforceable price-quantity agreements, there is a distinct possibility that output will settle at a level which is less than that at which the value of the marginal product of the upstream output is equal to the incremental cost of producing that output. Machlup and Taber have demonstrated that bilateral oligopoly is more likely to yield nonoptimal solutions than bilateral monopoly.[18] While negotiations between bilateral monopolists will usually include price *and* quantity, oligopolists are not able to specify *industry* quantities in their bargaining with adjacent oligopolists unless there is complete coordination among the firms. Since such coordination will be difficult to effect in many cases and probably illegal in nearly all cases, it is to be expected that a greater loss of efficiency will occur under bilateral oligopoly than under bilateral monopoly.

Crucial to the determination of market structure is the relationship between economies of large scale in production and market size. If minimum efficient scale in components markets were increasing at a rate greater than the market size, it might be expected that bilateral oligopoly would become more prevalent over time.[19] Studies by Leonward Weiss[20] and the present author[21] provide mild evidence that the minimum efficient scale in motor-vehicle production processes has no more than doubled since 1947 while total output of vehicles has trebled. Thus, it seems likely that the

[16] Meyer L. Burstein, 'A Theory of Full-Line Forcing', *Northwestern University Law Review*, 1960, pp. 62–95.

[17] Ibid.

[18] Fritz Machlup and Martha Taber, op. cit.

[19] See George Stigler, 'The Division of Labor is Limited by the Extent of the Market', *Journal of Political Economy*, June 1951, pp. 185–93 for a detailed examination of the relationship between scale economies and integration.

[20] Leonard Weiss, 'The Survival Technique and the Extent of Suboptimal Capacity', *Journal of Political Economy*, June 1964, pp. 246–61.

[21] Robert W. Crandall, *Vertical Integration in the U.S. Automobile Industry*, unpublished Ph.D. dissertation, Northwestern University, 1968.

problems of bilateral oligopoly have lessened rather than increased and that the recent trend in integration by assemblers cannot be explained on this basis.

The notion that assemblers have sought greater self-sufficiency in components due to technological joint economies in the production of various outputs may also be dismissed after examination of the distribution of production facilities in the industry. Assemblers typically maintain separate establishments for assembly, stamping, casting, transmission assembly and myriad other activities. The great variety in the activities undertaken in separate facilities of the Big Three assemblers leads one to the impression that joint economies in production are of minor importance.[22]

Some writers have seen vertical integration as a means to ensure more efficient interequilibrium adjustment.[23] A firm may even seek to expand into a competitive adjacent market if the absence of a futures market impedes adjustments of fixed plant and equipment to their equilibrium values. Thus, it may be that assemblers have sought improved coordination of markets through integration, but the economist trained in price theory may ask why these firms have not simply entered into long-term contracts with suppliers if certainty of future supply were desired. The answer may rest in the continual qualitative changes in components design, but then why is not style change limited to superficial changes in body parts and improvements of a few components while basic parts such as frame members, drive shafts, springs, shock absorbers and mufflers are produced to standardized patterns? The model provided in section III of this paper may serve to answer these questions.

We are left with two theoretical constructs: price discrimination and forestalling entry. These constructs are intimately related in the automobile industry as the remainder of this paper demonstrates.

III. INTEGRATION AND PRICE DISCRIMINATION

We begin with the assumption that each of the Big Three assemblers has considerable market power and, hence, faces a downward-sloping demand curve for new automobiles. It is in each firm's interest to construct a discriminatory pricing scheme in which each consumer pays his maximum reservation price for each automobile he purchases. Arbitrage makes such an aspiration impossible, of

[22] See John Menge, *Internal Transfer Pricing and Vertical Integration in the Automobile Industry*, unpublished Ph.D. dissertation, M.I.T., 1959, pp. 343–8.

[23] Tibor Scitovsky, 'Two Concepts of External Economies', *Journal of Political Economy*, April 1954, pp. 143–51; J. N. Wolfe, 'Coordination Assumptions and Equilibria', *Quarterly Journal of Economics*, May 1961, pp. 262–77.

course, but if this reservation price is a direct function of intensity in use why not develop a rental system in which consumers pay identical *rates per mile* but different *total* payments for utilizing a vehicle? Problems of coordination, the difficulty in inducing consumers to properly maintain rented vehicles, the huge capital costs of owning such a fleet and the added vulnerability to antitrust litigation militate against such a scheme. If a rental system is not possible, the assembler might find a suitable alternative in tying the consumer to a complementary product whose consumption varies directly with intensity of use of the vehicle. For example, the vehicle assembler may produce an automobile which requires a special variety of fuel which can only be obtained from the assembler's outlets. If all assemblers developed such a device, the consumer would be unable to avoid the implicit tying arrangement. Does the possibility of formally or informally tying a complement to the use of a vehicle exist? We shall argue that it does although its efficacy may be evaporating with time.

Every motor vehicle requires maintenance in order to function properly. Lubrication must be applied periodically, ignition parts must be changed and various other components wear out. If all components had equal longevity under any set of environmental conditions, maintenance might not be a common phenomenon as vehicles would operate for a certain number of miles and be relegated to scrap. But components have unequal durability, and maintenance is an important part of vehicle operation, requiring a large share of the vehicle consumer's total expenditure on transportation.[24] Since much of this maintenance is directly related to the mileage amassed by the vehicle, the provision of maintenance is an ideal method by which assemblers may meter the demand for vehicles if we accept the premise that the consumer's demand for automobiles is related to intensity of use.

Automobile producers could sell their vehicles under an arrangement which ties the consumer to their local service facility and thus extract part of the consumers' surplus by charging prices for servicing which are considerably above marginal cost. It turns out that not even this is necessary, however, for all that is required is for assemblers to sell the replacement parts required in repair to service outlets—dealerships, garages and gasoline stations—at prices above marginal cost.

In fact, all assemblers sell large quantities repair parts to their

[24] According to O.B.E. estimates, consumer expenditures on 'Repairs, Greasing, Washing, Parking, and Rental' were $5.5 billion in 1963 while consumer expenditures on automobiles totalled $20.7 billion.

own dealerships and other repair outlets, and this practice has persisted throughout the history of the industry. In earlier years, assemblers even provided a great deal of the actual servicing due to a fear that the absence of mechanics trained in repairing *their* automobiles would detract from their goodwill. As repair markets have broadened and the number of assemblers has contracted, servicing has been left more to the assemblers' franchised dealers and to other repair establishments. Yet, during this period assemblers have not reduced their share of parts sales. If these sales are made at prices considerably in excess of incremental cost, it may be argued that assemblers have developed and maintained a method of 'metering' the demand for vehicles.

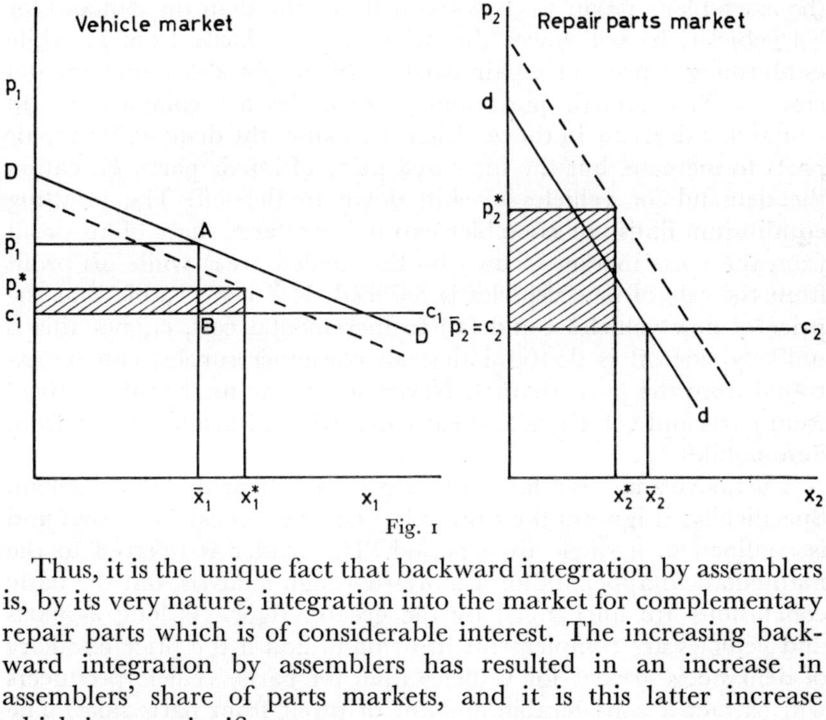

Fig. 1

Thus, it is the unique fact that backward integration by assemblers is, by its very nature, integration into the market for complementary repair parts which is of considerable interest. The increasing backward integration by assemblers has resulted in an increase in assemblers' share of parts markets, and it is this latter increase which is most significant.

The efficacy of metering vehicle demand through the sale of repair parts can be demonstrated with the aid of Figure 1. A representative assembler is assumed to produce new vehicles, x_1, and repair parts, x_2.[25] The demand for the assembler's vehicles, assuming a price of repair parts equal to $\bar{p}_2$, is given by DD; and the demand for the

[25] Of course, there exists a myriad of repair parts for each vehicle model. This fact need not trouble us, however, since we can view x_2 as a vector of repair parts for the assembler's vehicle.

assembler's repair parts, given that new vehicles are priced at $\bar{p}_1$, is depicted by *dd*. Per-unit costs of producing each output are assumed to be constant and equal to c_1 and $c_2(=\bar{p}_2)$, respectively, since the particular form of the cost functions does not influence the argument.

If the assembler were only a producer of new vehicles and repair-parts markets were competitive, the assembler would sell vehicles at a price of $c_1 + x_1/a_{11}$ where a_{11} equals $-dx/dp_1$. This 'simple monopoly' price is represented by $\bar{p}_1$ in Figure 1, and the monopoly rent accruing to the assembler is the area $c_1\bar{p}_1AB$.

Now assume that the assembler is able to establish market power in the distribution of repair parts for his vehicles. If the demand for the assembler's repair parts is less price elastic than the demand for his vehicles, he will lower the price of the vehicles from $\bar{p}_1$ while establishing a price of repair parts considerably above incremental cost, c_2. Since repair parts and automobiles are complements in demand, a decrease in the vehicle price causes the demand for repair parts to increase, but the increased price of repair parts, p_2^*, causes the demand for vehicles to shift down to the left. The resulting equilibrium finds the assembler extracting a large share of his profit from the parts market (shown by the shaded area) while his profit from the sale of new vehicles is reduced. It is conceivable that the price of new vehicles could fall to incremental cost, c_1, but this is unlikely since it is doubtful that all consumer surplus can be extrated from the parts market. Nevertheless, the total profit derived from parts and vehicle sales greatly exceeds that available only from automobiles.

The above analysis is far from a rigorous statement of the problem. Specifically, it ignores the distinction between stocks and flows and is confined to a single time period. The reader is referred to the mathematical appendix for a more thorough analysis, but the basic conclusions are unchanged by the greater rigor. As long as parts and vehicles are complements in demand and if the price elasticity of demand is greater for vehicles than for parts, vehicle producers will extract a considerable amount of profit from parts sales. The price of vehicles will be lower than that which would obtain if the repair-parts market were competitive. Finally, the higher the ratio of parts sales to vehicle sales, the lower will be the ratio of the price of parts to the price of vehicles, and the greater will be the share of assemblers' profit accruing from parts sales.

The major requirement of our model is that assemblers be able to increase the price of repair parts without inducing substitution of independently produced and distributed parts for their own by consumers or repair mechanics. Since entry barriers would seem to be lower for parts production than vehicle production, how can assemblers hope to extract such rents from parts markets? The answer to this question turns on a myriad of assembler practices, the most important of which are (a) differentiation of franchised dealers' repair services, (b) ownership of special tools, dies, jigs and fixtures utilized in producing components for assembly, (c) frequent variation of components, and (d) vertical integration.

(a) Since the earliest years of the motor-vehicle industry, assemblers have sought to provide service for their makes of vehicles through franchised dealerships, actively promoting their dealers' 'factory authorized service' despite pressures toward substitution. Elsewhere, this author has shown that prices of repair parts sold by assemblers to dealers are higher than prices obtainable through independent channels; that the price of repair in dealers' garages is significantly higher than the price in independent garages and service stations; and that dealers purchase a very large percentage of parts from assemblers (over 80 per cent) while independent garages purchase no more than 40 per cent of their requirements from assembler channels.[26] The reason for this combination of phenomena is not difficult to explain—the dealer must purchase his parts from the assembler or face retribution since the dealer depends upon the assembler for timely delivery of vehicles and certain parts, for warrantee adjustments, and myriad other services. Moreover, the requirement that warrantee work be performed with 'genuine factory parts' forces the dealer to duplicate inventories if he wishes to stock the rival part. This aspect of assembler power in parts markets is diminishing in importance, however, as dealers are losing their share of repair markets.[27] Apparently consumers are reacting to price differentials as alternative outlets become more readily available with the growth of the market. Nevertheless, this source of control of the parts market cannot be ignored, for dealers still vend at least 30 per cent of all repair parts.

(b) Assemblers have always insisted upon ownership of all special tooling utilized by suppliers in fabricating parts for the vehicle companies. Even if the supplier manufactures the tooling himself, it immediately becomes the property of the assembler. This practice has been justified on grounds of flexibility since the assembler can conceivably move these tools from one establishment to another if the supplier's production is interrupted by, say, a strike. But perhaps

[26] Robert Crandall, op. cit., ch. 6.

[27] Ibid. This author has found that dealers' share of total vehicle repair has declined by 25 to 30 per cent in the past fifteen years.

more important is the effect of the ownership of these tools upon entry into parts production for each supplier must contemplate complete retooling in order to produce for replacement markets. Since assemblers require large volumes of each component for original assembly, they are able to amortize these tools over many units of output. Independent firms seeking to enter the repair market must amortize these expenses over a smaller volume of output, and this initial tooling requirement may serve as a potent entry barrier indeed. Due to limited possibilities for substituting less durable tooling as the anticipated volume of components is reduced and because assemblers alter component design so frequently, the disadvantage faced by an independent producer of repair parts is extreme. Where tooling expenses are the greatest—in automotive stampings—assemblers have a virtual monopoly in repair-parts distribution. If their suppliers were able to use the special tools and dies utilized in stamping units for original equipment in further production of parts for repair, this monopoly would erode rapidly.[28]

(c) Automobile companies have practiced frequent qualitative product changes in order to differentiate their outputs from rivals, but this practice has extended to even the most minute components. There is strong evidence that the large assemblers have always opposed standardization of basic automobile parts despite the obvious advantages of standardization in improving the performance of upstream markets and permitting greater flexibility in the short run. Thompson[29] noted that the Society of Automotive Engineers failed in its attempts to provide standardization for the industry due to the large companies' refusal to agree to such homogeneity except for thread sizes and other minor matters. As a result, a majority of components are unique to that make to which they attach. Potential rivals in replacement-parts markets must face the task of investing in special tooling to accommodate this multitude of products and

[28] The testimony of Mr. Dodge of the Dana Corporation, a large parts supplier, before the Senate Antitrust Subcommittee (*Hearings, A Study of the Antitrust Laws*, 84th Congress, 1st Session, 1956, pp. 2974–5) is illustrative. The questioning by Mr. McHugh of the Subcommittee staff resulted in the following dialogue:

Mr. McHugh: 'Why would you not sell to these warehouse distributors in the replacement market items which have been particularly tailored for the General Motors car?'

Mr. Dodge: 'We would if General Motors had not paid for the tooling.'

Mr. McHugh: 'Would you explain what you mean by that?'

Mr. Dodge: 'There are certain articles that you manufacture which are peculiar for a vehicle whereby the customer pays (sic.) for the tooling required to produce those parts, and when in that case we will retain and only sell those particular items to that customer'... Therefore, that particular part we would not make over. If we wanted to make some other tools and make that part we could, but *we could not afford it.*' [emphasis supplied].

[29] George V. Thompson, 'Standardization in the Automobile Industry', *Journal of Economic History*, winter 1954, pp. 11–12.

must calculate the potential volume over which this tooling may be amortized. Thus, by restricting the size of the market for each component, assemblers can force independent suppliers to incur even larger tooling costs per unit output and further restrict entry.

(d) Where the ownership of special tooling is not important, integration by assemblers may serve to impede entry into parts production. The requirement that an expensive special tool or die be amortized over a large *volume*[30] of output may forestall entry into repair-parts production when the assembler owns the special tooling even if the economies of large *scale*, measured in terms of flow-rate of output, are not important. However, where dies are inexpensive, but there are considerable economies of large-scale output, backward integration may serve to discourage independent producers from attempting to serve repair-parts markets. An excellent example of this phenomenon is to be found in small body-trim items, which, despite the relatively small die expense, are typically produced only by assemblers. If independent producers are unable to realize the economies of large scale without original-equipment contracts, backward integration by assemblers is a convenient method of eliminating competition in repair-parts markets as well. When Monroe lost its original-equipment contracts for spark plugs, it abandoned producing them for replacement, and Eltra Corporation has found replacement-market distribution of spark plugs difficult after losing Chrysler's original-equipment contract.[31] In short, it can be argued that integration by the Big Three into parts production has served to forestall competition in repair-parts markets. For many components, the vehicle repairman finds few alternative sources of supply. For a full 25 per cent (in value terms) of all components, he faces *no* alternative.[32] As long as original-equipment contracts are the *sine qua non* for repair-parts production, integration by assemblers reduces competition in certain parts markets and erects barriers to future competition.

Our model is complete: assemblers may exploit the consumers' surplus which attaches to the sale of new automobiles through integration into parts supply and the consequent extension of market power in parts markets. It is precisely because the original component and the repair part are identical that *backward* integration results in market power in repair-parts markets. We can expect this mechanism to be successful as long as special tooling is expensive

[30] *Volume* is defined as $\int_0^t x(t)dt$ where $x(t)$ is the *rate* of output.

[31] Lincoln Freeman, 'The $7 Billion Aftermarket Gets an Overhaul', *Fortune*, March 1962, p. 228.

[32] Ward's *Automotive Yearbook*, 1966, p. 13.

and long lived, until repair markets and become so large that entrants scamper over the artificial entry barriers, and until the artificial distinction between 'genuine factory parts' in dealers' repair garages and other parts at independent garages is completely ignored by consumers.

IV. EMPIRICAL SUPPORT FOR THE MODEL

As there are no satisfactory time-series data for estimating the price-elasticity of demand for repair, it is fruitless to test the assumptions of our model: namely, that the own-price effect for repair parts is much lower than for new vehicles and that the cross effect is quite large.[33] It is even quite difficult to estimate the relative scale of replacement-parts sales to new vehicle sales for each assembler.

We propose to test the implications of the model: that a large share of profits of assemblers comes from repair-parts sales and that, despite the apparently competitive conditions in components markets, the price of repair parts is considerably above assembler's incremental cost of production. Such a test is more easily effected if one is willing to settle for limited postwar data and more complete pre-World War II data.

The 1939 Federal Trade Commission *Report on Motor Vehicles*[34] presented considerably detailed income statements for the largest assemblers. Unfortunately, General Motors' total parts sales to repair markets were not estimated due to the Company's organization into both parts and vehicle divisions. Using the A.M.A. data for total assembler parts sales[35] for the years 1929, 1932 and 1934–37, and subtracting the F.T.C. data for other assembler's parts sales, we were able to arrive at estimates of G.M.'s annual parts sales for the period. These appear in Table III along with other assemblers' parts sales for the period. The profit datum for G.M. was estimated by assuming that non-repair parts sales were mere intracorporate transfers at a shadow profit margin of 6 per cent.[36] As a result, the 35 per cent profit margin for repair-parts sales may be biased

[33] Estimation of the own-price elasticity of demand for new vehicles and parts would be helpful but not conclusive since we require these data for each motor-vehicle producer. Houthakker and Taylor (*Consumer Demand in the United States, 1929–1970, Analyses and Projections*, Cambridge: Harvard University Press, 1966, p. 115) have estimated the price coefficient for the demand for 'repairs, washing, greasing, parking, storage, and rentals', but the O.B.E. data which they utilize are constructed from two of the independent variables in their regressions—price and vehicle stocks—rendering these estimates of dubious validity.

[34] U.S. Federal Trade Commission, *Report on Motor Vehicles*, 1939, chs. XII–XV.

[35] Automobile Manufacturers' Association, *Automobile Facts and Figures*, annual issues.

[36] John Menge, op. cit., p. 65, states that a 6 per cent margin is typical for internal transfer pricing at G.M. although there is considerable variance about this average.

upward since parts sales to other assemblers are ignored, but the magnitude of this upward bias is probably small, given that sales by the vehicle divisions realized 24.85 per cent margins in addition to the intracorporate transfer margin of at least 6 per cent. While the average profit margin for parts sales may not have been five times that for the sale of G.M. motor vehicles, it was at least four times that margin.

For every firm but Packard, the profit margins in parts sales were very large compared to that for motor vehicles. In order to translate these data into rates of return upon capital, it is necessary to have some measure of the sales/capital ratios, and the *pro forma* balance-sheet divisions performed by the F.C.C. analysts result in sales/capital ratios of 2.35/1 for G.M. in both parts production and vehicle assembly.[37] The inclusion of some parts manufacture in the

TABLE III

AVERAGE ANNUAL DATA FOR ASSEMBLERS, 1929–37

Firm	*Vehicle sales* ($000)	*Parts sales* ($000)	*Net profit on vehicles* ($000)	%	*Net profit on parts* ($000)	%
G.M.[a]	881,166	(167,619)	63,286	7.18	(58,718)	(35.0)
Ford[b]	462,372	64,817	−1,674	−0.36	7,826	12.07
Chrysler	335,960	13,857	22,219	6.60	2,406	17.36
Hudson[c]	86,015	3,387	1,841	2.14	862	25.45
Nash[d]	32,408	1,610	2,145	6.62	295	18.32
Packard	48,434	3,662	3,259	6.73	215	5.87
Studebaker[c]	74,702	1,450	2,824	3.78	430	29.73

[a] General Motors data for the years 1929, 1932, 1934–37 only. Parts data estimated ( ).
[b] Ford data exclude foreign sales.
[c] Studebaker and Hudson data are for 1927–37, inclusive.
[d] Nash data are for domestic sales only.

vehicle divisions leads to a bias in this result, however, and it is likely that vehicle assembly and unit subassembly as well as distribution facilities accounted for capital investment of about one-third of average sales while parts production may have encountered a sales to capital ratio of closer to 2/1. It would be impossible to improve upon the accuracy of these ratios without further evidence, and even then the distinction between capital required for producing vehicles and that invested to produce for repair markets would be difficult to distinguish. If we take the sales/capital ratios as 3/1 and 2/1 for vehicles and parts, respectively, rates of return on capital become 70 per cent for parts production and 14.36 per cent for vehicle sales. Since the other firms are considerably less integrated, their sales/

[37] These capital data are total assets valued at historical cost and therefore represent an understatement of the current value of capital.

capital ratios in parts production will be lower, and the differences in profit margins shown in Table III for each firm's two activities will perhaps understate the differences in rates of return on capital. Of course, it is not contended that Ford produced vehicles at a loss throughout the Company's prewar history. It was a period of severe disequilibrium for Ford due to the changing over from a long run of Model Ts.

One should not view the data in Table III as a result of the particular period chosen, for even in years of high new automobile demand, the results were very similar. During 1937, for example, the vehicle divisions of General Motors earned but 6.39 per cent on vehicle sales while realizing nearly 36 per cent on parts sales. Moreover, earlier data for Ford reveal that in 1917, a year of high Model-T demand, repair parts sales resulted in over 26 per cent of the firm's total profit. In fact, Ford's margin on repair parts, 26.1 per cent, was greater in this era than in the period 1929–37.[38] By failing to change models for so long, the Company had made entry into Ford parts production too easy. Chilton's *Automotive Buyers' Guide* for the 1920s was usually divided into two fairly equal sections—those for general parts producers and those for producers of parts and accessories especially for the Model T!

More recent data are difficult to obtain because of the firms' refusal to divulge parts sales and profits data, but it should be noticed that assemblers' share of the parts market has increased since 1938 quite considerably. In 1938, assemblers accounted for 33.8 per cent of repair parts sales according to A.M.A. data,[39] but the 1958 Census data show that assemblers shipped 47.6 per cent of all automobile parts and accessories for repair (S.I.C. no. 37176),[40] a percentage which increased to 49.1 in the 1963 Census.[41] Moreover, this may be an understatement of these firms' share because engine electrical equipment, headlights and automotive stampings are excluded, and these are markets in which assemblers are quite dominant.

The president of Diamond T Motor Car Company, a truck assembler of moderate size, testified before Congress that parts sales were a most important source of profits for his company, and he submitted income-statement breakdowns for 1946–50.[42] These

[38] U.S. Board of Tax Appeals, *James Couzens et al. v. Commissioner of Internal Revenue*, Docket 10438 et al., Exhibits.

[39] A.M.A., op. cit.

[40] U.S. Bureau of the Census, 1958 *Census of Manufactures*, Industry Statistics.

[41] Ibid., 1963 *Census of Manufactures*, Industry Statistics.

[42] U.S. House of Representatives, Subcommittee of the Committee on Expenditures in the Executive Departments, *Inquiry into the Procurement of Automotive Spare Parts by the United States Government*, 82nd Congress, 1st Session, 1951, p. 683 ff.

showed that although parts sales were only 30 per cent of vehicle sales in an average year, they resulted in nearly the same total flow of after-tax profits. The profit margin on parts was 11.4 per cent while vehicles realized only 3.7 per cent on sales. Given that Diamond T is only lightly integrated, these data translate into a rate of return of perhaps 34.2 to 45.6 per cent on capital for parts production and about 7.4 per cent on capital for vehicle production.

Thus, scattered evidence from three separate time periods reveals the same pattern—assemblers extract far greater rates of return upon capital in parts production than in vehicle assembly. This is accomplished through raising the barriers to entry in the supplying of parts for their vehicles to repair markets and through integration. As the ability to preclude entry through continual change in components design, ownership of tooling and preempting the share of the repair market represented by dealer garages has begun to wane, assemblers have sought greater integration in order to prevent rivals in repair-parts manufacture from obtaining sufficient scale for efficient operation through original-equipment contracts.

V. IMPLICATIONS OF THE MODEL

There are two final implications of the model of section III which deserve examination. First, the data for parts and vehicle sales for 1929–37 presented in Table III reveal that there is a strong correlation between size of assembler and the ratio of parts sales to vehicle sales. For General Motors, for instance, this ratio was slightly less than 1 to 5, declining to less than 1 to 7 for Ford, the second largest assembler, and to 1 to 25 for Chrysler. Since we have seen that the relative price ratio p_1^*/p_2^* is inversely related to the ratio of parts sales (x_2) to vehicle sales (x_1), the largest assembler will always wish a lower price of vehicles, *ceteris paribus*, than its rivals, and it is not surprising that General Motors has become the price leader in the automobile industry with the other members of the Big Three often reluctantly following General Motors' lower prices and gratefully accepting G.M.'s decisions to raise prices. The problem of conjectural interdependence is largely avoided within a wide range on the matter of vehicle prices if the most integrated assembler continues to attract relatively larger parts demand than its rivals.

Although there are no data available for parts sales by each assembler since World War II, one observer claims that General Motors vends at least $1 million in repair parts through nondealer channels alone.[43] If this estimate is valid General Motors certainly

[43] Freeman Lincoln, 'How General Motors Did It', *Fortune*, June 1963, p. 67 ff.

accounts for considerably more than half of assembler parts sales, and its ratio of parts sales to vehicle sales would continue to be above that of its rivals. Thus, there is reason to believe that General Motors prefers the lowest price for automobiles among the Big Three. The price which G.M. establishes each year places its less integrated rivals at a relative disadvantage—one which is often attributed to the firm's lower costs of production. But the reader should note that even if all assemblers have identical cost functions, the assembler who vends the greatest quantity of parts per new vehicle assembled will be the low-price preference firm and will extract greater monopoly rents at the established prices. Rivals can only hope to achieve similar success in selling repair parts or to settle for lower returns upon capital.

Second, the pricing model of section III bodes ill for potential entrants. Since such entities cannot hope to enter the industry as fully integrated as any of the Big Three, they must depend upon independent suppliers *and* Big Three firms for parts requirements. As a result, these firms are able to successfully tap the repair-parts market demand for parts from the entrant, reducing his ability to capture rents from these markets. But at the same time the entrant must compete for buyers of new vehicles at the prices established by the larger firms which are depressed to p_1^* in order to stimulate a large market for repair parts. If the entrant cannot gain a large share of the parts demand generated by his vehicles, profit margins in vehicle supply may be so low as to forbid his continued production, especially given the natural cost disadvantages of low-scale production faced by the nascent producer. In short, the pricing mechanism developed by the large assemblers may serve to impede entry at the assembly stage.

VI. SUMMARY AND CONCLUSIONS

From a profit-maximization model of a firm producing complementary products, we have developed a model explaining the desire by assemblers to produce large amounts of their components requirements which might easily be produced in competitive markets. In addition to impeding entry into repair-parts markets, this integration and the pricing pattern which evolves from it are seen to erect higher barriers to entry into assembly. The social cost of assembler integration into and dominance of repair markets cannot be evaluated here, but it is worth mentioning that if assemblers were forbidden from marketing repair parts, much greater standardization of components would probably exist. This would undoubtedly result in considerable improvement in resource allocation although, for the same market structure at the assembly stage, new car prices would be higher. But the major effect might be to encourage entry into a market which has been completely closed from potential entry for at least twenty years and into which no venturesome entrepreneur would dare tread. The only possible social cost of disallowing integration into components production and marketing by assemblers might be a loss in intertemporal efficiency caused by a resort to the price mechanism for investment decisions. Even this loss could be compensated for by a gravitation toward long-term contracts with suppliers, totally lacking at this time.

MASSACHUSETTS INSTITUTE OF TECHNOLOGY

Appendix

In order to provide greater rigor to the analysis of the joint-monopoly problem outlined above, we begin with a model similar to that found in Allen.[44] The demand functions are written:

(1) $$x_1 = x_1(p_1, p_2) \qquad \partial x_1/\partial p_1 < 0$$

(2) $$x_2 = x_2(p_1, p_2) \qquad \partial x_2/\partial p_2 < 0$$

where the p_i's are relative prices. The cost functions are given by (3) and (4), reflecting the innocuous assumption of constant costs.

(3) $$C_1 = C_1(x_1) = c_1 x_1$$

(4) $$C_2 = C_2(x_2) = c_2 x_2$$

The c_i's are the per unit costs of production. If the market for repair parts were competitive and assemblers did not sell in repair markets, it is easily verified that the relative prices would be

(5) $$\bar{p}_1 = c_1 + x_1/a_{11}$$

(6) $$\bar{p}_2 = c_2$$

where $a_{11} = -\partial x_1/\partial p_1$. If there are several assemblers, each facing a demand function of the form (1), the price, $\bar{p}_1$, obtains if it can be assumed that assemblers face downward-sloping demand curves.

In the absence of assembler integration, there is strong reason to believe that a competitive parts market would exist and that the price of repair parts would be equal to c_2. But if an assembler seeks

44 R. G. D. Allen, *Mathematical Analysis for Economists*, New York: St. Martin's Press, 1964, pp. 359–62.

to produce for the repair market, his net revenue function becomes

$$\pi = p_1x_1(p_1, p_2)+p_2x_2(p_1, p_2)-c_1x_1(p_1, p_2)-c_2x_2(p_1, p_2) \tag{7}$$

The assembler's maximum net-revenue prices are obtained through differentiating (7) partially with respect to p_1 and p_2 and setting the partials equal to zero:

$$\partial\pi/\partial p_1 = -a_{11}(p_1-c_1)+x_1-a_{21}(p_2-c_2) = 0 \tag{8}$$

$$\partial\pi/\partial p_2 = -a_{12}(p_1-c_1)+x_2-a_{22}(p_2-c_2) = 0 \tag{9}$$

where all a_{ij}'s are equal to $-\partial x_i/\partial p_j$. Solving for p_1 and p_2, we obtain

$$p_1 = c_1+\frac{a_{22}x_1-a_{21}x_2}{(a_{11}a_{22}-a_{12}a_{21})} \tag{10}$$

$$p_2 = c_2+\frac{a_{11}x_2-a_{12}x_1}{(a_{11}a_{22}-a_{12}a_{21})} \tag{11}$$

The relative prices of vehicles and parts are dependent upon the a_{ij}'s and scale of demand, x_1 and x_2. The greater is the ratio of a_{11} to a_{22}, the higher will be the ratio of repair-parts prices to vehicle prices. In addition, the ratio of p_2/p_1 is directly related to the ratio of the scales of demand, x_2/x_1. If a_{21} is relatively large and positive, reflecting complementarity between vehicles and parts, vehicle firms may extract a large share of the monopoly rents deriving from their positions in the automobile market from the market for repair parts. Since this ability depends upon the assembler's being able to thwart substitution against his repair part, i.e. preventing a_{22} from rising and a_{21} from falling, the assembler will be careful to structure his procurement policies so as to impede suppliers' entry into distribution of parts for repair

Thus far we have implicitly assumed that both outputs are flow variables and that the magnitude of x_2, parts demand, is dependent only upon *current* demand for automobiles, x_1. In fact, the demand for repair parts is a function of relative prices and the *stock* of vehicles in operation and the flow demand for vehicles is derived from consumers' demand for the stock.

The model is reformulated in a partial stock-flow framework, requiring that (1) and (2) be rewritten as

$$x_1 = k(X_1-X_1^0) = k[X_1(p_1, p_2)-X_1^{(-1)}]+\delta X_1^{(-1)} \tag{12}$$

and

$$x_2 = x_2(X_1, p_1, p_2) \tag{13}$$

where X_1 is the desired stock of vehicles, X_1^0 is the existing stock of vehicles, k is a consumer-investment coefficient, δ is the annual rate of depreciation, and $X_1^{(-1)}$ is the stock of vehicles from the previous year. The demand relation for new vehicles expresses the relationship between the flow demand for new vehicles and the stock demand. If relative prices are unchanged, only $\delta X_1^{(-1)}$ of new vehicles are demanded by consumers. We are interested only in equilibrium states; hence, the flow demand equation which is relevant takes the form

$$x_1 = \delta X_1(p_1, p_2) \tag{12'}$$

That is, a change in relative prices will lead to an increase in the equilibrium value of X_1, but the change in equilibrium flows will only be δ times that change. The magnitudes a_{11} and a_{12} must now be interpreted as $-\delta(\partial X_1/\partial p_1)$ and $-\delta(\partial X_1/\partial p_2)$.

The effects of changed relative prices upon equilibrium flows of x_2 are more drastically altered, however, since the demand for parts is not only a function of relative prices but of the *stock* of new automobiles. Thus, we write the differential of x_2:

$$\mathrm{d}x_2 = (\partial x_2/\partial p_1)\mathrm{d}p_1 + (\partial x_2/\partial p_2)\mathrm{d}p_2 + (\partial x_2/\partial X_1)\mathrm{d}X_1 \tag{14}$$

From this expression, we may derive the derivatives $\mathrm{d}x_2/\mathrm{d}p_1$ and $\mathrm{d}x_2/\mathrm{d}p_2$:

$$\mathrm{d}x_2/\mathrm{d}p_1 = \partial x_2/\partial p_1 + (\partial x_2/\partial X_1)(\mathrm{d}X_1/\mathrm{d}p_1 \tag{ 5}$$

$$\mathrm{d}x_2/\mathrm{d}p_2 = \partial x_2/\partial p_2 + (\partial x_2/\partial X_1)(\mathrm{d}X_1/\mathrm{d}p_2) \tag{16}$$

The effect of a change in relative prices upon the demand for parts is divided into two segments, one reflecting the effect of the change in the stock of vehicles upon parts demand and the other representing the substitution of parts for new automobiles (or vice versa) for a *given* automobile stock. It is to be expected that $\mathrm{d}x_2/\mathrm{d}p_1$ is negative, reflecting complementarity, since the change in parts demand induced by an increase or decrease in the stock of automobiles surely outweighs the substitution effected by buyers between repair parts and new vehicles.

The assembler's equilibrium can now be reassessed by writing the differential $\mathrm{d}\pi$:

$$\begin{aligned} \mathrm{d}\pi = {} & p_1(\partial x_1/\partial p_1)\mathrm{d}p_1 + x_1\mathrm{d}p_1 + p_1(\partial x_1/\partial p_2)\mathrm{d}p_2 + p_2(\partial x_2/\partial p_1)\mathrm{d}p_1 + \\ & p_2(\partial x_2/\partial X_1)\mathrm{d}X_1 + p_2(\partial x_2/\partial p_2)\mathrm{d}p_2 - c_1(\partial x_1/\partial p_1)\mathrm{d}p_1 - \\ & c_2(\partial x_2/\partial p_1)\mathrm{d}p_1 - c_1(\partial x_1/\partial p_2)\mathrm{d}p_2 - c_2(\partial x_2/\partial X_1)\mathrm{d}X_1 - \\ & c_2(\partial x_2/\partial p_2)\mathrm{d}p_2 \end{aligned} \tag{17}$$

Setting the derivatives $d\pi/dp_1$ and $d\pi/dp_2$ equal to zero and solving, we obtain:

$$p_1^* = c_1 + \frac{A_{22}x_1 - A_{21}x_2}{(A_{22}a_{11} - A_{21}a_{12})} \tag{18}$$

and

$$p_2^* = c_2 + \frac{a_{11}x_2 - a_{12}x_1}{(A_{22}a_{11} - A_{21}a_{12})} \tag{19}$$

where $A_{ij} = -dx_i/dp_j$.

It comes as no great surprise that the only change in the equilibrium prices is a substitution of the total derivatives, A_{ij}, for the partial derivatives, a_{21} and a_{22}. There is no corresponding change in a_{11} and a_{12} since the demand for vehicles is not a function of the 'stock' of repair parts.

Only one minor qualification remains to be expressed. The demand for parts is registered over a considerable period after the original vehicle is sold, and the effect of a change in prices upon repair parts demand, A_{21} and A_{22}, must be adjusted accordingly. For given demand and cost conditions, this is not a serious problem in the statement of equilibrium prices. The derivatives A_{21} and A_{22} are simply reduced in value by weighting future parts sales during the t periods by $1/(1+r)^t$ where r is the firm's appropriate discount rate. Thus A_{21} and A_{22} must be understood to be

(20)

$$A_{21}^* = -\sum_{t=1}^{n} \{1/(1+r)^{t-1}\}\{[\partial x_2^t/\partial X_1][dX_1/dp_1] + \partial x_2^t/\partial p_1\} \qquad t = 1, \ldots, n$$

and

(21)

$$A_{22}^* = -\sum_{t=1}^{n} \{1/(1+r)^{t-1}\}\{[\partial x_2^t/\partial X_1][dX_1/dp_2] + \partial x_2^t/\partial p_2\} \qquad t = 1, \ldots, n$$

This adjustment is not of major importance in interpreting the model since assemblers realize a large share of their repair parts sales in the first few years of the vehicle's life. Thereafter, competitive parts suppliers capture increasing shares of the market as the automobile owner obtains repair services at those outlets which are less the 'captives' of the assembler—i.e. nondealer garages.

PUBLICATIONS RECEIVED

Adjustment of Workers to Technical Change at Plant Level, Final Report International Conference, Amsterdam November 15th–18th, 1966, Organization for Economic Co-operation and Development, $1.80, 12s., F. 7, Sw. Fr. 7, DM 5.80; and supplement to Final Report.

After the Common Market, by Douglas Jay, Penguin Books, April 25th, 1968, 4s.

American Science Manpower 1966, a report of the National Register of Scientific and Technical Personnel, National Science Foundation, NSF 68–7.

Basic Statistical Tables for Science and Engineering, by John Murdoch and John Barnes (College of Aeronautics, Cranfield), Macmillan & Co. Ltd., February 1968, 6s.

Changements Industriels et Productivité, by Daniel Vidal, Mouton & Co., Le Haye.

The Consequences of Games Playing in the British Political Economy, by William Allen, Industrial Educational, and Research Foundation, 1968, 6s.

Corporate Planning in Industry, by Aris Presanis, Business Publications Ltd., 1968, 55s.

The Corporate Private Sector, a study of Concentration Ownership Control, by R. K. Hazari, Asia Publishing House, 55s.

Creating a Market, Publications of the International Labour Office, Geneva, 1968, Sw. Fr. 7, U.S. $1.75, U.K. 13s. 6d.

Crucial Issues in Industrial Relations in Singapore, by W. Ellison Chalmers, Donald Moore Press Ltd., 1968, $4.50.

Demand for Energy in North West India, by P. N. Dhar and D. U. Sastry, Asia Publishing House, 1968.

The Economic Approach to Social Questions, by Harry G. Johnson, Weidenfeld & Nicolson, 1968, 6s.

Economic Dimensions of Major Metropolitan Areas, by Juan Torres, Technical Paper Number 18, The National Industrial Conference Board, New York.

Emigrant Workers Returning to Their Home Country, International Management Seminar 1966, Final Report, Organization for Economic Co-operation and Development; and supplement to Final Report.

The Euro-Dollar Market: An Interpretation, by Alexander K. Swoboda, International Finance Section, Princeton University, February 1968.

Fluttuazioni E sviluppo Nella Dinamica Di Squilibrio Di Sistema Economico, by Giovanni Caravale, Instituto Per La Contabilita Nazionale, 1967.

The Gold Trap and the Dollar, by Xenophon Zolotas, Victor Papasissis Publishers, Athens, 1968.

Halifax and Calder Valley, an Area Study, Yorkshire and Humberside Economic Planning Council and Board, H.M.S.O., 17s. 6d.

Industria, Commercio e Banca in Lombardia Nel XVIII Secolo, by Bruno Caizzi, Banca Commerciale Italiana, Milano, 1968.

Investment Decision-making, by Albert I. A. Bookbinder, Ph.D. Programmed Press, 2301; Baylis Avenue, Elmont, N.Y. 11003, 1968.

Industry and Empire, by E. J. Hobsbawm, Weidenfeld & Nicolson, April 1968, 50s. net U.K. only.

Justice or Prejudice, report published by the National Federation of Business and Professional Women's Clubs, March 1968, 3s. 6d.

Kreditmarknaden Och Industrins Investeringar, by Gunnar Eliasson, Almqvist & Wiksell, Stockholm, with summary in English, 1968.

Lancashire Textiles, a Case Study of Industrial Change, by Caroline Miles, Cambridge University Press, National Institute of Economic and Industrial Research, April 1968, U.K. 21s., U.S.A. $3.75.

Il Marketing dei beni industriali, by Ignio Lagioni, Società Editrice Vita e Pensiero, Milan.

Mathematical Model Building in Economics and Industry, a Series of Papers by various authors sponsored by C-E-I-R Ltd., Charles Griffin & Co. Ltd. 45s.

Moderna Organizacija, published by the School for the Organization of Work at Kranj, Moderna organizacija, Cesta Staneta Zagarja 33, Kranj.

Money and Inflation, by Emile Burns, Lawrence & Wishart 1968, 5s.

I Problemi Dell'Economia Mondiale Alla Luce Della Populorum Progressio, Società Editrice Vita e Pensiero, Milano.

Proposals for Re-organization Affecting the Company's Ordinary Shares, Preference Shares and Debenture Stocks and Providing for the Establishment of International Computers (Holdings) Limited, I.C.T., May 1968.

R & D Activities in State Government Agencies, Fiscal Years 1964 and 1965, National Science Foundation 1967.

Reparations in the Postwar Period, a Survey by Benjamin J. Cohen, Princeton University, February 1968.

Report From Iron Mountain, on the Possibility and Desirability of Peace, with introductory material by Leonard C. Lewin, MacDonald & Co. (Publishing) Ltd., 1968, 18s.

Research Papers 2 (Part 2), Disputes Procedures in Britain, by A. I. Marsh and W. E. J. McCarthy, Royal Commission on Trade Unions and Employers Associations, H.M.S.O., 11s. od.

Research Papers 9, Royal Commission on Trade Unions and Employers' Associations, *Overtime Working in Britain*, by E. C. Whybrew, 1968, H.M.S.O., 8s. 6d.

Research Papers 10, *Shop Stewards and Workshop Relations*, by W. E. McCarthy and S. R. Parker, April 1968, H.M.S.O., 13s.

Reviews of Manpower and Social Policies—Austria, Organization for Economic Co-operation and Development, Paris, 1967, $2.50, 15s. F. 10, Sw. Fr. 10, DM 18.30.

Reviews of Manpower and Social Policies—Netherlands, Organization for Economic Co-operation and Development, Paris, 1967, $4.80, 27s. 6d. F. 19, Sw. Fr. 19, DM 15.80.

Royal Commission on Trade Unions and Employers' Associations 1965–68, Report June 1968, H.M.S.O., £1.

Saving and Economic Development, by Balbir S. Sahni, Scientific Book Agency, Calcutta, Rs. 18.

Science Technology and Public Policy, The National Science Foundation and the Department of Government, Indiana University.

Scientific Activities of Non-Profit Institutions 1964 Expenditures and January 1965 Manpower, National Science Foundation, NSF 67–17, U.S. Government Printing Office, 60 cents.

Scientific and Technical Personnel in the Federal Government 1964, National Science Foundation NSF 67–21, 30 cents.